CONTENTS

INTRODUCTION

When Jack Burke told the fellow members of the 'Thursday Group' that he had been busy collecting data re the history of a local athletic club he had belonged to since the 1930s, and which was approaching its centenary, the decision to help him create a history of that club, Sutton Harriers, was taken.

More formally known as St Helens association for research into Local History, the group meet each Thursday in St Helens Local History and Archives Library. They are the research branch of St Helens Historical Society, which Jack joined at its inception in 1959.

Full of enthusiasm, the group sought and received a grant from Awards for All to assist their efforts. Little did they realise how their project would expand or the time it would take as they began to plumb the depths of the sports pages of a century's local papers on the Library's machines, and to pore over whichever Sutton Harriers' minute books had survived. News of their activities spread and exhibitions of harriers' memorabilia were held in the Library and at the World of Glass. Thanks to Jack's many contacts, long-standing club members began to drop in on the group's activities, some becoming permanent members of the team.

Harriers further afield helped by contributing articles, reminiscences, lending their personal scrapbooks, photographs and programmes of athletic events. Indeed so many have assisted in their way that the group can really only give a general 'thank you' to them all.

Sadly the team has had its losses:- Reg Lowe, who was a great organiser of any photographs that came the group's way, Ron Welding, whose own research into his Sutton Harrier father Sam (winner of the club's great international race in Paris in 1907) helped considerably, and Jack Burke himself, the group's source of wisdom and inspiration. He died in November 2000. Two contributors, Allan Morris and Roy Ashley have also passed away, whilst an unintended boost to the group's efforts came when various Harriers gathered for Alf Tyrer's funeral and heard of the planned volume.

Much writing and re-writing has proved necessary as fresh information appeared (some from Spain!) and sections needed expanding or amending. Here thanks are particularly due to team member Dorothy Hughes, not only for word-processing but also for patient acceptance of multiple amendments to the script and the re-printing involved. Thanks must also go to our meticulous proof-reader Lucy McConnell, who enjoyed her tasks and learned from it about the Harriers and their home town - real people in a real place! An especial 'thank-you' is truly deserved by Vivien Hainsworth (Senior Heritage Officer) and her staff at the St Helens Local History and Archives Library for their unfailing helpfulness and their ability to meet requests and to make a necessarily talkative group so welcome.

Sutton Harriers' earliest motto was 'Paucillatim' - little by little. Thus the club grew and thus, too, the team have recorded the progress during the century since its foundation in 1899. Inevitably some information has proved scarce, and there are gaps. With luck, readers will be able to fill in some of these. The tree depicted on the club's stationery and blazer badge denoted their more familiar motto, 'from Acorn to Mighty Oak'. The group hope that developing from the acorn of Jack Burke's initiative they have done justice to the achievements of the St Helens, Lancashire, athletics club which has richly lived up to both its mottoes.

Mary Presland, (General Editor)
Ken Wilcock and Allan Moore, (Associate Editors)

From Acorn to Oak

A History of
Sutton Harriers and Athletic Club (St Helens)

Published March 2007
by St Helens Association for Research into Local History

Editorial Team : Mary Presland (General Editor)
                 Ken Wilcock and Allan Moore (Associate Editors)

ISBN 978-09536904-1-1

Produced in Great Britain by Old Roan Graphics

Chapter One

THE PLANTING OF THE ACORN

When Sutton Harriers and Athletic Club was established in 1899 it never occurred to its members to include 'St Helens' in the club's title. The Sutton in which they met, trained and ran was one of Lancashire's ancient townships - 3708 acres of it - which with three others had been merged in 1868 to form the borough of St Helens (named after the former chapel of ease that once stood near where the townships' boundaries converged).

Half a century later, during which period Sutton Harriers had been competing successfully in local, regional and national events, and had produced several international runners, action was needed. The club had won the National Cross-Country Senior Championship - but journalists, faced with England's many Suttons, were giving Sutton Harriers the wrong geographical location. It was unanimously decided at the 1949 AGM that the club's title should be 'Sutton Harriers and Athletic Club (St Helens)'.

Even today, in the minds of many St Helens' residents, Sutton does not start at the 'Hotties' (that town centre stretch of the canal into which Pilkington's glassworks discharged boiling water) but means the district that evolved from the small clusters of dwellings at the southern edge of Sutton township - Sutton Leach, Sutton Oak, Sutton Manor and the Junction (born in January 1832 when St Helens' railway link to the Liverpool-Manchester line was completed).

It was lanes rather than roads that linked these settlements. Today's road names - Leach Lane, Robins Lane, Lancots Lane etc show their rural origins. Farmland and mossland lay all around - much of it was, or had been, part of two major estates.

Until it was auctioned in 1860 the great Bold Hall estate had for centures included some of Sutton, as well as most of Bold township and part of Burtonwood. In Sutton, the Clock Face Inn and about sixty acres of land 'well worthy of the speculative builder' adjoining or close to St Helens Junction Station were among the lots listed by the auctioneer.

Further to the west lay the Sherdley Hall estate, built up by the Welsh industrialist, Michael Hughes, who had come to St Helens in 1780 to manage the Parys Mine Company's copper works newly set up beside the canal at Ravenhead, near Sutton's northern extremity. He prospered, made judicious land purchases, built a handsome mansion, Sherdley Hall, as his home and laid out parkland around it (now Sherdley Park). In 1886 his grandson and namesake, Michael Hughes III, then a lieutenant in the 2nd Life Guards, inherited the estate. Ten years later, with thirteen years' service behind him and with the rank of captain, he retired from the army. Moneyed and educated, interested in Sutton and in sport, Captain Hughes was destined to be very important when local athletic enthusiasts brought Sutton Harriers and Athletic Club into being in 1899.

For Elizabethans, three hundred years earlier, the word 'harriers' would have meant hounds, smaller than foxhounds, used for hunting the hare. Gradually it came to mean a pack of such hounds, including the huntsmen and those following the chase on foot and, eventually, the members of a hare and hounds team.

To play at 'hare and hounds', or have a 'paperchase', would have been well established by the time Thomas Hughes, writing *Tom Brown's Schooldays* made his hero plead: 'Please sir, we've been out Big Side at hare and hounds and lost our way'.

The nineteenth century, which saw Tom Brown's school at Rugby develop a new form of football and W G Grace score 49,645 runs and take 2,684 wickets, was one of increasing interest in and opportunity for sport.

In 1867 one enthusiast, Walter Rye, encouraged his fellow oarsmen of the Thames Rowing Club into a winter training scheme of cross-country running. Their appropriately named Thames Hare and Hounds Club resulted.

Other clubs were started and competitions held. In the North, with the intention of building up Manchester businessmen's fitness in readiness for summer sports, the Cheshire Tally-Ho Hare and Hounds Club was created in 1877 by amalgamating the Manchester Athenaeum Gymnastic and the Sale and the Wilmslow Hare and Hounds Clubs.

Five years later the first successful national event took place at Roehampton. Regional associations of clubs were set up. The Northern Counties Cross-Country Association, covering Cheshire, Cumberland, Derbyshire, Durham, Lancashire, Northumberland, Westmorland and Yorkshire, dates from 1882. When, a year later, the National Cross-Country Union was formed the same Walter Rye was made its first president.

Cross-country running well suited the winter months when there were few growing crops to trample in farm fields. It was a cheap pursuit - needing no more than singlet, trunks, plimsolls and determination, and offering fitness, competition and comradeship. Only dense fog would prevent runners turning out. Otherwise cross-country was, and is, an all-weather, any-weather activity.

Things could go wrong. When, according to the *St Helens Reporter*, Prescot Harriers went to Sutton for a Saturday afternoon race in November 1900, the trail led from their hosts' Sutton HQ at the *Red Lion* in Robins Lane to Burtonwood and Bold, and then via Clock Face and Marshalls Cross home. The weather was good, but the fields and brooks were flooded, and when several of the pack got up to the neck in ditches the race was declared off, though some of the pack kept on running.

'Pack', 'trail' and many other cross-country terms come directly from the sport's hunting background. Before an event the trail would be laid by the host club along a pre-determined course. Incidentally, it was F W Webber (described on another occasion as 'the little Sutton man') who finished first on that watery day in 1900 and who had suggested to the club's committee a year earlier that Messrs Beechams be approached to provide strips of paper for laying a trail when having an inter-club run.

Seconding Webber's proposal, and second, too, on that water-logged course, came George Southward, who was made sub-captain in August 1899 and would turn out successfully on many occasions. Samuel Colville, who had finished third, must surely have played a major part in founding Sutton Harriers.

There is no information of any inaugural meeting - but from the earliest surviving records (March 1899) onwards Sammy Colville was an active committee member and athlete.

A small plaque presented by Captain Michael Hughes commemorates Colville's success in the one mile open race at sports held at Sherdley Hall the previous year. In November 1899 Colville was made club captain.Was it through him that Captain Hughes became the Harriers' first president? This surely gave kudos to the infant club.

In 1947 Colville's almost half-century of service and support was marked by the committee when he was awarded life membership of Sutton Harriers. So, too, on that occasion, (and for the second time) was William 'Billy' Brough, trainer to the club since its formation and seen posing, towel over his arm, in many team pictures. Two years later, as the club reached its half century, a press photographer captured them both with other senior Harriers congratulating that season's team on their National Championship victory.

Though Colville, Webber and Southward (of Ellamsbridge Road, the *Red Rat Hotel* and Edgeworth Street respectively) were all Sutton men, two-thirds of the fifty members recorded on 1899-1905 subscription lists lived further afield. With their HQ invariably in Sutton, the Harriers have always attracted members from all round the district.

They were by no means the first St Helens cross-country club. By 1899 Sacred Heart Harriers were well established, but St Helens Harriers, formed from a rambling club in 1886, had vanished. 180 entrants from 15 clubs competed in the 8-mile Liverpool and District Cross-Country Championship, held at Parkgate in early March 1900, in which Sutton were described as a new club, finished 6th and were awarded 'novice' medals - indicating that the team had not previously competed in that or any other recognised event.

By the time Sutton Harriers were formed the athletic year had taken on a pattern. Cross-country running occupied the winter months, and track events the summer. Between the two, in autumn and late spring, came the road running. There would be a monster meet in the autumn and friendly inter-club events. Then came the inter-club cross-country meetings - some in early days ending, if Sutton were hosts, with a social and a hot-pot supper.

The Christmas Handicap (part cross-country and part road race) began in the club's very first season. Commencing at the *Red Lion*, the course was 6½ miles long. Starting times were staggered according to each entrant's ability. Southward, described in the press as 'a youth in his first season' won by 200 yards, having had a 2 minute start. Webber, starting last, at scratch, was second, and Colville, beginning with a 2½ minute lead, came in third.

In golf a handicap measures each player's expertise and enables him to play on equal terms against players of greater or lesser skill.

For Sutton Harriers, each December, handicapping meant that experienced largely non-running members, wise as to each runner's capability, would decide the distances, or as in 1899 the times, at which each entrant would start in front of the ablest, who would be at 'scratch'. This gave all an equal chance of the prizes donated for the occasion. In one case the winner's fine turkey was still flourishing in its farmyard when the race ended.

Much depended on the experienced, non-competing members of the club - especially those stationed at the finish of an event - when time and finishing position had to be known for each runner (and records carefully compiled). Sometimes a club, local, regional or national record might be broken. More often runners might beat their own personal bests - or have an off day!

In rugby football victory goes to the team scoring most points, and while individual players' personal point scoring is acclaimed, all the team have contributed. The reverse applies in athletics. In senior competitions (and junior until 1951) only the achievements of the first six team members to finish count, whilst in youths', boys' and (from 1952) junior events it is the first four of the team to complete the course who matter. The finishing positions of these 'counting' runners or 'counters' are totalled, and the team with the lowest total is the winner. (NB the positions of individual runners are discounted when calculating the team points, as their clubs are not competing for the team event.)

Purchases of rough towels, jerseys for the trainers and occasionally an ankle band for a runner are recorded in the committee's early minutes. Stop-watches - essential for time-keeping - are never mentioned, and must have been personal possessions. In the late 1800s cheap ones were being made in Prescot by the Lancashire Watch Company. Were some of these used by the Harriers?

The starting signal for an informal training run could be as simple as a white handkerchief dropped by an obliging onlooker. On formal occasions a starting gun was needed - which emitted a flash as well as the subsequent 'bang'. On seeing the flash the time-keepers positioned at the finish simultaneously started their stop-watches.

The starter's familiar 'On your marks; get set' would precede the starting shot, words which would be highly compressed by one well-known local starter, Mr Knapper, if ever a false start had occurred. He owned several ancient blunderbusses any of which would give out smoke, flame and shreds of newspaper when fired - sufficient force to get the runners away to a good start. On one occasion, anxious as ever to avoid a false start, he told one Harrier, who was 'back-marker' and positioned to the rear of all the other runners, 'I'll bang it when thee guz'.

Each New Year, club teams became involved in the sequence of cross-country championships:- the Liverpool and District (held much later in 1900 than became usual), the Lancashire (an individual and not a team event, to select the county entrants for the Inter-Counties Championships), the West Lancashire, then the Northern Counties and finally, in early March, the National.

Matching the club's motto 'Paucillatim' (or 'little by little') the Harriers gradually notched up successes in these events.

J W (Bill) Bailey

In this, the earliest Sutton Harriers' team photo extant, Bill Bailey sits cross-legged behind the cup. Bill joined the club in July 1901, so that when he died in September 1976 he had been a member for three quarters of a century. Other new members in 1901 were Jimmy Morris, who sits at Bill Bailey's left, and

Hubert Wilcox, who stands to his right. Thomas Thomley, landlord of the *Glassmakers Arms*, is at Wilcox' right, and seated between them is Sammy Colville, whilst George Southward stands between Bailey and Morris. Suited and with his medals on his watch-chain F W Webber, who is at Southward's left, was to earn an international vest in 1904 when work commitments had cause him briefly to quit Sutton for Crewe AC. Back again, he finally retired south in 1906.

During the decade in which he competed for the club Bill Bailey was an integral member of the teams which won the Liverpool and District in 1902, the Norther Junior in 1904 and the English National Cross-Country Championships in 1906. A tenacious runner, always determined to stay the course, he shared in Sutton Harriers' triumph in Paris, and then, during Charlie Straw's suspension and Sammy Welding's temporary retirement, Bill was consistently one of the club's leading runners - putting in his best performance in the Northern Senior in 1908 when he finished 5th.

His many medals included one for achieving a standard time in an AAA 10 Mile Track Championship at Fallowfield, Manchester, completing the distance in 57 minutes and in pouring rain.

In September 1958 Bill, by then living in the Isle of Man, was made a life member of Sutton Harriers, to whom in 1974 he generously donated the trophy that bears his name, and is awarded to the track and field athlete of the year.

As The Athletic Field and Swimming World reported on April 9, 1910:- *'The Club's first real championship of note was achieved in 1901, when they won the Liverpool and District Novice Championship, their first man home finishing*

second to such sterling runners as *Jimmy Roberts* and *J.Tennant*. This was followed up the next year, when they were placed third, to *Sefton* and *Farnworth*, in the senior event, and their first man home, *F.W.Webber*, finished second to *J.Roberts*.

THEY WIN THE NORTHERN JUNIOR

It was these triumphs that whetted their appetite for further glory. They did not rest on their laurels. "We have done well," said these boys, "but we can do better".

But the club had set its very united heart on winning the Northern Junior Championship, and their president of 1904 *Captain Michael Hughes*, (a sportsman out and out and through and through) had set his heart on their winning it too.

They had just obtained the third position in the Liverpool Senior.

"Well done, my lads!" said the president. "But neither third place nor second place either are good enough for the fellows who sport the oak. Away you go, lads, for a sea trip. Clear out to the Isle of Man for a few days. I'll foot the bill."

So away to the Isle of Man they went, and they came back like giants refreshed with new wine.

"You've got to win the Northern Junior," said the president. "We will win the Northern Junior," replied the runners. And they did.

And the year after that they were runners up to the Farnworth

Officials and runners with the 1904 Northern Juniors winners shield

Harriers in the Liverpool Championships, and came in third in the Northern Senior. The club's best man, *Sam Welding*, ran second then to *F.J.Whittle* (then a Farnworth man) and second to *Hooker* in the Northern Senior.

THE SUTTON'S YEAR.

But 1906 was the Sutton's year. It was the year they won the Liverpool Senior event with a score of 33 points the team finishing: *J.Bailey, H. Wilcox, S. Welding, J.Morris, J.W.Bailey* and *J.Chapman*.

In the Northern, which the club was expected to win, many of the team were unable to show their best form and they were unable to finish nearer than second to *Crewe*, who beat them by 8 points. However, they had the satisfaction of sending the first two men home in the persons of *C.J. Straw* and *S.Welding*.

THE GRAND NATIONAL

But the Club's crowning feat came two weeks later, when they won the National Championship. It was no chance victory either. It was a victory achieved by sterling running and splendid pluck. The club really entered this event believing they had a good sporting chance of winning the bronze medals, for that year the Birchfield Harriers were extremely strong and big favourites. Having, however, conceived a wish to take tea with the winners, they fixed up such a banquet with the Midland champions.

When the race was over it appeared as if Highgate Harriers had won, with Haddington Harriers (Ireland) second, and Birchfield Harriers third. In fact, many Press telegrams were despatched by representatives to this effect, and most of the Sutton supporters were consoling themselves with the knowledge that one of their men - viz. *C.J. Straw* - had been first man home.

The Club's secretary, *Mr.H.S.Finney*, was quietly reckoning up the score when suddenly just as the gorgeous truth had flashed upon him, he heard *Mr.Hardwick* exclaim:"I really do believe Sutton have won!" "By Jove! they have," cried *Mr.Finney*, jumping up from his seat.

And they had.

In the words of the poet, "It was a glorious victory". The club entered in the hope of securing the bronze medals for third place. They brought away the gold medals and the Frank Wynne shield. So they really did have tea with the winners, and the Birchfielders were their guests!

THE BONAPARTE BIRCHFIELDERS

It was whilst at tea they discovered that the Birchfielders had out-Napoleoned Napoleon Bonaparte, who, you will remember had medals prepared for the winners before the Battle of Waterloo. They had printed slips announcing them as 'National Champions'. Rough luck, wasn't it? The team which accomplished this performance scored as follows: C.J.Straw 1, S.Welding 6, J.Bailey 18, H.Wilcox 22, J.W.Bailey 33, J.Morris 40 - total 120 points. Highgate H.scored 125 points, and Haddington scored 127 points, which is about the closest scoring there has ever been in this race, while it is also marvellous to narrate that the placed teams finished the first men home in the same positions:- I. C.J.Straw (Sutton), 2. G.Pearce (Highgate) , 3. T.Hughes, (Haddington)'

Sitting rigidly for the photographer to take this celebratory picture, the Harriers' National Championship Team are: *(l t r)* Wilcox, Morris, Straw, Welding, J W (Bill) Bailey and J (Joe) Bailey. Apart from Straw and Welding, who as international runners are clad in their England vests, all the Harriers shown wear the turkey red vests with black 2 inch hoops, and the white pants, chosen by the committee in 1904. They had yet to adopt the diamond-shaped badge with the oak and acorn emblem that shows up clearly in shows up clearly in later photographs.

C J (Charlie) Straw

Neither in the National, in which he had led the Harriers to victory, nor in other events, could Charlie Straw rely on hearing the starter's gun. Childhood meningitis had left him virtually stone deaf - and dependent on a colleague's tap on his back to signal the start of a race.

He must have felt among friends when, having won the Northern Counties Junior Championship 1903, 04 and 05, he left Warrington Athletic Club to join Sutton Harriers, whose success in the 1904 Northern Junior had moved them on into the Senior competition. Webber, Southward, Morris and Wilcox had all run against him in the 1903 event. Now apart from Webber, who had moved south, but plus Sammy Welding, who had joined Harriers in September 1904 and six months later achieved seventh place in the International at Dublin, they were his team mates, and runners of high calibre.

An agricultural worker who lived all his life in Winwick, Straw, a big man, was indefatigable, whatever the weather or terrain. His action, according to one reporter, was neither the most graceful nor the most ungainly 'but a perfectly natural manner of getting over the ground at the highest speed'.

1906 was Charlie Straw's great season. In February he won the Northern Senior (Sutton were placed 2nd); in March he led his clubmates to victory in the National, thus earning the international vest in which he went on to win the International at Caerleon racecourse, (and thus became one of the rare athletes to do so at their first attempt), a contest in which Sammy Welding again came seventh. The three gold medals won at these events were to adorn his watch-chain throughout his life - and are now much treasured family heirlooms.

Off days can happen, even to champions, but Straw's unexpected failure to win the Liverpool and District Championship soon afterwards was alleged - though he strenuously denied it - to be through 'running for the bookies'. The consequent two year ban from competititive running imposed by the Northern Cross-Country Association, did not stop him from training, nor the Harriers' committee from urging the lifting of the ban.

However, the suspension did deprive Straw of running for the club on that very special occasion when they represented their country overseas.

Taking on the French

Was Sutton's National success the magnet that attracted two international runners to the club a few months later? Previously members respectively of Farnworth Harriers and St Helens St Joseph's, F J Whittle and T Greenall had been part of the English team that Charlie Straw had led to victory in the International at Caerleon that March, finishing 12th and 22nd, and with Sammy Welding in 7th place.

The additional strength their membership gave to the team became especially significant in November 1906 when the club were invited by *L'Auto and Sporting Life* to compete in an international cross-country championship in Paris the following January. These two leading French journals had in 1905 set up a contest to be staged between major French clubs and the winning club in the English National Championship. Thus Highgate Harriers had taken part in 1905 and 1906 and been victorious. Now it was Sutton's turn.

The club committee accepted the invitation. Planning began at once for the race which was to be held at St.Cloud, Paris, on Sunday January 20th 1907. Quotations were sought for travel. The party was to set off on Friday 25th, and it was decided that 'the £1.0.0d extra which is left after allowing each man £3.0.0d towards expenses be for their tea in London'. Seven runners were immediately selected. Three club events were then used as trials to select the remaining three team members.

In all, the Sutton contingent numbered thirty - including the Club President, Captain Michael Hughes, who had broken off his holiday in Egypt to come to support his club. Dr Baker Bates, the

S Welding, J Bailey, T Greenall and C Straw, all England internationals, pictured in 1908

Vice-President, was there too, as were the secretary, treasurer, trainers and others of the committee. Seven ordinary members completed the party, including Charlie Straw. His special role on the day would be, with a well-known non-competing French runner, to lay the trail immediately in advance of the race.

In the words of 'One who went' (as printed in the St Helens Reporter) :- *'The Sutton Harriers and their supporters left St. Helens station per L. and N.W. saloon, at 1 p.m. on Friday, January 18th, and arrived at London after an uneventful journey. Tea was provided for the party at the Boddington Hotel, after which they proceeded to Victoria Station, where carriages were reserved in the boat train for Newhaven. The passage across the Channel to Dieppe*

Officials at the winning post, Paris 1907

was all that could be desired. The party retired to the cabin and rested. Arriving at Dieppe, passing through the Customs, and entering train for Paris, the party here had their first glimpse of French people, and were very much amused by the attempts made by various members to negotiate bargains for pictorial post cards, fruit etc. Daylight had not dawned, they were therefore unable to see the country on the way to Paris, so again settled down to rest. St. Lazare Station, Paris was reached at 7.05 a.m. and here the party was met by the kind, genial and attentive sportsman, Monsieur Costa, of the Stade Francais, who directed them to the carriages which were waiting to convey them to their hotel "La Grande Bretagne". Their curiosity had now reached boiling point. They were very anxious to investigate their surroundings as quickly as possible but nature (in the way of their appetites) asserted herself, and they therefore adjourned for breakfast. The appearance of the long, thin French rolls as bread caused much amusement, but when the egg and bacon arrived everyone enquired for the bacon, which was found hidden away in small pieces in the white of the poached egg. Breakfast over it was decided by the trainers, Messrs Colville and Brough, to give the team a little exercise.

It was decided to visit the "Louvre" and view the pictures, sculpturing, etc. After lunch it was thought advisable to visit the course, so a train was taken to St. Cloud, and amusement was great at the peculiar railway carriages with their upper decks reminding one of the days of the old steam tram in St. Helens. The course lay in an ideal spot and the scenery was magnificent to view, but when it came to the walk round, well, the supporters at any rate had quite sufficient by the time they had gone half round. It must be seen to appreciate the difficulties: true, there were not hedges or ditches, but it was one continual climb for about three miles. Then one had to make one's way through trees, plantations, with an undergrowth of brambles, numerous cross paths in all directions, naturally tempting one to deviate from the centre to find oneself lost from the rest of the party. We were then taken by our French companions to the dressing rooms at the hotel. They insisted upon our accepting their hospitality, at the termination of which the party returned to Paris, the team retiring early to rest before the great event.

Sunday afternoon duly arrived and found us at St. Cloud. We were received by Monsieur Maix, the representative of the "Sporting Life" who explained explicitly the whole of the conditions, course, requirements, etc. Mons. Guervin, president of the Club Amical Sportif de Saint Mande; Mons. Etling, President of the Stade Francais and Mons. Costa, secretary. The team was trimmed up by the trainers and looked in the pink of condition when they went to the post. No sooner had they arrived on the course than hundreds of French men and women surrounded them, cheering them enthusiastically, and one could hear comments in broken English on all sides. The opinion seemed to be that it would prove an exciting race between the Stade Francais and the Sutton Harriers and that every inch of the ground would be combatted by the champions of both teams.'

Let a French journalist, writing in "L'Auto" describe the scene and the race:- *'Ten thousand persons profiting by the beautiful weather we had yesterday, witnessed the cross country international at Saint Cloud. When I fixed the number of spectators at 10,000 I am certainly below the mark, but it is impossible to estimate the real number who went to see the best clubs of France and England contest for the "Open Air" Life Cup. There were people everywhere; at the starting place; in the woods; and at the most distant corner of the course. In order to obtain a good view of the runners, men and women alike proceeded with all speed, and risked their necks in climbing points of vantage on the borders of the park, which they quickly forsook to find fresh ones as the runners passed. As the finish drew near thousands assembled, in the twinkling of an eye, round the barriers which enclosed the finishing post. The finishing course had been railed off in a straight line for a long distance, and this gave the men a chance of coming in without obstruction. From a sporting point of view the day was good, in spite of the absence of one of our best clubs.*

Victory fell to one of the most celebrated English pedestrians, Samuel Welding, who triumphed with much ease over his club comrades. It was to Drouet of the S.F. that the honour fell of being the first of the French runners, he being followed by Cousin. The French runners gave their English friends a very keen race... ...

But let us return to a more detailed account of the day. At one o'clock in the afternoon the Palais Avenue and the lower Park present a scene of great animation. All is ready for the race. The course had been marked out, and as an extra precaution Messrs. L. Maertens and Straw act as trail-layers. The finishing post is beautifully decorated with flags; there is a special enclosure for the officials; and a body of gendarmes keep the course clear. The splendid Band of the 101st Regiment plays delightful selections of music, which are received with great applause. At 3 o'clock the Central Avenue is black with people and the gendarmes have great difficulty in keeping a clear passage.'

Names having been given and the course cleared all the runners are off to a splendid start in excellent weather, and the spectators rush to vantage points. It is necessary to climb up a steep bank in order to see the runners pass, and the ladies, who are as anxious as anyone to see them, are kindly assisted by their gentlemen friends. There is a great shout as the men appear. Welding leads in front of Guesnon, Rax and Delmotte and he appears to be going very easily. Quickly the people get down, for the runners will soon pass the starting place... ...

Six kilometres are covered, and Welding is ahead, followed by J. Bailey, and with Whittle 20 metres behind. Then come Cousin, Doublet, Bradshaw, Drouet, Guesnon, Chapman, J.W. Bailey, Lutz etc. The French runners are evidently in good condition. At the "Hunting Star" the order of the runners is altered slightly. Welding leads with J. Bailey, but Drouet and Cousin have drawn together and have passed Whittle. Then come Chapman, Doublet, W. Bailey, Whittle, Bradshaw etc.

The runners are about to re-pass quite near to the finishing point. The road opens out and they come near the "Diogene's Lantern" in front of a terrible descent of 100 metres. Here are 2,000 spectators. The English runners are always in front, Welding leading by 50 metres.

Sam Welding wins the Paris race

People run from all sides to watch the finish. The straight finishing course is surrounded by spectators ten deep. The first runner is announced. It is Samuel Welding and he seems to cover the last mile in a remarkably easy fashion. He is received with tremendous cheers by the spectators. The 12 kilometres (7½ miles) have been accomplished in 47 minutes. The other runners come in quickly, and thanks to the good organisation, it is possible to see all of them finish without the spectators being crowded.'

As the placings show, the last of his twenty-four competitors completed the 7½ mile course barely four minutes behind Sammy Welding.

INDIVIDUAL PLACINGS

Place	Name	Min	Sec	Place	Name	Min	Sec
1	Welding, Sutton (1)	47	45	14	Lutz, Stade Francais	49	37
2	Joe Bailey, Sutton (3)	47	51	15	Keller, Stade Francais	49	51
3	Drouet, Stade Francais	48	12	16	Morris, Sutton (7)	49	53
4	Cousin, Stade Francais	48	18	17	Vedal, CAS de St Mande	51	12
5	Whitttle, Sutton (2)	48	24	18	Bonvicini, C A S de St Mande	51	15
6	Chapman, Sutton (6)	48	27	19	Pascal, C A S de St Mande	51	17
7	Doublet, Stade Francais	48	41	20	Wilcox, Sutton (5)	51	31
8	Guesnon, C A S de St Mande	48	52	21	A Rax, Stade Francais	51	32
9	Landriot, C A S de St Mande	48	54	22	Webster, Sutton (8)	51	35
10	J W Bailey, Sutton (4)	49	14	23	Liptrot, Sutton (10)	51	50
11	Bradshaw, Sutton (9)	49	15	24	Gaudichard, C A S de St Mande	51	51
12	Rax, Stade Francais	49	30	25	Berjean, C A S de St Mande	51	59
13	Delmotte, C A S de St Mande	49	33				

CLUB PLACINGS

Sutton Harriers 35 points; Stade Francais 55 points; Club Amical Sportif de Saint Mande, 84 points.

Their team numbers (beside their names in the placings), clearly identify the Sutton runners in this pre-race photograph. Tall and bowler-hatted, Michael Hughes stands centrally behind them.

The victory, according to 'One Who Went' was *'well received by the French spectators, the military band in attendance playing the National Anthem, "God save the King." at the conclusion of which the spectators gave three hearty cheers for the "Sutton Harriers", the force of which re-echoed through the fine woods, and positively made the ground shake.*

SUTTON HARRIERS. NATIONAL CHAMPIONS. ST CLOUD JAN. 20TH 1907.

The competitors were escorted back to their dressing rooms by an admiring crowd. A large room had been specially reserved for congratulatory speeches. Mons. Etling proposed the toast to the Sutton Harriers. This was responded to by their president, who, to the astonishment of all, both English and French, spoke for nearly half an hour in French, making many witty and suitable hits. We had this time to follow the lead of the Frenchmen, and applaud when they applauded'. Captain Hughes was a 'tower of strength in himself, and I am informed by several Frenchmen, who could speak a little English, that the speech was a masterpiece. During his remarks he invited the French teams to come over to St. Helens and retrieve, if possible, their losses. They were delighted with his invitation, and negotiations are on foot for obtaining Haydock Park, if possible, for the last Saturday in January 1908 for the French Champions to visit us.

In the evening the teams and their supporters were entertained to dinner at the "Restaurant Ronteray" and Welding, as champion, was presented with a beautiful bronze trophy. The Auto cup and medals are to be sent on in due course. This terminated the official programme and was a real Entente Cordiale.

Work having been finished the team was liberated for amusements. Through the generosity of Captain Hughes a wagonette was chartered on Monday morning and the harriers shown all the places of interest in Paris. As they were now playing off their own bat, many funny experiences occurred. I am told that in order to obtain milk at one restaurant the individual imitated the 'milking of a cow', much to the amusement of the French waitress. Another in purchasing an article, put his money in his hand to allow the shopkeeper to help himself. Another paid two francs (1s 0d) (5p) for a real red rose. (The same sum could have purchased 4 lbs Golden Syrup or 3 lbs of cod, or 2½ lbs of acid drops in St Helens.)

Trophy awarded to Sam Welding in Paris

The French Minister of Agriculture came after the race to congratulate the President, (Captain Hughes) on the success of his team. The party had a splendid send off on Monday evening at 9.20 p.m. from St. Lazare Station by many of their French Admirers and although their stay had been brief many acquaintances had been made, and the good feeling existing between the two nations was forcibly shown, and contrasted marvellously with the feeling that existed during the late Boer war. I was in Paris at that time, and all an Englishman expected was an exhibition of bad feeling almost wherever he went. We must not forget that our nation owes a deep debt of gratitude to our King, Edward VII for this wonderful change, and all honour is due to him for promoting and strengthening the Entente Cordiale with the most polite nation in the world.

Arrived at Dieppe midnight boat was taken for Newhaven. Favoured by a good passage, our men arrived, fit and well, once more in "Dear Old England" where they spoke more French than ever they did in France.

I must here deliver a message from the steward of the boat. He said we should not only be proud of the boys for the victory they had won, but that it was a credit to see men flushed with success return in such a steady and sober manner.

London reached, luggage placed in custody at Euston. The party walked to Gattie's in the Strand, and had a real good old English feed. They were then taken to see the Sights of London and visited Whitehall, saw the Guards changed at the Palace, listened to the Band of the Guards, Westminster Abbey, Houses of Parliament, Cleopatra's Needle, Somerset House, along the Thames Embankment to St. Paul's, thence to the Bank of England, Mansion House and Exchange, took the 2d. (1p.) tube from Bank Station to Shepherds Bush, back by motor 'bus through the residential part of the city to Oxford Circus; from here to Euston and joined their saloon to good old St. Helens.'

According to the St Helens Reporter 'The victors and their friends arrived back at St Helens about 7 o'clock on Tuesday night, and they had a splendid reception. Hundreds of people assembled in the vicinity of the railway station and there was tremendous excitement. The runners were met on the platform by officials and personal friends, and they were warmly congratulated on their success. As S. Welding, the captain, came out of the station carrying a massive bronze statue, the trophy given to the first man in the race, deafening cheers were given, and there was a great waving of flags and hats.

Dr. Bates and the other members of the party were also given a rousing greeting as they made their appearance. The Sutton-road Prize Band and several wagonettes were waiting and the runners were escorted round the streets of the town and everywhere there was enthusiasm. A torch light contingent added a great deal to the general rejoicings. The reception was very well arranged and Mr. Arthur Royle. who had it in hand, is to be complimented on the success of his efforts. After parading the principal streets of the town, with the bronze trophy held on high and the band playing "See the Conquering Hero Comes" the party proceeded to Sutton where the inhabitants turned out to renew the welcome given in St. Helens. The headquarters of the Club, the Glassmakers Arms was eventually arrived at, and there was hand shaking all round.'

Sandwiches were quickly disposed of by the hungry travellers and then (as described in the *St Helens Newspaper and Advertiser*) *'the members, runners and a few friends adjourned to the club room where Mr.George Southward proposed that Mr.A.Royle take the chair.*

After everyone had settled down, the Chairman rose to make a few remarks in which he said he had great pleasure in rising on this occasion to thank the runners, who had taken part in the great race, and on behalf of the members who did not go, he thanked all who had taken part in helping them to gain this grand victory. He hoped the runners would have health and strength to run this race again next year.

They had kept to their training grandly, and were bent on winning when they left St.Helens last Friday. They all had willing hearts and a willing heart went further than one that was downhearted.

They were now the champions of the world (applause). The members thanked the runners heartily for defeating the French champions and they could have no better success or title than that which they now had. He thanked Sutton-road Band for meeting the runners and if it ever came their way to do them a good turn, they would gladly do it. He proposed a vote of thanks to the band, which was carried unanimously. Mr.Royle then called upon Mr.S.Welding to give his experiences on the race, and also on Mr.C.Rigby a non-runner to say a few words.

Mr.S.Welding on rising, was greeted with "For he's a jolly good fellow". He said that speech-making was not in his line at all, but he had one thing to say, and that was they had run as hard as they could, and the people of France had seen them at their best. The course was the hardest one they had ever run on, and if the race had been at Sutton, he would say the French would have had the hardest job in the world to get one home in the first ten. He thanked all those who had given them this rousing reception. (Applause)

Mr.C.Rigby said the way the Frenchmen had treated them was remarkably good, and when Welding was finishing, he was cheered by them as loud as they could shout. Captain Michael Hughes was very pleased to see them win, and he told the Frenchmen that he would pay all their expenses to come to Sutton next January, if they thought they could win the cup back again, but he (Mr.Rigby) thought that it would be useless for them to come, but after all they would like to see the Frenchmen in St.Helens. (Applause).

Mr.A.Royle said he was very pleased to hear what Mr.Rigby had said about Captain Michael Hughes paying the Frenchmen's expenses. They would give them a rousing reception. He could not promise as much as Captain Hughes, but he could promise that they would have a very good time whilst they were here. He asked Mr.Platt of the St.Helens A.C., to say a few words. Mr.Platt, on behalf of the St.Helens Harriers, thanked the Sutton lads for gaining this victory.

Songs were rendered during the evening by Messrs.V.Wainwright, G.Southward, T.Arnold, F.J.Whittle, J.Chapman, J.Wilson, G.Barnes and J.Travis.'

No subsequent event in the Harriers' long history has ever received such lengthy press coverage. Regrettably, the suggested visit by Stade to run against the Harriers at Haydock Park never materialised.

Back to earth from their heady experience, or - as with Jimmy Morris, Sammy Welding and the club's many other coal-mining members - back beneath the earth, normality returned. The committee were quick to express their thanks to Captain Hughes and Dr Bates for all their support. Greenall's bill of 7s 6d (37½ p) for the wagonette from the station was paid. Their attention then turned to fixtures and team selections.

The gold medals that were the winners' due must have been slow to arrive. Two letters to Paris enquiring about them from the secretary, and then one from Dr Bates, are mentioned. While they waited did his team-mates wonder if the only tangible evidence of their great achievement was to be the bronze statuette carried back triumphantly by Sammy Welding, and still much revered by his descendants? In fact, the medals did materialise. One is known still to survive and be cherished in Canada by a descendant of Jimmy Morris.

Michael Hughes

Captain Michael Hughes' role in the Harriers' Paris triumph highlighted his concern for and generous support of the club. He had been its president almost continuously since its creation eight years earlier, only relinquishing office briefly when military duties took him to South Africa and the Boer War, during which his wife became matron of No.9 Hospital in Bloemfontein.

Even though he gave up the presidency later in 1907 and after World War I, (in which he served as major in the Suffolk Regiment, before commanding the 7th Service Battalion of the Royal Iniskillin Fusiliers), he and his wife moved to Thornham Hall in Suffolk, Michael Hughes never lost touch with the Harriers. His subscriptions of £5 0s 0d, where other patrons managed £1 1s 0d, 10s or 5s (£1 05, 50p or 25p), appear regularly in the club accounts. In March 1937 this letter of congratulation and support reached the Club Secretary shortly after Sutton had, at Worsley, won the Northern Cross-Country Senior Championship for the first time, and before they were to take part in the National Championship at Stratford-on-Avon, in which they came third.

> *Stowlangtoft Hall*
> *Bury-St-Edmunds*
> *SUFFOLK*
> *March 9th 1937*
>
> *To Mr W F Glover*
>
> *My very heartiest congratulations to you and all your colleagues over the great success of the Sutton Harriers in winning the Northern Senior Championship. It must have been most exciting and I much wish that I could have been present at Worsley at the end of last month.*
>
> *It is some years now when I was a schoolboy I captained a team to play cricket at Stratford-on-Avon and I remember hitting a ball for 6 into the river; may the Sutton Harriers meet with the success they deserve there; I shall eagerly look out for your letter telling me how they fare after the 13th.*
>
> *Faithfully yours*
>
> *Michael Hughes*

That September the committee sent Michael (by then Colonel) Hughes a vote of thanks for his subscription. It proved to be his last. He died at Stowlangtoft Hall, Suffolk, on August 21st 1938, aged 77, and on August 25th was interred in the family grave at St Nicholas, Sutton, where his wife had been buried in September 1922.

The club's AGM, held on August 31st, 'opened with the members standing for one minute's silence as a token of respect to the Col M Hughes our late Patron'. Monies collected and spent on a wreath show in the 1938-9 accounts. So also did a 'grant' of 4s 0d (20p) for a wedding present for Jim Forshaw, a long-standing member, who had served as secretary and was to be important in helping the Harriers re-establish themselves after World War II.

Michael Hughes would have been delighted to know that two years later, at Leyland in 1939, victory in the Northern Senior Championships again came Sutton's way. Three members of that winning team were destined to share in the 'glory days' the Harriers would enjoy once Hitler had been defeated and cross-country running could return to normality.

Hubert Wilcox

Sadly, helping Sutton Harriers achieve their great victory in Paris proved to be Hubert Wilcox's last appearance for the club. Born in 1880 and having run as a schoolboy in Herefordshire and later with Birchfield AC, he came to St.Helens in 1901. So began what turned out to be his 43 years as a joiner at Pilkington's Ravenhead works, and his time as a Sutton Harrier.

A key member of the cross-country team, he was Club Captain 1904-5. Most important to him of his track successes (which included gaining most points in the club sports in 1903 and 4) was winning the Bollington mile, which he reckoned was then the premier event in the country at that distance.

However, before that, the committee had already granted him a guinea (£1.05p) towards consulting a specialist, and provided him with an elastic stocking. The Paris photo shows him bandaged, and by the time the club's 1907 Bollington team was selected Hubert Wilcox's increasing leg problem had caused his retirement from running - but not his interest in Sutton Harriers. Present at several of the celebratory events during the club's 'golden years' post World War II, he was made a life member of the club in September 1958.

He took up bowls, and after his death in 1974 his family presented his handsome Bollington trophy to Sutton Harriers. This generous gift, held by the athlete at the right-hand of the Club President, Eddie Stubbs, can be seen in the photo (page 116) of the 1983 awards presentation.

Lost and Found A Father

My early childhood was spent in the Broad Oak Road area of Parr, St Helens. Born on the 21st December 1927, I was the youngest child of Samuel and Ellen Welding then living in Nicholson Street, Parr. I was to learn some years later that my father died on the 30th July 1928. So he was the father I never knew.

It also became clear some years later that the family I lived with in Broad Oak road were in fact foster parents. Jack and Elizabeth Bate, whom I called Father and Mother, along with their four children, would look after me for some years and would eventually tell me of my true father and mother and the other children of that marriage.

Now I needed to find out more about my true family and with the help of my foster-parents, I traced my mother who had re-married and was living with my brother and sister in Haydock. Although at this point in time, aged six, I returned to my mother in Haydock, at every opportunity I would return to Parr.

Each weekend and school holidays would be spent with the Bate family, and on more than one occasion I left home to go back to Parr. So it was that I began to learn about my father Sammy Welding and his athletic feats and his association with Sutton Harriers. Most of the information came from people I got to know in Parr, along with members of the Bate family who would on occasion suggest that I should do well in school sports as my father was a famous runner, or ask, "Where did all your Dad's trophies go? Your front room was full of them."

The facts are I only ever saw a couple of trophies in the family home and these disappeared in later years. Mother was not very forthcoming about the father we didn't know. The truth is that we as children were not allowed to ask questions at that time.

So it was that some sixty years later, with the help of a cousin I got to know purely by chance, I started to research and ask questions about my father and his association with Sutton Harriers. I was able to make contact with Jack Burke who was the first to show me Sutton records of my father not only joining the Harriers, but the involvement of my grandfather and his six sons with the club from 1904 onwards.

During my research I, along with my brother and sister, have looked with pride and astonishment at club and newspaper records of our father's achievements as a runner. When I think of him working in the mines of Parr in those days, and then being called on by his country as a cross-country International on five occasions over seven years and being reserve once, plus his championship appearances for his club, and winning the team International in Paris, then I can only say it gave me great satisfaction and enormous pride to uncover so much detail after so many years of not knowing. I feel now that we have found our father again at last.

We do at least have one trophy in the family and that is the famous bronze statuette Sammy my father won in Paris in 1907. This is in the safe keeping of his granddaughter Betty. Thankfully the St Helens Historical Society's Thursday Group and some former Harriers have created this book which puts on record the exploits of this famous Harriers club and its many great runners.

Ron Welding.

NB In addition, Ron's own tribute to his father: Sam Welding: Sutton Harrier Parr Excellence was published in 2002.

Chapter Two

IN AND OUT OF THE DOLDRUMS (1919 - 39)

Not all the Harriers survived the tremendous slaughter of World War I. Some, like Sammy Welding's brother, Alfred, who lost a leg, had their athletic careers abruptly ended by injury.

Nevertheless, on January 15th 1919, barely two months after the Armistice, nine Harriers got together and appointed a committee of six, whose officers, Councillor W Bell, Sammy Colville and Charles Rigby, were appointed to their respective pre-war posts of President, Secretary and Treasurer.

The club was back in being - a fund-raising dinner and dance was planned, and a dozen running shirts were ordered. A further dozen were ordered on September 3rd at the AGM when twenty-three new members were elected and the year's subscription fixed at 1/6d (7½ p) for those under eighteen and 3/- (15p) for those over.

On September 30th two packs turned out for a seven-mile club run. The Harriers really were ready for the resumption that season of the customary pattern of club, inter-club and championship events suspended during the war. They proved this by winning both the West Lancashire Cross-Country Novice Championship that December, and the Junior Championship (in which competitors were between 18 and 21) eight weeks later. In the Northern Championships Sutton's senior team came 5th, and the juniors were 3rd.

Two of Sammy Welding's brothers, Arthur and Abraham, were in the West Lancs junior team. Together with a third brother, two Morrisses and three Hughes they had been among the new 1919 intake. Family links like these, sometimes spanning several generations, have always been part of the club's life.

At the AGM in May 1920 members presented Sammy Colville with an inscribed gold watch (still treasured by his grandson) in appreciation of his twenty-plus years' work on behalf of the club. Robert Fowles, son of another pre-World War I stalwart, succeeded him as Club Secretary - whilst Colville returned to being a very active committee member. He was by then landlord of the *Red Rat Inn*, in Ellamsbridge Road, Sutton. Hence it was no surprise that the inn bcame the meeting place for the committee, and the starting point for some club events.

Their Own H Q

The *Red Lion* in Robins Lane and the *Glassmakers' Arms* nearby at Ditch Hillock, where the Paris victory was celebrated in 1907, had also served their turn as venues for committee, training, club and inter-club activities.

However, Sutton Harriers really did need a home of their own, and plans for one had seemed well in hand in February 1914 when the committee decided that the opening run for the 'New Headquarters' would be left in the hands of Messrs Colville, Rigby and Brough.

This event would presumably have started off the 1914-5 season had war not intervened. Concluding the AGM, held a fortnight after hostilities had begun, the Club President, Cllr Bell, thanked all the members and 'hoped they would attend to their training in their new headquarters'. What then occurred was not recorded. However, something certainly happened, for the AGM in August 1922 was held at 'the Pavilion'. Amongst the business was the passing of the building account - the only mention this item ever got.

The committee again met at the Pavilion at the end of August, but thereafter, with one exception, reverted to the Red Rat until the following summer.Was the new HQ, which they resolved to call the

'Morris Pavilion', in Jimmy's honour, draughtier or less hospitable than the *Red Rat?* Sammy Colville had left the *Red Rat* by 1924, and after October 1923 the minutes cease to show where the committee met.

The influx of new members and the acquisition of a much needed HQ must have encouraged the old athletic hands whose pre-World War I experience was providing the continuity that took Sutton successfully into the 1920s. Some, like Sammy Welding, made a life member in 1920, were still running. Jimmy Morris became a 'back-room' boy - handicapping, organising events, representing the club at meetings of various cross-country bodies. Ernie Harrison, a pre-war vice-captain, succeeded Jimmy Morris as Club Captain, and Joe Hughes, whose war service had earned him the Military Medal, became a vice-captain. Messrs Brough, Massey and Lowcock continued in their invaluable roles as trainers.

Meanwhile, in 1921, having moved up to 3rd place in the Northern Senior Cross-Country Championship, a slot they again filled the following year, Sutton Harriers managed a creditable 7th position in the National Championship, whilst in 1923 Arthur Welding won the West Lancs Senior Championship.

How long Jim Kelly, the Irish athlete who joined Sutton in 1921, spent with the club is unrecorded - but 1924 was certainly his year. Not only did he lead the senior team to victory in the West Lancs Cross-Country Championship, but also came in first himself. On the track he won the Northern Counties Steeplechase, and achieved international status when he ran for Eire in the Olympics in Paris.

Similarly unmentioned is the date when the future English international cross-country runner, Albert Worrall, joined the Harriers, but in 1924 their records show him as winning the Novice Championship.

By then the Northern Cross-Country Association had initiated a Youths' Championship in which teams needed four 'counters' and not the usual six. With February 1st as the crucial date 'youths' were defined as 16-17 year olds, and 'juniors' as the 18-21s. However, for the Senior Championship entrants could be 18 or over - enabling clubs to enter junior runners if they so wished, or needed to.

The concept of 'senior' and 'junior' had certainly changed since the Harriers proudly won senior status in 1904, the success which had prompted Charlie Straw to join them.

In 1925, aged 22, Albert Worrall ran for Harriers in the West Lancs Senior Championship - not one of their successes. But, as the photo shows, the club did win the Junior Championship, and standing to the right of the trophy is Myles Morris - Jimmy's son. His, and his team-mates', running shoes seem far more supple and much less savagely spiked than those worn in the early team photographs.

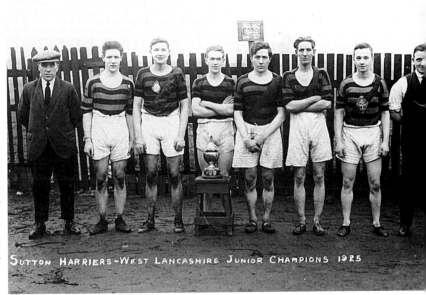

Sutton Harriers - West Lancashire Junior Champions 1925

The 1925 junior team can be spotted amongst this larger group, all, judging by their muddied legs, fresh from the day's event. Half-kneeling, centre front, is Albert Worrall.

Knees and shorts were spotless when the club members posed outside this unidentified building. There are no trophies on display, but a range of medals for second and third places, and individual successes grace a large board. Behind this and beaming sits Albert Worrall (by then a club vice-captain) wearing the England international vest he was awarded in 1928. He had finished 23rd, and 6th counter, in the International Cross-Country Championship at Ayr - having also that season come 3rd in both the National and the Northern Championships.

It seems sad that, soon after Albert Worrall achieved international recognition, Sammy Welding, still a club supporter and with pre-World War I international honours, contracted pneumonia, which in an era before penicillin rapidly proved fatal.

Neither the committee's minutes nor local press reports make any mention of Albert Worrall's representing England. Over the years he is referred to in club team selections. He was certainly an active

committee member and also captained the club. Three other members of the Worrall family belonged to the club. One, Albert's brother Frank, ran and had invaluable skills as a masseur, whilst Albert's sister Edna, later Mrs Duckworth, deserves special recognition as an athlete of high calibre - and the Harriers' first woman member.

In 1929 when the Harriers again won the West Lancs Senior Cross-Country Championship, it was another St Helens' club, Ravenhead, who won the Junior event. They had done so twice before, as had another local club, Sacred Heart, and between them these two clubs had produced six individual winners since the championships were introduced in 1911. Amongst the Sacred Heart West Lancs medal winners were amateur boxer Harry Tipping and W 'Bill' Maleedy, winners respectively of the Junior Championship in 1920 and the Senior in 1924. Since neither Sacred Heart nor Ravenhead survived into the 1930s, it was in the Harriers' colours that future Tippings and Maleedys were destined to achieve their many successes. Another migrant from Sacred Heart was W 'Bill' Glover, West Lancs Junior Champion in 1926 and 1927, who not only ran for Sutton but was also to serve as Club Secretary - an office Robert Fowles had held for most of the 1920s, relinquishing it in September 1929 to club newcomer Eddie Stubbs.

Robert Fowles, who continued to serve as the Harriers' treasurer, was in addition honorary secretary of both the United Alkali Harriers and the St Helens and District Cross-Country Association. He was vice-president of the West Lancs Cross-Country Association and a member of the Northern Counties Cross-Country Committee. As such, when in November 1929 the combination of influenza and long-suffered war injuries resulted in Robert Fowles' death, this touched the whole of the athletic world in the North of England.

Perhaps appropriately, it was Eddie Stubbs who was doubling the roles of secretary and treasurer as the decade ended, thereby beginning his own long period of service to Sutton Harriers.

Sutton Harriers' sole achievement, when the West Lancs Cross-Country Championships were held at Makerfield AC's ground in Newton-le-Willows in February 1930, was to be the only competing club to be placed in each event, their senior, junior and youths' teams having finished 3rd, 2nd and 3rd respectively.

The later years of the 1920s had brought Sutton Harriers very little success. Both Sammy Colville and Jimmy Morris, pre-World War I veterans, busy as officals at the various championships, and their contemporaries Hubert Wilcox and Charlie Straw, present there among many other Sutton supporters, must have wondered about the club's future. They'd seen Jackie Meadows run splendidly against Makerfield's Alf Tyrer in the youth's race, but also had to watch Albert Worrall, who had led Sutton to victory the previous year, only finish 23rd in the senior championship. Though unfit, he had turned out to help the club, thus making his initial appearance in a season in which he had been dogged by ill-health.

In the subsequent Northern Cross-Country Championships Sutton's seniors finished 11th and the juniors 9th - the position they also achieved in the National Championships, for which the club entered no senior team.

It was becoming clear that, since the senior members of the club were reaching the twilight of their running careers, to attract a new intake at youth and junior level was essential. That this was gradually achieved is demonstrated by Sutton's results in the West Lancashire Cross-Country Championships.

The junior team started the sequence of successes by winning the team race in 1931 and again in 1933, 34, 35 and 37, with Tommy Lee the individual winner in 1935 and Peter McGovern in 1937. The youths' team were successful in winning the championship in 1932, 33, 38 and 39, with Eddie Wakefield winning the individual title in 1933 and Tom Fillingham in 1939. In the senior event Sutton won the team race in 1932, 33, 35, 36, 37, 38 and 39. Arthur Williams won the individual championship for four consecutive years 1935-38, and Alf Tyrer succeeded him as champion in 1939.

In the 1933 Northern Counties Cross-Country Championships the youths' team won the championship with Eddie Wakefield 3rd, R Singleton 5th, H Morgan 9th and W Williams 34th, whilst the junior team finished in third position. Two years later (1935) it was the junior team (T Lee 9th, J Cunliffe 19th, W Highcock 21st, J T Harrison 29th, H Morgan 32nd and J Banks 37th) who were victorious.

Proudest of the Sutton Harriers photographed with their trophies inside the Morris Pavilion at the end of the 1935 cross-country season must have been Jimmy Morris *(seated left)* and Billy Brough *(standing extreme right)*. Each, as runner and trainer respectively, had helped the club win the Northern Counties

Junior Cross Country Championship in 1904. Now the trophy, the large framed shield, was in Sutton again. Seated between Jimmy and the trophy is Tommy Lee, who had led the team to success, and immediately behind it stands senior team member Arthur Williams, wearing his Welsh International vest.

In this, the only surviving photograph of the interior of the Morris Pavilion, large photographs of the 1904 and 1906 club teams can just be seen on the wall behind the 1935 group.

As these results show, the Harriers were gaining in strength throughout the club, and by the mid 1930s their need for enough senior members able to achieve success in the Northern and National Championships was steadily being met.

Club Captain from 1933-5 was Jackie Meadows, who had come 7th in the National Youths' Championship in 1930. Another Harrier, Arthur Williams, thanks to being entered by the club secretary, Bill Glover, as an individual in the Welsh National Cross-Country Championship, and his expenses being met by a collection from club members, was selected to run in the International Championship in Paris, where he finished 29th, and 2nd counter for Wales in March 1935.

Meanwhile in 1934, Alf Tyrer, West Lancs Youth Champion in 1930, and Junior Champion in both 1932 and '33, transferred from Makerfield AC to Sutton. Together with Jackie Meadows, Arthur Williams and Tommy Lee (whose junior, senior and international successes lay ahead), Alf was selected for the Manchester-Blackpool Road Relay Race in October 1934, as they all were again in 1935 - the last occasion on which Albert Worrall and Sammy Salmon competed in this event.

The following year Douglas Gordon Edgar, a Liverpool postman, was included in the team and was allotted the 10th leg in the relay. He had transferred to Sutton from Liverpool Harriers where he had been their half mile, one mile and ten miles champion. Finally, in January 1937 when Bill McMinnis was listed as running for Sutton, the club's senior competition strength had become something to reckon with.

The season had started with Alf Tyrer and Arthur Williams finishing first and second in the St Helens and District Cross-Country Senior Championship and Tom Fillingham winning the Youths' event. Then, in the West Lancashire Cross-Country Championships at Lancaster on 6th February 1937, Sutton won the Senior team championship, with the individual winner, Arthur Williams, followed home by Gordon Edgar 2nd, Bill McMinnis 3rd, Jackie Meadows 8th and Alf Tyrer, who was suffering from influenza, 11th. They had looked easy winners but Tommy Lee, who had led early in the race, started to suffer owing to the stiff breeze and heavy course, eventually finishing a tired 26th but enabling Sutton to win the team race from Liverpool Pembroke. Sutton Harriers' junior team's packing was excellent and had their six runners in the first twenty-one finishers with Peter McGovern the winner. The youths' team managed a creditable 3rd place in their race.

Three weeks later, on 27th February, the Northern Counties Cross-Country Championships took place at Worsley, and Sutton Harriers were there. The club had never won the senior team race in this championship but having finished third the previous year they were hoping to better that performance.

Northern Counties winning team and trophies, 1937

The start was inches deep in mud and the ploughed area was in places calf deep. In addition there was a strong cold wind blowing across the course, together with an occasional heavy shower of sleet and snow. The ground for the senior race was made worse through the youths' and junior races having been run beforehand. However, Sutton did indeed win the Senior team championship with 54 points, convincingly ahead of Salford Harriers with 146 points. Arthur Williams finished 1st, Alf Tyrer 3rd, Jackie Meadows 7th, Gordon Edgar 9th, Tommy Lee 12th and Bill McMinnis 22nd. In the junior race Sutton were 4th and in the youths' race 5th.

When the National Cross-Country Championships were held at Stratford-upon-Avon on 13th March the course had to be changed because of the previous week's inclement weather. But even this did not improve conditions under foot. The race was over one lap of 1¼ miles and four laps of 2 miles 330 yards, and resulted in Birchfield Harriers winning the team event for the sixteenth time since 1918. It proved a very close race as the winners only had a four point difference over Belgrave Harriers with Sutton 3rd. Sutton's team was Arthur Williams 4th, Tommy Lee 7th, Alf Tyrer 16th, Jackie Meadows 19th, Gordon Edgar 37th and Bill McMinnis 79th. All in all, Sutton had done very well in the 1937 cross-country season, and defied the weather which had made the going in the championships very bad indeed.

After the National Tommy Lee was selected to run in the England team in the International Cross-Country Championship at Brussels and Arthur Williams was chosen for the Welsh team. Their selection prompted a special meeting of the club committee, at which it was decided that as *'A Williams, having been selected to run for Wales in the International, had been requested to contribute 30 shillings (£1.50 - three days' wages for a collier in 1938) towards his expenses , the club should stand this amount and a collection be made afterwards among the members'. Also, 'T Lee, travelling with the English International team, and not having received his railway ticket up to the meeting was to be lent 30 shillings in case he has to pay his own fare and wait until getting to London to have it refunded'.*

In Brussels, Tommy Lee, making his international debut, helped England to victory by coming in 18th (and 6th counter) in 51 min 50secs, whilst Arthur Williams, running for Wales for the third time, came in 35th (and 4th counter), just 95 seconds behind his clubmate.

That same weekend, and nearer home on the fell course at Horwich, Jackie Meadows came second to Pat Campbell of Salford Harriers in the Rivington Pike Fell Race. A big surprise in the handicap was provided by the youngster, Tom Fillingham, also from Sutton, who was first on handicap. This was a fine performance when one considers he had been too young to run in the West Lancashire Cross-Country Championship race a few months earlier.

During the 1938 cross-country season the same six senior runners won the West Lancashire Championship, with Arthur Williams again being the individual winner. In the Northern Counties Championships the junior team gained a creditable fourth place, but the seniors, winners in 1937, were disappointed only to finish third, and then to come fourth in the National Championship, a place lower then the previous year. However, Gordon Edgar won selection for Eire, and took part in the International Championship at Belfast on April 2nd.

This was the first of Eire's two appearances in the International Championships. In 1937 the Amateur Athletic Union of Eire had gained affiliation to the International Amateur Athletic Federation, and the International Cross-Country Union immediately gave the AAUE the right to compete.

After World War II the ICCU were asked, and agreed, that the Northern Ireland's AAA and Eire's AAU should join forces to form one Ireland team. This first took place in 1948 - making Gordon Edgar's honour rare indeed.

An interesting incident occurred during the summer of 1938 at Widnes Police Sports when Sutton Harriers and Salford Harriers tied for second place behind Liverpool Pembroke in the two miles team race. There was some discussion as to what should be done to decide the second place. The Sutton captain, Gordon Edgar, declined to toss a coin for the prizes and suggested a run-off, which Salford accepted. This was staged at the close of the meeting and a very thrilling race resulted in Sutton winning with 10 points to Salford's 11. In later years the problem would have been resolved by the positions of the clubs' fourth runners being the deciding factor.

1939 saw Sutton Harriers looking to improve on the club's performances. Alf Tyrer won the West Lancashire Cross-Country Championship and Sutton won the team race. A few weeks later Alf won the Northern Counties Cross-Country Championship individual medal over a 9 miles course at Leyland, beating Jack Potts (Saltwell Harriers), the winner for the previous three years, into second place. This was the first time Sutton had had the individual winner since Sammy Welding's victory in 1907. Forty-seven clubs took part in the senior race and Potts held a slight lead over the first two laps, before being overtaken by Alf, who was never extended and finished comparatively fresh. Arthur Williams finished 4th, followed by Fred McMinnis 9th, Bill McMinnis 16th, Gordon Edgar 23rd and Tommy Lee 31st, thus winning the team race with 84 points from Salford Harriers and Liverpool Pembroke, with 108 points and 143 points respectively.

The National Cross-Country Championships were held at Grange Farm, Worsley, on Saturday 11th March 1939 in terrible weather. The Northern Cross-Country Championship had been held on this course two years earlier in similar conditions. From the start in the senior event Jack Holden (Tipton Harriers) was in the lead along with Alf Tyrer (Sutton), Reeve (RAF), Noble (Hallamshire Harriers), Penny (Belgrave Harriers) and Etheridge (South London Harriers). This order was maintained during the first two laps, after which Tyrer and Reeve gained a very slight lead which they retained until the last lap, when Holden made a supreme effort to pass them both and eventually win by twenty yards with Alf Tyrer 2nd and Reeve 3rd. Halfway through it appeared that Sutton Harriers were winning the team race, with Belgrave Harriers and Mitcham Harriers close on their heels. However, on the last lap, Belgrave Harriers, Birchfield Harriers and Mitcham Harriers pulled back a lot of ground to finish in that order with Sutton pushed down into fourth position. Nevertheless, Sutton did win the Charles Ottway Memorial Cup, awarded to the club whose full team of nine runners completed the course with the best aggregate points.

Following the National Alf Tyrer was selected for the England team in the International Cross-Country Championship at Cardiff, where he finished 15th, being the second English runner to finish and enabling the England team to be runners-up to France in the team race.

As usual throughout this very successful cross-country season Harrier members of the Territorial Army, such as Tommy Lee, J T Harrison, Bert Lee and Bill Glover had also been maintaining their stamina by very successfully representing their units at cross-country events.

That summer three of the club's victorious Northern team won Lancashire selection for track events - Alf Tyrer *(No 14 in picture below)* for the 2 mile Steeplechase at the White City, and Gordon Edgar and Fred McMinnis for the 3 miles. Meanwhile, Tom Fillingham came 2nd in the Lancashire one mile Junior Championship in Manchester.

Regular sporting activities went into abeyance nationwide following the declaration of war against Germany on 3rd September 1939. Call-up, war-work, bombing and evacuation disrupted clubs, teams, training and venues. 'Ad hoc' matches and competitions certainly took place - but it was only after the cessation of hostilities in 1945 that the normal pattern of events could gradually be resumed.

During the war one sad event did bring three of the successful six together. In July 1944 Alf Tyrer, Jackie Meadows and Arthur Williams (together with club-mates Jimmy Moore, Albert Lowcock and Ernie Henderson) were bearers at the funeral at St.Nicholas', Sutton, of Jimmy Morris, whose running had helped Sutton to victory in the National in 1906 and in Paris in 1907, and after whom the Morris Pavilion had been named. As Club Captain he had done much to ensure the club's resurgence after World War I, and he remained a very valued and useful committee member until World War II broke out, abruptly halting athletic activities.

Three months earlier, also at St.Nicholas, athletes and colleagues from his workplace at the L.M.S. Stores Department had gathered for the funeral of 'Ham' Finney, a very early club member and former Club Secretary.

All had probably read this tribute to 'Ham' by *'Onlooker'*, printed in the *St Helens Newspaper* on April 7, 1944.

'THE FINAL WHISTLE - Ham. Finney

"Yours until the final whistle" wrote 'H.A.Milton' styled Hamilton Stevenson Finney, at the conclusion of his letters to me while in hospital,' writes "Onlooker". This was typical of the spirit which kept him to his three score years and ten before passing out on Tuesday, 4th April last.

"Ham" Finney loved sport of all kinds, and his powerful personality endeared him to all in the boxing, bowling, soccer and athletic world. For many years he was a firm favourite at the Stadium while Manchester and other cities saw his interest. His chief connection was with the Northern Counties Cross-Country Association, the West Lancashire C.C.A and the Amateur Athletic Association. His life was spent in the work and only a fortnight ago he was responsible for a West Lancashire meeting at Whiston.

His career commenced with the famous Sutton Harriers and his work constituted a record of unremitting labour. He went to France with that famous band of athletes in 1907 to bring honour to the town. When Sutton failed to muster a team he joined up with Makerfield, but from time to time he tried to revive flickering embers that smoulder in the hearts of cross-country lovers. In later years "Ham" is said to have donned the shorts to lay trail when no one else could be found.

He served on the Olympic Committee and attended many Olympic events in foreign countries. "Ham" rarely missed a sports meeting in this area, acting in every capacity, of the game. In later years he helped East Lancashire Cross-Country Association.

He voiced charitable ideals and his influence was the means of organising events to this end. In 1939, through his endeavours, the Ladies' Match, Preston v.Bolton, was staged at City Road Ground, the proceeds of which were devoted to the local Hospitals.

He never took an active part in soccer, but was a great devotee of St.Helens Football Combination, for it was due to him that the Combination was born.

He was a lover of Shakespearian prose as well as being versed with wit and good humour, and it was this which brought him in touch with thousands of sports friends and made him so likeable.

Thus, another colleague from the sports arena passes on, but in doing so he left a final message with me: "Stick to the authorities about the sports stadium. Other towns have one and St.Helens is worthy of one."

Almost exactly forty years had passed since Ham Finney, seconded by Jimmy Morris, had successfully proposed to the committee that turkey red vests with black hoops and white pants should be Sutton Harriers' club colours.

Now faded and tattered but still surviving, Jimmy Morris's striped vest, worn by him when Sutton Harriers won the National in 1906 was passed on by Jimmy to Bill McMinnis, who wore it in the club's National victories in 1947, 49, 1950 and 51.

Arthur Williams

In an athletic career which spanned the 1930s Arthur Williams led the Sutton Harriers to their first Northern win in 1937, when, coming 2nd himself, he lost narrowly to Jack Potts. He ran for Wales on four occasions and, four times also, both won and led the club to victory in the West Lancs Championships.

When, in 1939, the club again won the Northern, it was only the brilliance of his club-mate Alf Tyrer (winner of both the West Lancs and the Northern and placed 2nd in the National) that prevented Arthur from equalling Sammy Dodd's record of five successive West Lancs victories.

This failure, and his defeat by Potts, he was to recall with equanimity in later years - feeling there was no disgrace in losing to the better man, especially if the team carried the day.

The war against Hitler took five years from Arthur's running career, and though he earned a medal in the Northern Counties Victory Championships in 1946 he gladly allowed others to carry Sutton's colours in the post-war period.

Almost half a century after he had become the first Sutton Harrier to represent Wales, and shortly before his death in January 1983, Arthur Williams was presented with a NCAA Centenary medal. This award he regarded with pride, and with gratitude that he should have been remembered for his contribution to a sport he had graced.

Chapter 3

CROSS-COUNTRY - THE GOLDEN YEARS

It was totally appropriate that, 50 years old in 1949, Sutton Harriers should celebrate their Golden Jubilee almost mid-way within their 'Golden Years' of cross-country running.

Yet four years earlier, at the end of World War II, only the most optimistic and the most determined could have envisaged any future at all for the club. There was no clubhouse; the foremost senior member and backbone of the club, Jimmy Morris, had died; both military service, which had taken Harrier lives including that of Bill Glover, and war work had scattered the pre-war runners. Of these Tommy Lee, who never rejoined the club, was to achieve local fame when, returning from work at Laporte Chemicals, Warrington, he dived in and rescued a man from the Manchester Ship Canal.

Coming home after their war experiences, servicemen everywhere were trying to adjust to a 'normal' life - in which clothes, food and coal rationing still continued. In many places there was renewed interest in cross-country running, and locally Sutton Harriers were like UGB Sports Club, Pilkingtons Recreation Athletic Club and Earlestown Viaduct AC in attempting to revive club membership.

Determined to get cross-country and road running organised again three Harriers, Jim Forshaw, Alf Tyrer and Tom Fillingham, made contact with other Lancashire clubs, such as Winton Harriers (based at Eccles), with the result that a programme of events and venues was established. It was certainly also thanks to the efforts of the same trio in gathering the support of former members and securing temporary accommodation at East Sutton Labour Club that Sutton's situation began to improve.

Working locally in engineering Alf Tyrer, who had won the Northern in 1939, had managed to train regularly at Ruskin Drive - but like the other returning club members had lost six years of competitive running. However, by himself finishing 2nd and leading the club team to 2nd place in the Northern Counties Victory Cross-Country Championship at Radcliffe in February 1946, Alf signalled that Sutton Harriers were back in business.

That autumn, 1946, a cross-country race held on November 2nd by the West Lancs Cross-Country Association in conjunction with the UGB Sports Club's Chrysanthemum, Poultry and Pigeon Show at the UGB Sports Ground in Bobbys Lane, Eccleston, ushered in the cross-country season. The race was run for a distance of four miles over the country and the runners were stopped at the *Stanley Arms Hotel* in readiness for a one-mile break race back to the club grounds. Joe Harrison, running for Pilkingtons, finished 1st with Alf Tyrer 3rd.

In the same month Sutton were victorious in three triangular matches against Earlestown Viaduct and Pilkingtons, and in December came 6th out of sixteen competing teams in the West Lancs Novices Race, held at the UGB ground over a two lap course of five miles which included some heavy going over ploughed fields. It was eighteen-year-old Mick Maleedy, nephew of Billy and running for UGB, who finished in 6th place, and that same month joined Sutton Harriers, as also did Joe Harrison.

On December 28th the Northern Counties held a trial to select a team to compete against the Universities Athletic Union at Sheffield the following month. The race, over eight miles at Sutton, was between the ten best West Lancs runners and the ten best East Lancs runners. Tom Fillingham, Fred and Bill McMinnis, Arthur Williams and Ernie Henderson were selected for West Lancs as well as Joe Harrison, who was not available, and Alf Tyrer, who had an injured tendon and could not run. Tom and Fred finished 1st and 3rd respectively and, at Sheffield on January 18th, together with Joe Harrison, justified their Northern Counties selection by finishing 8th, 10th and 14th in the race against the UAU, especially considering that all three had been demobbed during the previous twelve months.

Winter had really set in when the West Lancs Championships were held at Woolton on February 8th. Sutton, winning the Senior event by five points from Pembroke, proved they had as strong a team as pre-war. Tom Fillingham, the individual winner, who ran an exceptionally well-judged race, finishing 100 yards ahead of the second runner, led the team to victory - achieved despite the adverse weather conditions and with regular team member Ernie Henderson down with 'flu. Their finishing positions were: Tom Fillingham 1st, Fred McMinnis 3rd, Joe Harrison 6th, Bill McMinnis 10th, Alf Tyrer 12th and Eddy McMinnis 37th.

Meanwhile, in the Junior event, in which Sutton had no team, Mick Maleedy finished 2nd in only his second race and D Saunders was 7th, whilst the club's young inexperienced youths' team finished a creditable 4th.

Two weeks later conditions had worsened when the Northern Counties Cross-Country Championships were held at Gosforth Park, Newcastle, on Saturday 22nd February 1947. Sutton scored a magnificent victory - *'a victory'* (according to the *St Helens Reporter*) *'which will go down in the club annals as one of the greatest, if not the greatest, of their many triumphs so far'.*

'In years to come the members of Sutton who travelled to Newcastle will tell younger generations all about this race. It was surely a magnificent display of courage and team spirit, the like of which has not been seen for many a day and carried Sutton from what seemed certain defeat to a convincing win.

DOGGED DOES IT

Sutton's fight for victory began at six o'clock on Saturday morning when the team and officials and supporters left St.Helens to travel to Newcastle by road. Arriving in Manchester it was found that the Oldham-Huddersfield road over the Pennines was blocked. A long detour was made through Rochdale and Halifax. Along the whole route the roads were ice-bound and sudden snow squalls were frequently encountered. It was two o'clock when they eventually reached Newcastle and there is no doubt that the runners felt the effects of this long and tiring journey so much that at the end of the first lap of two miles Sutton's hopes of winning were nil.

RACE THROUGH SNOW

A carpet of snow a foot deep covered the Gosforth racecourse but this did not deter the runners. Over 200 faced the starter, Sutton were drawn badly and suffered for it, Tom Fillingham being spiked and Fred McMinnis knocked over at the start. At the end of the two miles lap the team positions were Hallamshire 129 points Sutton 185 points. It was evident that the Sutton lads were feeling the effects of the long journey and that a supreme effort was needed to beat Hallamshire. At this stage Alf Tyrer in 24th position had lost one running shoe and so decided to kick the other off and carry on in his bare feet.

After five miles the Sutton team, with Fillingham lying 3rd, had settled down to their running and having been acquainted of the effort needed to win responded magnificently.

BAREFOOT RUNNER'S PLUCK

Alf Tyrer, in bare feet, had moved up from 24th position to 6th and Fred McMinnis had run through the field from 40th to 8th position with the team position being Hallamshire 157 points Sutton 168 points.

With two miles to go Hallamshire had been cut down to five points and it became a grim fight for supremacy. While the Sutton officials had their fingers crossed the Sutton athletes set about the task of making up the necessary positions to assure victory.

When the final count began Sutton's hopes soared having 56 points for five men whereas Hallamshire had counted 145 points for their full team of six. As in the West Lancs everything now depended on Sutton's sixth man and a rousing cheer went up when Ernie Henderson handed in disc number 79 to give Sutton 135 points and victory by ten points.

TEAM SPIRIT TRIUMPHS

It would be difficult to single out any individual performances as this was a triumph for six men who put their team before themselves. Tom Fillingham, who ran on after being spiked to finish third, Alf Tyrer losing both shoes finishing fifth, Fred McMinnis after being knocked over at the start and running through the field to finish ninth, Joe Harrison 6th and Bill McMinnis 33rd ran their usual stouthearted race and Ernie Henderson's gallant performance after being ill with influenza to finish 79th and make the sixth counting position for Sutton.

Backing up the six were Eddy McMinnis 87th, Mick Maleedy 92nd and Denis Saunders 100th who all had youth on their side to be able to play their part in future championships.'

It must largely be left to Bill McMinnis, surviving member of the Sutton Harriers' contingent that returned in triumph from the National Cross-Country Championship, held at Apsley, (near Watford) , on March 8th, to describe the occasion:

'The winter of 1947 was a very bitter one with several heavy falls of snow, one and two feet deep in places. This obviously made cross-country races exceptionally hard going. In February 1947, Sutton Harriers had already won the West Lancs and Northern Senior. The week before the National Cross-Country Championships saw more heavy snow, putting a question mark over whether the race should take place. It was organised at Watford, and on Friday prior to the Saturday race, all the Sutton senior team held a meeting at Secretary, Harry Wilson's home, in Ormskirk Street, St Helens, to decide whether we

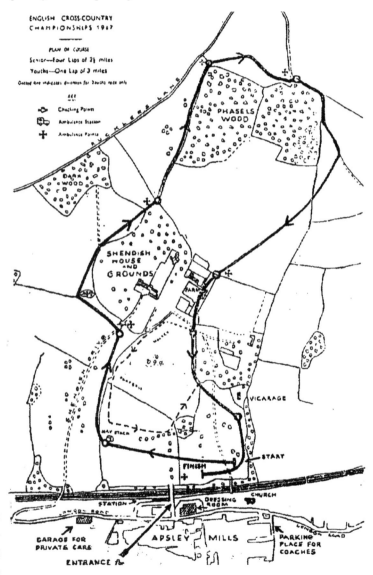

should, or should not, go. Was the race still on? Was it worth the (personal) expense of a Watford train trip? After much discussion, we decided to risk it, and arranged to meet again on that same Friday night at Lime Street Railway station, Liverpool, in time for the midnight train to London, via Watford, where we were to stop. After an uncomfortable trip of about four hours, we landed at Watford, and made our way to what was apparently a bakery, where we were allowed the use of a large room which had hot water pipes all round the walls at floor level. Everyone then sat down on the floor and *started hugging the pipes, and, of course, going to sleep in the comfortably heated room. This was at around four to five am. We stayed until 8 or 9 am, eating our sandwiches and drinking coffee as a makeshift breakfast. Later in the morning we made our way to the course at Apsley, and found that it was 1½ to 2 feet deep in snow.*

What happened after that, in the races, is now history, especially as a very well known athletics reporter said Sutton Harriers' win was a fluke, since lots of other teams never arrived because of the snow. To prove the reporter was ill-informed, Sutton Harriers, over the next four years, won the National Championship a further three times, and were second once - SOME FLUKE!'

Certainly both Birchfield Harriers and Tipton Harriers, whose HQs were 100 miles nearer Apsley than was Sutton's, arrived too late to run. However, Sutton did effectively beat the previous holders and favourites, Belgrave Harriers, Sutton's scoring six being Tom Fillingham 11th, Alf Tyrer 13th, Joe Harrison 14th, Fred McMinnis 24th, Bill McMinnis 30th and Ernie Henderson 68th. Tom Fillingham thus missed by one position selection for the International Championships held in Paris three weeks later, in which Norman Ashcroft, then running for Manchester AC - came in 30th - the 7th English team member to finish.

Winning English National Cross Country team and trophy, 1947

In September 1947 the club formed a special section for boys 14-16 years of age to help build up the club's future and to assist in this formation a Club Novices Race was held on Saturday, November 22nd.

This attracted over 30 youths from all districts of St.Helens and from Prescot, Whiston, Rainford and Runcorn. In presenting medals and prizes to the first three in each age group, (who included G Horsfall, Dennis Wilson, Roy Ashley, Gratton Purcell, John Orrell, Bob Maleedy and George Gabbott), Mr E J Stubbs, Club President, congratulated the entrants upon their showing in this the first Club Novice Race for many years and remarked on how closely contested were the

Group including the 1947 National team and trophies

races. It was quite evident that with the enthusiasm displayed Sutton had no worries with regard to the immediate future. Here was the material to carry on the great traditions and achievements of Sutton Harriers.

He was to be proved right. While two under-eighteen Sutton teams were gaining experience in the West Lancs C C Novice Race at Preston on December 6th, the club's senior runners were taking part in a Lancashire County trial race - won by Fred McMinnis, with his brother Bill 3rd, Joe Harrison 5th, Alf Tyrer 6th, Mick Maleedy 8th and Bill Burrows 13th.

A week later Sutton travelled to Horwich for a match involving Horwich, Manchester AC, Bolton, Radcliffe, London and Leigh. It was rare that so many clubs got together for a friendly inter-club race, and a novel feature was the tea and social evening which followed the run, especially as food rationing was still in force. Having stolen the limelight in the afternoon by taking the 1st, 2nd, 3rd, 4th, 5th, 9th, 10th and 13th finishing positions Sutton carried this into the evening thanks to the singing of Mick Maleedy.

A personal account follows of the next challenge taken on by three Sutton stalwarts and its consequences.

THE ONE THAT GOT AWAY

'In the cross-country season of 1947/8, Alf Tyrer and Joe Harrison suggested that we three should enter the Morpeth to Newcastle Road Race, 14 plus miles, to be run on New Year's Day 1948. We duly entered as individuals, and as Sutton Harriers as a team in the 'three-to-count-race'. After much train travelling we landed and had overnight accommodation in Whitley Bay. It was a bitterly cold winter and I remember waking in the middle of the night to find Joe Harrison wandering about in pyjamas and a waistcoat (not a pretty sight).

After my falling asleep on the platform at Newcastle Station during a long wait for a Morpeth train (New Year's Day travel) Alf suggested that I would probably run well after my little snooze. At 1 pm the race from Morpeth to Newcastle got under way, and true to Alf Tyrer's prediction I found myself in front of around 200 runners. They included the formidable Jack Holden, who one month later won the Empire Games Marathon in New Zealand, and who, in 1939 had beaten Alf Tyrer into 2nd place in the National Championship.

Sutton Harriers were, as usual, well placed in the team race and towards the end of the race, at around eleven or twelve miles, we were placed 1st, 5th and 6th, and at the finish we had easily won the team race, with positions 3rd, 5th and 6th, with a team total of 14 points.

After the race, we found out that our prizes were:

Bill McMinnis   3rd and first team, and first novice

Alf Tyrer   5th and first team

Joe Harrison   6th and first team

making a total of seven prizes in all, plus an enormous silver trophy for the team race.

Alf then suggested that, since he and Joe had to be in work at 8 am on the 2nd January, and I had a day off, I should stay and collect all the prizes, and return home the next day. They, in the meantime, would catch the next train from Newcastle to Manchester. I duly did this and found myself in RAF uniform in Newcastle on a dark, wet, night, with a grip full of running gear, plus two cardboard cartons containing seven prizes and one large valuable silver team trophy. Very uncertain of what to do next, since I had to find overnight accommodation, I called into a police station to explain my situation. The police constable asked, 'Did you run in today's race from Morpeth to Newcastle?' I said, 'Yes. I was third', and he explained that he'd been the motor cycle escort.

I then described my dilemma, ie safeguarding overnight one valuable silver cup and seven prizes, four of which belonged to my team mates. He then suggested we made a list and put everything in a police cell overnight (but not me). Everything was then fully organised, and all mine and Sutton Harriers' worldly goods were locked up in a police cell for the night. I was given a written list to produce next day to collect them. I then left the police station to find myself accommodation in the local Salvation Army Hostel for the night.

After a good night's sleep, I returned to the police station, collected the cartons and my belongings, and caught a train for Manchester and on to St. Helens. (In those days, if you didn't travel by train everywhere you just didn't go).

On my arriving home, my parents opened the door, and said, 'We know you won. It was on the wireless. Let's see your prizes'. We opened up one of the cartons, and a wee mouse jumped out. We never did find that Geordie mouse!'

Bill McMinnis

On January 10th 1948 there were four Sutton runners in the Lancashire team which finished 4th in the Inter-Counties Cross-Country Championships at Horsham, Sussex:- Fred McMinnis, first Lancastrian in 10th position, Bill McMinnis, Joe Harrison and Tom Fillingham. Mick Maleedy, passed over by the Lancashire selectors as too young, Alf Tyrer, selected but unable to undertake the journey, and Fred McMinnis were all chosen to represent Northern Counties in a cross-country match in which Bill McMinnis was part of the RAF team.

When the West Lancs Cross-Country Championships were held at Sherdley Park on February 14th, Sutton Harriers were delighted to win the Senior race - with Fred, Tom, Bill and Alf in the first four positions.

In the Junior race Mick Maleedy was first, winning very easily, though there was no Sutton team. However, in the Youths' Race the club's team (F Tootill, Bob Maleedy, G Purcell, J Orrell) finished 2nd, behind Liverpool Harriers who had been the 1947 Youth Champions.

On Saturday February 28th the enterprise in which almost every club member had been involved came to fruition when Sutton Harriers hosted the Northern Counties' Cross-Country Championships. Planning for this event had begun with an Extraordinary General Meeting held, as the club had no HQ, at East Sutton Labour Club in October 1947.

When the day came, all the members' planning and hard work was well rewarded - for in the Senior Championship Fred McMinnis was first to finish with his five Harrier team-mates sufficiently close to ensure Sutton were again the winning Championship team, whilst Mick Maleedy finished 3rd in the Junior event.

It was probably as well, though, that the Committee decided to postpone the dance initially planned for the evening of the Championship!

Two weeks later, on March 14th, in contrast to 1947's icy conditions, the National Cross-Country Championships were decided in glorious weather in Sheffield and - as reported in the *St Helens Reporter*: '*Sutton Harriers, the 1947 champions, failed by 20 points to retain their title, being beaten by Belgrave Harriers who were second to Sutton last year.*

From start to finish it was impossible to say who would win the individual or team race, so gruelling was the course. It was a case of who would crack first and several fancied runners came to grief early on.

With the exception of Joe Harrison and Ernie Henderson the Sutton team was away to a good start. At the end of the first mile Sutton had Fred McMinnis, Bill McMinnis and Tom Fillingham in the first fifteen places, Mick Maleedy 30th, Alf Tyrer 42nd with Ernie Henderson and Joe Harrison well down the field followed by Bill Burrows and G. Reid.

Even at this early stage it was evident that the team race would be fought out by Belgrave, Blackheath and Sutton with Blackheath, led by Sydney Wooderson, favourites. The race was both won and lost in the next three miles. It was at this stage that ill-luck dogged Sutton. Fred McMinnis, who had strained an ankle tendon winning the Northern, felt his ankle giving trouble and had to slacken his pace, thus losing all hopes of the individual title. He finished well up however to give Sutton a chance.

Sutton's second man at this stage was Mick Maleedy, who was running a grand race in 20th position, Tom Fillingham had dropped back to 39th and Bill McMinnis was running in the 70s with Alf Tyrer close behind and Joe Harrison 95th.

It seemed that the race was left between Belgrave and Blackheath because with the exception of Mick Maleedy the Sutton team were having a hard time. Then, as suddenly as they had lost ground, the Sutton boys struck their real form and at the seven miles stage they were back in the race with a chance.

Fred McMinnis was running a fairly comfortable 12th, Mick Maleedy 27th, Tom Fillingharn 32nd, Bill

McMinnis 36th, Alf Tyrer 45th and Joe Harrison 87th and all were running strongly. So well were the Sutton boys running on the last lap that they very nearly pulled the race out of the fire and people who had written them off early were made to change their tune. However well they did run on that last lap, Belgrave had seized their chance on the second lap and ran out worthy winners with 154 points to Sutton's 174 points and Blackheath's 183.

Sutton's counting six were:- 11th Fred McMinnis, 17th Bill McMinnis, 20th Tom Fillingham, 24th Mick Maleedy, 37th Alf Tyrer and 65th Joe Harrison, who had injured a foot early in the race.'

After the National Fred McMinnis was selected as a reserve for England in the International race at Reading on April 3rd, whilst as a result of their consistent performances throughout the cross-country season Fred McMinnis, Tom Fillingham and Mick Maleedy were in the Northern Counties team against the Combined Services team, which included Bill McMinnis, at Timperley, Sale, on 28th March. Fred was selected to run for an England team at an international cross-country race in Belgium on April 11th 1948 which was won by Emil Zatopek of Czechoslovakia, who later in the year achieved Olympic glory.

With a team which must have been the youngest ever to represent the club, Sutton Harriers won the West Lancs Cross-Country Novice team race at Runcorn on Saturday, December 4th 1948. Aged 16 and 17, the seven boys did not seem to worry that the majority of the competitors were much older and bigger. The team and positions were:- R Williams 2nd, D Wilson 3rd, T Welton 8th, G Burke 10th, G Horsfall 25th, A Cowell 38th and R Ashley 41st. The winner, R K ('Bob') Meadows, then running for Pilkington Recs , joined Sutton during the late 1950s whilst serving in the Royal Navy and with a frigate's boat deck as his training course. Bob would have been a great asset to the club had he joined earlier, especially as Pilkingtons could never field a team in major cross-country championships.

Following the Lancashire County Cross-Country Championships held at Childwall on New Year's Day 1949, in which Fred McMinnis finished 3rd, Fred, Tom Fillingham, and Joe Harrison were selected (with Mick Maleedy as reserve) to run in the Inter-Counties Cross-Country Championships at Worsley two weeks later. Lancashire won the team title with Joe, Fred and Tom at 11th, 12th and 13th being in the winning counters. (Unable to get into the Lancashire team, and having been born at Port Sunlight, on this occasion Alf Tyrer chose to represent Cheshire.)

Lancashire team, including Sutton runners, which won the Intercounties 1949 cross country championship

From Sutton Harriers' point of view, the West Lancs Cross-Country Championships at Croston turned out as expected! Their teams won both Senior and Junior races, with Fred McMinnis and Mick Maleedy retaining their respective titles. Also as expected, in the Youths' race Liverpool Harriers had a narrow 8 points win over the Sutton youngsters.

The team positions were:

Seniors:- Fred McMinnis 1st, Tom Fillingham 3rd, Joe Harrison 5th, Alf Tyrer 8th, Bill McMinnis 9th, Les Lamb 13th.

Juniors:- Mick Maleedy 1st, G Burke 2nd, R (Bob) Maleedy 4th, F Tootill 10th.

Youths:- D Wilson 3rd, R Williams 4th, R Ashley 8th, T Welton 13th.

It augured well for the Northern Counties Cross-Country Championship, held at York on February 25th, as described in the *St Helens Reporter*: *'In winning this championship for the third successive year, the Sutton Harriers' runners gave a perfect example of team running. Frank Aaron (Leeds) led throughout and won easily. Mick Maleedy was one of four runners racing together fighting for second place and only five yards separated them at the finish. Mick, still only 20 years of age, was 5th. Fred McMinnis, who had won the race at Sherdley Park twelve months earlier, never seemed happy through stomach trouble and was content to run 6th all the way, only to be passed near the finish and did well to finish 7th. Just behind came Sutton's next four runners Joe Harrison 8th, Tom Fillingham 9th, Bill McMinnis 11th and Alf Tyrer 12th. This wasn't because they waited for each other but through excellent teamwork, with each one making the running in turn. Ably supporting the winning six were Les Lamb 54th, in his first year with the club, and Ernie Henderson 112th, as reliable as ever.'*

The club's youngsters, lacking Tony Welton injured in a car accident, did well to finish in fourth place, whilst Bob Maleedy came 19th in the Junior event.

Next came the National Cross-Country Championships, held at Birmingham on March 12th, and - to quote the *St Helens Reporter* once more: *'What better way could any club find to celebrate their Golden Jubilee than by winning the highest honour in that particular sport in which they take part? Such good fortune befell Sutton Harriers when they won the National Cross Country championships at Birmingham for the third time since the club was formed in 1899. Before the race the fancied teams were Belgrave (Southern Counties), Tipton (Midland Counties) and Sutton (Northern Counties) and if anything Sutton were the most fancied team on account of their brilliant showing in the Northern Championships at York a fortnight earlier.*

Four hundred and fifty runners faced the starter and by the time the one mile stage had been reached the Sutton team, led by Mick Maleedy, running full of confidence, had the race in their pocket counting six in the first fifty runners and being backed up by Les Lamb and Ernie Henderson. A check of the team positions at three miles showed Sutton well ahead of anyone else and barring accidents, certain champions.

Mick Maleedy, Fred McMinnis and Tom Fillingham were all within striking distance of international selection at this point and it was a question of who was going to be the first Sutton man to finish. Just behind, Joe Harrison, Bill McMinnis and Alf Tyrer were putting in some real stout running. With one lap to go to the finish Mick Maleedy was running ninth and looked to be qualifying for the international team even though there was a bunch of runners together, most of whom had already represented England.

Although tiring in the last half mile Mick hung on to finish 7th followed by Tom Fillingham 14th, Fred McMinnis 22nd, Joe Harrison 23rd, W.McMinnis 24th and Alf Tyrer 30th completing the six counting team runners.'

It was a magnificent finish to a memorable season.

Saturday, 19th November 1949 was Novices' day at Sutton when 22 youngsters, all keen to make a name for themselves, lined up for the start of the race for over-sixteens in Sherdley Park. It was no surprise that the favourite, Tom Mcintyre, running very strongly over the last mile, finished first, followed by Alec Griffin 2nd and T Duffy 3rd. The under-sixteen race result was G Rothwell 1st, Bob Maleedy 2nd and G Charnock 3rd.

Events clashed the following Saturday. At Birmingham Fred and Bill McMinnis, Mick Maleedy and Tom Fillingham all contributed to the Northern Counties' victory in a cross-country match against Midland Counties and the Universities Athletic Union. Meanwhile the host club, Wirral AC, beat a necessarily weakened Sutton team into second place in a cross-country match in which Joe Harrison finished 2nd, P Batterly 7th, D Friar 9th, G Burke 12th, T McIntyre 14th, L Lamb 15th, R Ashley 17th, J O'Neill 22nd and G Hughes 23rd.

In the West Lancs Novices Cross-Country race, held at West Derby over a 4½ mile water-logged course a week later, Sutton's 'A' and 'B' teams finished in 2nd and 8th positions respectively and on New Year's Day 1950 Bill McMinnis again came third in the Morpeth to Newcastle Road Race.

Lancashire County Cross-Country Championships were held at Culcheth on January 7th and nine Sutton Harriers, each vying for county selection, dominated the senior race. Tom Fillingham, Fred and Bill McMinnis and Mick Maleedy were selected, with Joe Harrison as reserve. When the Inter-Counties Championship took place at Leicester, Lancashire were again the winners with Tom at 9th, and Bill 10th, being the third and fourth counters, Fred finishing 16th and Mick 48th.

With Sutton Harriers counting six in the first eight runners to finish, and their seventh man coming 9th, the club made sure of victory in the West Lancs Senior Cross-Country race at Runcorn on February 11th, where Liverpool Harriers once more beat the club's junior team into 2nd place.

Sutton's youngsters, who had shown individual promise in the Lancashire Championships Youths' race, closely contested the Youths' event at Runcorn only conceding first place to Liverpool Harriers by a single point.

Two weeks later came the Northern Cross-Country Championships at Horwich. It had been assumed that Sutton Harriers would complete their post World War II hat-trick and win the Senior event, which they did- with Mick Mick Maleedy 4th, Bill McMinnis 5th, Joe Harrison 10th, Tom Fillingham 12th, Fred McMinnis 14th and Jack Chidlow 26th being the team counters, supported by Tom McIntyre 44th and Les Lamb 49th.

But it was the youngsters who stole the limelight, for, as readers of the *St Helens Reporter* were told:

Sutton team captain Fred McMinnis receiving Northern Senior Championship trophy at Horwich in 1950

'*Ardent followers of the cross-country sport are accustomed to the Sutton team-work by experts of the McMinnis, Fillingham, Harrison and Maleedy class, but when mere boys of under 18 not only take a leaf out of their book but go one better, then it is something to talk about.*

As the first dozen runners finished, the Sutton contingent at the finishing post had given up hopes of winning as not one Sutton boy was amongst them. Then the finishing straight was filled with red and black jerseys as no less than five Sutton boys raced to the finishing post. Only four could count in the team race so it became devil take the hindmost. The judges had difficulty sorting out who was who but placed them 14th, 15th, 16th, 17th and 18th with less than a yard separating them all. This was a field of over 200 runners and at the end of a gruelling three miles course which included everything - plough, three jumps, grazing land and cinderpaths. Sutton's winning team was 14th R.Williams, 15th D.Wilson, 16th F.Griffiths and 17th D.Friar, supported by A.Griffin 18th.'

Even greater glory awaited both teams. Competing in the National Cross-Country Championships at Aylesbury on March 11th 1950, they proved Sutton Harriers were without doubt the country's premier cross-country club by adding victory in both the English National Senior and Youths' Championships to the club's long list of successes.

It was the first time any club had achieved a double victory in the English National Championships, and though the senior team had been the favourites their win by a total of 99 points nevertheless staggered the experts.

Having benefited from an overnight stay in Oxford, the Harriers had gone to

Sutton Harriers in close finsih when winning Northern Youths Championship at Horwich in 1950

Aylesbury very fit and refreshed, joining the field of 400 runners, a record number, who started in the senior race. At the end of the first two miles, when the runners had sorted themselves out, the red and black vests of the Sutton contingent were well to the fore and moving forward. It was clear that, whilst the individual title was plainly in the pocket of the reigning champion Dr F Aaron (Leeds St Marks Harriers), the real question was how many points margin there would be between Sutton Harriers and the second team. The struggle for this position lay between Shettleston Harriers (Scotland), Birchfield Harriers and Leeds Harehills.

The combined efforts of the Sutton team, who all ran to form, made victory possible, and after the race Mick Maleedy, who finished 11th overall, was selected as reserve for the forthcoming International Cross-Country Championship in Brussels. Fred McMinnis and Joe Harrison, coming in 13th and 14th respectively, just missed selection. The team results, having discarded individual runners who did not count in the team scores, were: - 1st, Sutton Harriers (M Maleedy 8th, F McMinnis 10th, J Harrison 11th, T Fillingham 21st, W McMinnis 25th and J Chidlow 67th), 142 points; 2nd, Leeds Harehills, 241 points; 3rd, Shettleston Harriers, 242 points. Sutton runners T McIntyre and L Lamb finished 105th and 108th.

The Sutton youths, who rose to the occasion and pulled that little extra out of the bag, kept up the high tradition of the club in winning the Youths' Championship. At one time they were well back, but in the last mile or so they put in a lot of hard running to take the title from two other northern clubs - Winton Harriers and Liverpool Harriers. J Williams (Salford Harriers) took the individual title, thus making the race an all-northern triumph. The team positions for Sutton were:- R Williams 9th, D Wilson 11th, D Friar 16th and A Griffin 40th, the remaining Sutton runners being G Rothwell 51st, R Maleedy 93rd and E O'Brien 178th.

At the next meeting of St Helens County Borough Council on April 5th the then Mayor, Councillor E Price, made immediate reference to Sutton Harriers' prowess in the National Cross-Country Championships. His suggestion that the appropriate committee might consider what official recognition could be given the Harriers for having brought honour to the town met with general agreement.

Having acquitted themselves quite well in the West Lancs Novices Cross-Country race at Lancaster on December 2nd 1950, achieving 23rd and 26th positions, a week later, on December 9th, T Dearden and Ron Maleedy, plus Brian Parton, were only beaten by Bolton United Harriers, hosts of an inter-club event, when they finished 7th, 5th and 9th respectively in the youths' race. On the same occasion, Sutton's senior team - minus Jack Chidlow and Bill McMinnis, in training for the Morpeth-Newcastle race on New Year's Day, and Joe Harrison with an injured arm - nevertheless finished second, again to Bolton.

Following the Lancashire Cross-Country Championships, held at Childwall on January 6th, 1951 on a course part ankle-deep in mud and snow and with 70 contestants, Bill McMinnis won county selection together with Tom Fillingham, who was appointed team captain. Fred McMinnis and Jack Chidlow were to be second and third reserves. Victory was Lancashire's for the third successive year when the Inter-Counties Cross-Country Championship took place at Aylesford, Kent, on January 20th. Bill finished 13th and, as captain, Tom, though not one of Lancashire's six counters, had the privilege of receiving the trophy.

A recruiting appeal in the local press led, on February 3rd, to a club 2 miles cross-country trial in which a youths' team was beaten by recently joined 14-16 year olds.

When the West Lancs Cross-Country Championships took place at Moreton (Wallasey) on February 10th victory for the club in the Senior event was expected and accomplished - Sutton's counters occupying 2nd, 3rd, 4th, 5th, 6th and 7th positions! Quite unexpected was that Gerald Burke, G Hughes, Don Friar and John Orrell would become the Junior Champions.

Then, on February 24th, at the Northern Counties Cross-Country Championships at Gosforth Park, Newcastle (where in contrast to 1947's arctic conditions the weather was splendid), Sutton Harriers' senior team did it again! They won the Championship for the fifth consecutive year. Thus, having won it in 1939 and with no war-time races, the shield had been in the club's possession for twelve years. Moreover, with Bill McMinnis 7th, Joe Harrison 8th, Fred McMinnis 15th, Mick Maleedy 16th, Jack Chidlow 19th and Tom Fillingham 20th, Sutton Harriers won with a record number of points, their nearest rivals being Rotherham Harriers whose total was 114 points higher. Indeed, with Les Lamb 41st and Tom Mcintyre 50th, had Sutton counted eight men to every other team's six they would still have been victors.

Fortune also favoured Sutton's young recruits who, with Jimmy Doyle 4th, Ken Mather 8th, G Price 9th and T Charnock 15th, won the Boys' Championship. Less successful were the club's youths' and junior teams, whose members however, excelled themselve in the coach on the way home with their entertainment over the microphone.

The following week Bill McMinnis won the RAF Cross-Country Championship with Don Friar 28th, earning Bill selection as captain of the Combined Services' team to compete against North, South and Midland Counties at Sheffield. Joe Harrison was selected for the Northern Counties team.

On Tuesday, March 13th, readers of the *St Helens Reporter* were told:

'SUTTON HARRIERS ARE STILL CHAMPIONS

Sutton Harriers, English National Cross-Country champions, completed the hat-trick by retaining their title at Richmond, Yorkshire, on Saturday, 10th March 1951. Four of the five postwar races have been won by Sutton. On the other occasion at Sheffield in 1948 they were placed second and then only by 20 points. Five runners out of the six runners on Saturday have run in all of those events. The popularity of Sutton's win was shown at the presentation of trophies when they were cheered by their rivals from all over the country.

At the beginning of the race a disaster almost overtook Sutton. They were lined up just before the start in "Indian file" when Jack Chidlow had to make an adjustment to the lace of his shoe. While he was bent down the gun went and with half of the team in front of Jack and half behind it was a real scramble for the back half. Away they went with Jack still bent down tying his lace. Many an athlete would have considered the position hopeless but not Chidlow. Giving the whole field almost 100 yards start, he ran through the field of runners to finish in 51st place, sixth man for the Sutton team - a truly great performance.

At the end of the first lap Mick Maleedy was in the first dozen with Fred and Bill McMinnis and Tom Fillingham all together around the 25th position whilst Joe Harrison was just behind in the thirties. Sutton held their positions on the country lap after leaving the racecourse section and at this stage Sutton had five runners in the first twenty-six places as a result of strong running by Joe Harrison. On the last lap Mick Maleedy dropped back slightly to finish 18th with Joe Harrison 19th, Tom Fillingham 22nd, Bill McMinnis 36th, Fred McMinnis 37th and Jack Chidlow 51st completing the team.'

With neither Bill McMinnis nor Joe Harrison running, Jack Chidlow at 13th was the best placed Sutton Harrier in the Lancashire Cross-Country Championships on January 5th 1952, so that for the first time since 1947 the club had no representative in the Lancashire team for the Inter-Counties Championship.

A month later, however, at the West Lancs Cross-Country Championships held at Sherdley Park, Sutton Harriers could be justifiably proud of their achievements for they successfully defended their Senior title, won the Youths' event, finished second in the Junior and came third in the Boys' event. Proceedings started with the Boys' race and the strong field soon strung out with Les Laithwaite (Sutton) and Adams (Wirral) in the lead. After the lap in the country the runners had one lap of the starting field to cover before the finish. It seemed as though the Wirral boy was going to prove too strong for Laithwaite, but he made his effort too early and Les ran in a comfortable winner. The team race was won by Liverpool Harriers, 26 points, followed by Wirral AC, 33 points, and Sutton Harriers third with 52 points. Most of Sutton's team were new to championship running and put up a very creditable performance.

In the Youths' race there were two laps to complete and although Sutton had no-one in the first three places, their packing was good enough to beat the opposition. Ken Mather ran particularly well and was backed up by Sid Heesom, Jimmy Doyle and Brian Parton to score a total of 50 points, ahead of Liverpool Harriers and Waterloo Harriers, who both had 56 points.

Sutton's juniors, D Friar, J Hendry, G Hughes and Ron Maleedy, ably supported by G Carberry, who lost a shoe halfway through the race, came second.

As expected, Sutton won the Senior title again, but Wirral fought hard to try to bring about Sutton's first defeat in this event since the war. Sutton's team , W McMinnis 2nd, J Chidlow 5th, Bob Maleedy 6th, J Harrison 8th, T Fillingham 9th, F McMinnis 13th, (a grand effort considering he was still troubled with an injured ankle), scored 43 points. Wirral AC were second with 63 points and Sefton third with 110 points.

At Port Sunlight, on February 23rd 1952, Sutton's senior team's post-war reign as Northern Counties Cross-Country champions came to an end when, with 170 points, they finished third to Manchester AC (110 points) and Bolton (112 points). Even so, their first six men, Bill McMinnis, Joe Harrison, Jack Chidlow, Mick and Bob Maleedy and Tom Fillingham, were home before both Bolton and Manchester AC's sixth counters.

With J Hendry 20th, D Friar 29th, G Hughes 31st and G Carberry 32nd, Sutton's juniors also finished third - their packing being a delight to see. The youths' team came in fourth, led by Ken Mather in 14th place, and the boys' team were eighth in their race, with Les Laithwaite in 8th position.

Two weeks later, at the National Cross-Country Championship in Birmingham, Bill McMinnis's achieving international status by being placed 12th was Sutton's only good news. From early in the race it was clear that on the fast hilly course there would be a large total of points for whoever managed to win, and with Mick Maleedy well back through a twisted ankle Sutton's six counters with 394 points could only manage 6th position. Ken Mather did well, finishing 15th in the youths' race, but the team was unplaced.

Eleven Harriers took part in the Lancashire Cross-Country Championship at Liverpool on Saturday January 3rd 1953 in ideal conditions, overnight frost having hardened the fields and made the going fast. About 120 runners started in the senior seven miles race and Sutton's first to finish was Bill McMinnis whose 8th position should have guaranteed his selection for the Inter-Counties Championship. However the Lancashire County selection committee departed from precedent by selecting two Bolton runners, both internationals, despite their not being fit to run at Liverpool. In previous years the committee had refused to pick men who did not qualify through their performance in the county championship race - making it hard to understand why Bill was overlooked - particularly as he had been an international the previous season, and three weeks earlier had finished in front of one of the two in a cross-country race. Thus, for the second year, Sutton were unrepresented in the county team.

On the other hand, according to the *St Helens Reporter's* account: *'It was a good day for Sutton Harriers on Saturday 7th February 1953 at the West Lancashire Cross-Country Championships with three of their four teams returning as victors. They won the Senior, Junior and Youths' races, missing out in the Boys' event. However, Sutton's Boys' team member J.C.Pearson finished second, and gained a medal awarded to the first runner to finish whose team does not figure in the first three teams.*

In the Youths' race Sutton won without extending themselves. Ken Mather 4th, Jimmy Doyle 5th, Eddie Edwards 8th, and Les Laithwaite 16th, were the team counters, supported by Brian Parton.

As expected the Junior team also won. Ken Crouch ran a fine race to finish 2nd. George Carberry 4th, Don Friar 5th, and John Carberry in 11th position completed the team counters. Ron Maleedy, 13th, and Bert Holland, 35th, also ran.

What a surprise we received in the Senior race with Alf Tyrer, running his first championship since 1949, finishing 19th, sixth counter for Sutton, a considerable performance seeing that he won his first West Lancs medal 26 years ago in 1927 and is now 40 years old. Bill McMinnis won the race with Fred McMinnis 3rd, Jack Chidlow 5th, Mick Maleedy 9th, Tom Fillingham 18th, just a few yards ahead of Alf Tyrer. Others to finish were Tom Mcintyre 20th, Bob Maleedy 31st, Dick Howden 50th and Jimmy Bott.'

Having travelled along the Snake Pass on Saturday February 21st in thick mountain mist and with evidence of recent snowfalls lying around, Sutton Harriers were surprised to enter Sheffield, the venue for the Northern Counties Cross-Country Championships, in beautiful spring sunshine.

On a course consisting of springy turf for most of the lap, but with many hills to test the runners' stamina, Sutton did well. The senior team, which gained third place, again included Alf Tyrer, who with Tom McIntyre finished in the 80's, Sutton scoring six being Bill and Fred McMinnis, Bob and Mick Maleedy, Jack Chidlow and Tom Fillingham. With the same counters as in the West Lancs Championships, the club's youths team gained second place, whilst the juniors finished sixth.

When the National Cross-Country Championships took place at Reading on 7th March 1953 Sutton Harriers' senior team, so dominant during the years 1947-51, could only finish 7th, a position worse than the previous year's 3rd place. In the absence of Tom Fillingham and Alf Tyrer through illness and injury, Ken Crouch offered to run, instead of competing in the junior race and the opposition proved too tough for him. Individual placings were Bill McMinnis 19th, Fred McMinnis 45th,

Bob Maleedy 69th, Jack Chidlow 81st, Ken Crouch 93rd and Mick Maleedy 107th. The youths' team managed to keep the Sutton flag flying by being placed third, the team being Ken Mather 25th, Eddie Edwards 39th, Jimmy Doyle 56th and Les Laithwaite 59th. However, the junior team, minus Ken Crouch, had to be content with fourteenth position with G Carberry 62nd, J Carberry 75th, D Friar 100th and Ron Maleedy 132nd.

Although the junior team, Ken Crouch, George Carberry, Sid Heesom and Ken Mather, finished 3rd in the 1954 Northern Cross-Country Championship and 4th team in the National Cross-Country Championship at Arrowe Park, Birkenhead, the major cross-country successes they had enjoyed in their 'golden days' after World War II now eluded Sutton Harriers. Their teams only had minor success in Liverpool and District and West Lancashire Cross-Country championships and in 1960 they failed to have a runner in the National. The only individual successes were in 1958 when Bert Tebb gained selection for the Lancashire team for the Inter-Counties at Trentham Gardens, by finishing 8th at Leyland in the Lancashire County Cross-Country championship, and in 1960 when Bob Meadows also gained selection for Lancashire

Jimmy Bott

Jimmy Bott had joined Sutton Harriers in the late 1940s. Although both legs had been broken earlier in his life, he was nevertheless to become a most consistent and eager member of the Sutton Harriers' squad. For him, winning was not really important: taking part was his only concern. His interest in and dedication to all activities was an object lesson to other club members.

Jimmy was popular not only within his own club, but with other club members in the East and West Lancashire areas (examples of this were Salford, Manchester Athletics Club, East Cheshire Harriers, Pembroke AC (Liverpool) and Wirral AC.

He was the perfect clubman who always turned up for all events on the calendar where Sutton Harriers were competing. This included training sessions. These qualities were recognised at the Clock Face Colliery Sports, during 1950 when he was presented with a special cup for his athletic endeavours by Fred McMinnis, Club Captain, Lancashire County, and English International.

Jimmy Bott was Sutton Harriers' sportsperson of every year, for whom the club motto 'From the acorn grew the mighty oak' was true. This really was a man with a heart as big as the said mighty oak.

A SUPPORTER'S RECOLLECTIONS

In 2001 Allan Morris, a lifelong Sutton supporter, recalled the club's National Cross-Country successes he had witnessed as a teenager half a century earlier. *'I had been told by my father how my grandfather, Jimmy Morris, was one of the original Sutton Harriers and was the captain of the winning team in 1906 when they won the National. My father was the chairman of the club in 1947 and in his younger days had also run for Sutton.*

I was 14 years old when Sutton won the National in 1947 for the second time; that winter was a very severe one with heavy snowfalls. Some teams could not reach the venue and did not compete, so the win was a little devalued.

The next year, 1948, I accompanied my father, Myles Morris, to Sheffield to watch the National. The individual winner was the famous miler Sydney Wooderson and Sutton came second. The winners may have been Blackheath Harriers. I think the Sutton six that counted were Bill and Fred McMinnis, Tom Fillingham, Mick Maleedy, Joe Harrison and Alf Tyrer.

The start of the National was very spectacular, each team (ten runners to a team) lined up one behind the other with as many as five hundred runners starting the race. The course would be about three miles, with the youths doing one lap, the juniors two laps, and the seniors running three laps.

I was also a spectator in 1949 (Castle Bromwich), 1950 (Aylesbury), 1951 (Catterick), Sutton winning on all three occasions. 1951 saw the emergence of Gordon Pirie, the media's favourite for the junior title, but he was beaten by Walter Hesketh of Manchester Athletic Club to the delight of us northerners. Jack Chidlow had replaced Alf Tyrer in the six counters in these later years.

1952 was again in Birmingham. I think it was Perry Barr, with Sutton failing to add to their previous success.

The first ten runners to finish gained automatic selection to run for England in the International races, I think Bill and Fred McMinnis, Tom Fillingham, and Mick Maleedy achieved this. For such a small club all this was quite remarkable and I do not think the people of St Helens appreciated how good the Sutton Harriers were.'

Sutton's Golden Five

Tom Fillingham, 'Clubman I'

Begun formally in December 1936, when he was elected to club membership, Tom Fillingham's association with Sutton Harriers continued until his sudden death in December 1981.

A joiner by trade, Tom had attended Rivington Road School, where during 1935 he not only captained a very successful athletics team but also represented England Schoolboys at Rugby League.

Initially too young to compete in the club's youth teams in the cross-country championships, Tom revealed his prowess when he took part in, and won, the handicap section of the Rivington Pike Fell Race in March 1937. The following autumn he was allocated the 7th leg for the Manchester-Blackpool Road Relay. In 1938 Tom was a member of the Sutton Harriers' team which won the West Lancs Youths' Cross-Country Championship and competed in the Northern; whilst the following season he was the individual winner of the West Lancs event.

Unsurprisingly, in view of the comradeship which typified the club, linking the generations, Tom was joined in membership of Sutton Harriers both by his workmates and by his father and uncles. The older Fillinghams ably supported the club events and served on the committee for several years. In 1954 Tom's father, by then a vice-president, was appointed a life member in appreciation of his past work. This was an honour that had already been bestowed on another supporter-parent, Mr McMinnis, father of Bill, Fred and Eddie.

Wartime service interrupted what would certainly have been a successful period in Tom's athletic career, but upon the resumption of competition in 1947 it was Tom, who, leading Sutton Harriers to victory, himself won the West Lancs Senior Cross-Country Championship. He finished 3rd in the Northern Cross-Country Championship and 11th in the English National Cross-Country Championship, thereby gaining selection as a reserve for the International Championship in Paris.

In this and the following four seasons he was a member of the Sutton Harriers' team which dominated cross-country running, with four wins in five National Championships and a clean sweep in the Northern and West Lancs Championships. He represented Northern Counties in 1947/48/49 and Lancashire in 1948/49/50/51, being captain in 1951 when they won the Inter-Counties Cross-Country Championship at Aylesford.

On the track Tom was a regular member of the club's two-mile team which had many successes at the various athletic meetings in the north of England.

By 1949 Tom had joined the Club Committee, on which from 1950-3 he served as Assistant Secretary. Doubling the roles of Chairman and Treasurer 1956-7, he remained in the latter post almost continuously until 1972. Under the pseudonym 'Clubman' he became the club's press correspondent, providing the local newspapers each week with details of Sutton Harriers' activities and achievements (details which have greatly contributed to this volume).

Tom's joinery skills and work contacts (post-war he was employed by the electricity board) contributed much to his fellow Harriers' welfare. Thanks to his guidance and efforts, their initially grim quarters at the Powder Yard were rendered tolerably comfortable. It was he who submitted the plans for the Green Hut at Chester Lane for council approval - and simultaneously as Treasurer was ensuring that solid timber building could be financed.

Considerate at all times and to everyone (a photo shows him in heavy rain sharing his 'brolly' with a very junior member) Tom Fillingham was indeed a clubman.

Joe Harrison

A stalwart of the Sutton team which dominated cross-crountry running between 1947 and 1951, Joe Harrison was first recorded as participating in athletics when he ran in a 100 yards event at Pilkington Recs Sports on 9th July 1932. He had just turned sixteen.

Joe ran both track and cross-country for Pilkingtons, (where he was employed as a beveller throughout his working life) until World War II and service in the Royal Navy intervened.

1946 found him demobbed and running again with Pilkingtons, until in December he joined Sutton and became one of that illustrious quartet of runners - the others were Tom Fillingham, Fred McMinnis and Bill McMinnis - who were members of all the Sutton Harriers' teams which in 1947, 48, 49, 50 and 51 won both the West Lancashire and the Northern Counties Cross-Country Championships, and were the English National Champions in 1947, 49, 50 and 51, and came 2nd in 1948.

During this period Joe won many prizes on the track, in 880 yards and one mile races, as well as in the two mile team events, and in 1949 he was selected for Lancashire to compete in the Royal Ulster Constabulary sports in Belfast.

Joe missed the 1953 cross-country season through injury and from then concentrated on running long distance on the road, his first race being the Windsor to Chiswick Marathon in June 1954 when he finished 18th in 2 hours 37 mins 29 secs. Running in the London to Brighton 50 miles Road Race in 1956, he was struck a glancing blow by a taxi at a roundabout early in the race, injuring his shoulder. He continued and completed the distance, after feeling thirsty in the later stages and calling in a public house in Brighton for a pint before carrying on to the finish.

He seemed to enjoy these long distance races. In 1958 he came 2nd in the London to Brighton race and ran it again in 1959, and that same year first took part in the Liverpool to Blackpool 48 mile Road Race. Entering this for a second time in 1960 Joe finished 5th, and in 1962 he came in 4th. In 1959 he was selected to compete for Lancashire in the Inter-Counties 20 miles team race in Victoria Park, London.

Fred McMinnis and Joe Harrison running together in the Liverpool Pembroke 20 miles road race.

Just to show his versatility he competed for Lancashire during the summer of 1957 in a walking race!

A year after his elder brother, Bill, had joined Sutton Harriers and their father, too, had become a club supporter, Fred McMinnis, an all-round athlete, became a member during the winter of 1937-8. The following season he was one of the club's senior team which won the Northern and came third in the National Cross-Country Championships, and on the track won Lancashire selection for the three-mile event.

Like his four brothers and four sisters he had been brought up in Bronte Street, Newtown, St Helens. Here the McMinnis family's next-door-neighbour was Miss Nellie Cruise, who would eventually become head of Knowsley Road Infants' School, but was then an infant teacher at Rivington Road School, which she ensured all the McMinnis children entered. At that time Rivington was an all-age school, and, apart from their brother Ernest who passed the scholarship examination for Cowley Boys' School, the McMinnis children all remained there until they reached the school-leaving age of fourteen.

The family attended Newtown Congregational Church nearby, where Miss Cruise was in charge of the Sunday School, which ran a host of weekday activities, organised by Mr Stanley P Jones. These included snooker, billiards, rambling, drama (the Newtown Players originated from this, with Mr Jones their first president), the Band of Hope, football, cricket and athletics. Fred, also a keen cyclist, took part in many of the activities offered. Both left-handed and left-footed, a gift which was developed to an outstanding degree, Fred would surely have graduated to representative class in one or more of these sports but for the outbreak of hostilities in 1939.

Fred served in the Royal Navy during the war, and was wounded in one skirmish with the enemy in the Mediterranean. Having returned to civilian life he renewed contact with Sutton Harriers, and by December 1946 had won selection by Northern Counties to compete against a Universities Athletic team.

Teasing clubmates claimed that Fred, a town-centre window cleaner, trained and maintained his stamina by climbing up and down ladders. They enjoyed being told Tuesdays were his favourite working days - spent making pristine the windows at Greenall's brewery, and thereafter being invited to quaff their finest brew.

His achievements prove Fred's prowess in cross-country running. Not only was he a member of each of the Sutton teams that won both the West Lancs and the Northern Counties Cross-Country Championships each year from 1947 to 1951, but he himself won the West Lancs in 1948 and both championships in 1949 - each time over a 9 mile course. One of the counting six in all of Sutton's victories in the National Championships (1947, '49, '50 and '51), Fred came in 10th in 1950 and was 11th in 1948, when the club had had to be content with second place.

Selected for Lancashire in the Inter-Counties Cross-Country Championships in each year 1948 to 1951 Fred also represented England in Liege (Belgium) in 1948. There he ran against the redoubtable Emile Zatopek (Czecholslovakia), who was later to revolutionise thinking on training schedules for distance running.

Over the five-year period 1947-51 Fred McMinnis was a regular member of the club's 2 miles track team which won many races at various athletic meetings throughout the north of England, some times competing twice in the same afternoon, at different venues, for example in Liverpool and then in Manchester. On several occasions this team were invited to compete in the Birchfield Harriers' Waddilove Trophy at Perry Bar, Birmingham, where they came up against some of the best two-mile teams in the British Isles.

Fred won two one-mile races in Manchester in 1948 and at the Chester Autumn Sports in 1950 helped Sutton carry off the first three places in the Chester Five Mile, coming second to his brother Bill, and with Tom Fillingham in third place. It was Fred's turn to win the race in 1951, and in 1953 he came second to Ken Gates (Liverpool Pembroke's cross-country international) in the Lancashire County 6 miles Track Championship.

At his first attempt at the Liverpool City Marathon in 1954, Fred was forced to drop out in the later stages. However, the following year his successful completion of the couse helped Sutton to victory in the team race.

It was later said of Fred McMinnis that he was the right man in the right place at the right time - and from 1948-57 that place was as Club Captain. Thereafter he served for many years as Club Chairman. That he was elected to these posts for so long must be attributed to his popularity, sincerity and steadfast devotion to Sutton Harriers.

Bill McMinnis

Bill McMinnis seems almost to have begun his running career in the cradle. As a schoolboy at Rivington Road he ran for places in his class and school rugby teams. He held his own in Sunday School sports and relay races. Runs to Billinge and back from his Newtown home, sometimes propelling a hoop along the traffic-free roads, were holiday pleasures, and as a junior wage-earner , delivering groceries, he'd happily return at speed on two legs from Eccleston Park via Taylor Park rather than use public transport.

Enjoying sports, he played football and cricket with church teams and then, having begun work in the family window-cleaning business, he was to be found at Ruskin Drive at night in company with Jock Johnson and Sonny Doyle (who both went on to become first class Rugby League players), Tom and John Rimmer. All the youngsters were given encouragement by William Worsley, a senior Northern Counties official.

1936 was the year of the Berlin Olympics, and, enthused by Ernie Harper's performance in the Marathon, Bill joined Sutton Harriers that autumn - determined to emulate Ernie and not realising how long that might take.

He entered a world peopled by Harriers such as Sammy Salmon, Bill Glover, Jim Forshaw, Eddie Stubbs and the Club President, Jimmy Morris. Soon, at Norman's Lane he became accustomed to the Morris Pavilion's muddy bathwater, topped with coal dust, and to Walter Massey's harsh massaging hands, and Billy Brough's softer ones. Bill's potential was swiftly recognised, and he was immediately held back from other events to be able to compete in the West Lancs Novice Championship in Earlestown - an event for those who had never won a prize of any description. Luck was against Bill. Snow started as the race began. Conditions worsened and the officials abandoned the race at the end of the first of its two 2½ mile circuit laps, to avoid mishap to any inexperienced competitors.

Advised by Jimmy Morris that he needed to wear more than a singlet, Bill came by one of his most cherished possessions - a well-worn Harriers shirt given him by Jimmy Morris. By 1951, that shirt had taken part in the Harrier's five National victories!

By Boxing Day 1936 Bill had graduated to Sutton's senior team and won his first medal. Within three months he had helped the club win the West Lancs Senior event and its first-ever Northern Senior Championship, and taken part in the National Cross-Country Championship at Stratford-upon-Avon. Here the team came in third on a course which had included a foot deep water splash 100 yds long on each of its three laps.

Still unlucky in the National, Sutton again won the West Lancs in 1938, and in 1939, by which time Bill had been joined in the senior team by his brother Fred, the club enjoyed their second victory in the Northern Senior Championship.

The advent of war in September 1939 drew Bill into the Royal Air Force as a volunteer, where he became transformed into a PT instructor - toughening up the recruits. It was a service he would remain in until 1959, having become a regular at the end of the war. Chances to run were rare till in 1941 Bill was stationed at RAF Skegness. Forming the 1 mile part of the unit's track team Bill got his first silver cup in a RAF championship at Uxbridge. On leave occasional runs with Sutton were possible. Once, in Manchester, Bill ran against Sidney Wooderson who was in an Army team, and Bill had the satisfaction of finishing in front of him.

Then it was overseas - by troopship from Stranraer to an unknown destination, which turned out to be Bombay. Bill, now a flight-sergeant, became part of a medical mobile unit (shades of MASH ?), which, having reached the border with China and Nepal, gradually moved south through Burma's jungles as the Japanese forces retreated - eventually reaching the recently re-captured port of Rangoon.

Moving on from one impromptu airfield to the next (with Bill's jeep also his bedroom), the group's role had been to tend casualties awaiting air-lifting back to India and, in idle moments, to air-drop ammunition, food, clothing, mail and other supplies to otherwise isolated fighting units.

Now, herded from Rangoon on to a small cargo ship, the unit sailed south as part of a mighty flotilla intent on regaining Malaya. Suddenly, however, Bill's combat duties were ended by Japan's surrender, following the destruction of Hiroshima and Nagasaki by atomic bombs.

Unpleasantly familiar with dysentery, an almost 'normal' part of jungle life, Bill, now back with the RAF in the UK, succumbed to a serious attack of gastro-enteritis, rapidly losing weight and strength. Though re-invigorated after sick-leave Bill, now 32, felt himself too old to run again. However, in November 1946 Tom Fillingham, his pre-war Harrier team-mate, successfully nagged Bill into having a go. Still weak from the enteritis he ended his first training run by being walked in by Jim Forshaw.

Four months later Bill helped Sutton Harriers' tiny team to victory in the National Cross-Country Championships at Apsley. He had become a vital member of the club team that between 1947 and 1951 was to win four National, five Northern and five West Lancashire championships, and finishing 12th in the National in 1952 Bill won himself an English cross-country vest.

Within a year of the Apsley success Bill was representing the RAF in Group Command and Inter-Services teams at cross-country, track and road events, and whenever possible was running with Sutton at weekends. A physical training instructor, usually based at RAF Padgate (Warrington) Bill turned his daily journey between there and his home at Pewfall, some six miles away, into a valuable training opportunity by running it in each direction.

Long-distance running attracted and suited Bill. Be it taking part in road-relays, road races or marathons, his recollections are vivid ... *'Finchley 20 miles - in a leading group of about 8 one character forced me onto the pavement and then proceeded to moan about my foot in the kerb as it was a road race. This bellyaching annoyed me, so I went on the win the race in record time.'* ...

'Macclesfield 10 - one year it was a very slow time because a herd of cows blockd the road and runners had to find a way through.'...

Then there was being 'greeted by "boos" entering Anfield to win a Liverpool marathon - football spectators didn't like my RAF blue vest.'

In 1974, Bill, approaching sixty, completed two legs in the clubs's 75th Anniversary St Helens to London Relay. Norman Ashcroft successfully tempted Bill back into running and into veterans' events that in Toronto in 1977, at the first Veterans'World Athletic championships, Bill won the over-sixties 5000 m track, the 10,000 m track and the 1000 m cross-country World Championships. Within the next five years Bill crossed the continents and won seven world championships after which, having fulfilled his ambitions, he duly retired.

Blessed with longevity, and a lively memory, Bill has contributed much to this volume - vividly recalling athletic personalities and events over more than seventy years, and especially those concerning Sutton Harriers, whose Club President he has been since 1989.

Alf Tyrer - My Grandad

I am one of eight grandchildren of Alfred Tyrer, and due to circumstances I spent most of my time living with Grandad. During school holidays and at weekends at least five grandchildren would be at Toll Bar house (in Collins Green) and Grandad would take us for walks over the fields. We used to go to the Collins Green pit slack heaps. We called this the mountain. This was one of several walks, mostly taken on a Saturday afternoon before tea. Each time was like an adventure to us.

Most Sunday mornings Grandad would take us out in the car. We would go to Ainsdale beach, Hatchmere Lake in Delamere forest, Irlam baths and many other places. I can remember Grandad never having to tell us off, and never saying, 'Don't do that' etc.

I can't list all the things Grandad did for us. There are too many. He taught us to ride our bikes and when we were good enough to go fast on our own he would run alongside us, but we could never get in front of him.

When I got old enough to question Grandad about his running years I was interested and eventually put together his album 'Captured moments of an international Athlete'.

A couple of years ago I was talking to Ste, a lad from Collins Green who is about 15 years older than me. He told me that when he was a teenager he and his friend used to pass Toll Bar and when near to the house they used to torment Alf's dog. 'One day Alf seen us', he said, 'and told us to stop'. They gave him back chat and said, 'Come on then', thinking he would never catch them at his age, but Alf went speeding along the main road and caught them at the bottom of the lane. Ste recalled, 'We didn't know Alf had been an international runner for Sutton, for England. We was shocked when Alf was standing there waiting for us.'

In 1937 Alf was in a one mile track race organised by Manchester City Police Sports Club in Fallowfield, Manchester. The first prize was a display cabinet donated by the chief constable. Grandad told me he had entered mainly for the experience. There was a policeman entering the race, PC Scholey, from Huddersfield. Scholey, tipped to win, had come to the race in a police carrier van. Alf asked why had he come in a van. Someone said, 'To take home the first prize, the display cabinet'. In some cases, Grandad told me, he needed motivation to try harder. This was one occasion. Thereafter, the cabinet sat in Alf's living room displaying other trophies and prizes.

In 1939 Alf won the Rivington Pike Fell Race. It was a tough race and he had entered it about 3 times previously before winning. Alf had been talking to an ex-fell runner a few weeks before. Alf couldn't remember who it was but he gave Alf a tip and said, 'Don't try too hard on the way up'. Alf put this into practice, but he said, 'Runners were passing me, coming back down 30 yards before I got to the top: but when I got to the top I had lots of energy left and could jump down steep parts of the course instead of scrambling down them. I eventually passed the front runners to win.'

I'd like to mention Alf's best friend Jim Forshaw, who accompanied Alf to most of his Sutton Harrier meetings, actively helping and supporting the Club.

Tony Ashcroft

Following Sutton Harriers' success during the 1947 cross-country season the club were invited to host the Northern Counties Cross-Country Championships. They accepted and planning began with an Extraordinary General Meeting in October 1947, held, as the club had no HQ, at East Sutton Labour Club.

As Sherdley had never previously been a venue for the Northern much forethought was needed to ensure all went well. Everyone co-operated. Apart from detemining the actual course, decisions were needed on direction signs, car parking, changing facilities for competitors, sorting out programmes and tickets, and providing refreshments.

Experienced senior members were invaluable. Bob Maleedy was made Chief Clerk with Sammy Salmon and Jimmy Woods as his assistants. Ernie Owen and Arthur Dixon became Programme Stewards and Mr Fillingham and Alf Fillingham (Tom Fillingham's father and uncle) Competitors' Stewards, whilst Jim Forshaw and Arthur Fillingham (another uncle) formed the Refreshments Sub-Committee.

Problems were solved. Former RAF huts in Sherdley Park could provide changing facilities - with coal for boiling water and emergency lighting being provided by S Salmon and R Maleedy respectively. Meanwhile a request was made to the Director of Education to have Robins Lane School premises available as a standby. This was granted and the school premises used.

Printing went ahead:- 1000 programmes, 1250 admission tickets (to be on sale by January 17th), 750 competitors' tickets and 50 result sheets - with cardboard promised for the judges' cards.

Mr Knapper was asked to be starter and Joe White to tackle the announcing. Five more competitors' stewards were appointed:- H Shacklady (a TA sergeant at the Engineers' Hall on Croppers Hill pre World War II, and years later a Club Vice-President), Peter McGovern, Jim Moore, Arthur Williams and Horace Green.

Gatemen, essential to ensure that only ticket holders were admitted, were to be Fred Marsh, Bob Bridge, Wilfred Tyrer, Frank Tyrer and Bill Burrows. Clerks of the Course, whose job it was to direct the runners around the course, were named as Billy Lee, William Burrows, E Appleton, B Long, E Bailey, A Perry, H Elliott and W Bannerman.

The club became old hands at handling championship events. By 1985, Sherdley Park had nine times been the venue for the West Lancs Championships. The Lancashire Championships took place there in 1963, whilst in 1969 the club again hosted the Northern Championships. Competitors on that occasion long remembered the vast white towels and abundant hot water (even for the stragglers !) at Sutton Manor Colliery, their changing place.

Thus, having accepted the invitation to stage the 1986 Northern Cross-Country Championships, planning for that great day started in earnest in August 1985. The championships constituted such a big event that the club set up a sub-committee of five officers to co-ordinate the operation. Many meetings were held in various places, the most favoured being the home of the Club Captain, Frank Rimmer, who supplied varied refreshments and an invitation to the Mason's Arms after the meeting.

There had been changes at Sherdley Park since the Northern Championships were first held there in 1948. Gone were the park's high surrounding walls, gone, too, the World War II huts and rifle butts. The creation of a golf driving range and the municipal golf course necessitated modifications to the cross-country circuit, carefully mapped out for many of these occasions by Allan Moore and measured by Joe White and Frank Costello. Sutton High School had been built near the intersection of Eltonhead and Marshalls Cross Roads - but still lacked its promised all-weather track. Nearby, in

Chester Lane, lay Sutton Harriers' much improved clubhouse.

In the run-up to the Championships the whole club got involved as usual, along with the St Helens MBC Leisure Department. The Sutton Harriers' clubhouse and Robins Lane School were used for changing and presentations. On the day, the event went very well and was enjoyed by both competitors and spectators. The club was congratulated by the Northern officials at the presentation, and by many of the northern clubs that took part.

The success of the Northern Cross-Country Championships and the popularity of Sherdley Park resulted in an invitation to Sutton Harriers to stage the English Schools Cross-Country Boys' Championships in 1988, with the building of the course as the main task for the club to concentrate on. Some of the local clubs helped with other responsibilities, and the St Helens Education and Leisure Departments assisted by fencing off various part of the park and allowing the use of the Sports Hall in the Leisure Centre for the presentation.

Once again, on the day, the whole club came together to deliver an event that ran smoothly - much to the satisfaction of the club members, the competitors and the spectators, and congratulations to Sutton Harriers, especially on providing the finest course ever seen, were given by members of the English Schools Committee.

Among My Many Memories

Battling through blizzards to get to some Cross-Country events - on one occasion the team bus going straight across a traffic island because of fog and snow restricting visibility.

The back seat of coach always reserved on way back from major championships because Mick Maleedy would be ill after 'giving his all' to get international honours.

Meeting up with rest of youth team at the Savoy Cinema after competing on the Saturday afternoon, most of us jumping up with cramp at some time in the performance much to the amusement of other patrons.

The accelerator pedal cable of my van snapping when transporting the girls' cross-country team to Rawtenstall with the girls having to run the last half mile to the venue.

Roy Ashley

During Christmas 1957 I was working for the Post Office sorting parcels. On the Saturday afternoon the Harriers had their Christmas Handicap race. I managed to get away for a short time and won a large box of chocolates. When I got back to the sorting office in Copperas Hill I took the box in with me in one of the mail sacks. There were a group of young ladies near to me who were sorting letters. During a lull in the sorting I took the chocolates round. One of the sorters, Sylvia, was a student from I.M.Marsh, the P E college. We got talking a arranged to meet after our shift of work.

Two years later we were married. So the Harriers have many fond memories for me.

Bert Tebb

Jim Forshaw is remembered by Gratton Pursell as 'the guy who insisted you wore a newspaper between your vest and shirt whilst running to keep the cold out. Gratton recalls the club's post WWII base at the East Sutton Labour Club in Ellen Street as having 'no amenities, but plenty of Elliman's Athletic Rub. Still treasured, his first medal was actually donated by Alf Tyrer, the Club Captain, and had been inscribed 'News of the World - my first success'.

Chapter 4

AROUND THE TRACKS, 1947-1962

Following their great cross-country achievements in the winter of 1947, and despite being so few in number, Sutton Harriers went on to enjoy a very successful track season. They dominated the two miles team races throughout Merseyside and Lancashire, with any four of the five runners Bill McMinnis, Fred McMinnis, Tom Fillingham, Mick Maleedy or Joe Harrison, and this domination continued over the five year period 1947-51. Success was also gained in Yorkshire and the Midlands but Birchfield Harriers did manage to beat them at Rochdale and at Bradford Police Sports during 1948.

Fred McMinnis won the one mile event at two Manchester meetings and was placed in three others whilst Mick Maleedy had two wins over the same distance at Pilkingtons and Earlestown Viaduct. Tom Fillingham also had a couple of one mile wins and at Liverpool & District Track Championship won the one mile and three miles events. Meanwhile, Bill McMinnis represented the Combined Services against AAA , running the three miles in the Olympic Games trials meeting at the White City, London.

A young athlete, Tom Hackett, although at a teachers' training college near London, joined the club whilst home during his 1947 summer vacation and performed well in 880 yards races, even though basically a sprinter. During the following year he showed potential over 440 yards with some very good performances against international athletes. Another newcomer was John Orrell, who came 2nd in the club's 16-18 Novice Race in November 1947 and was 2nd reserve for the Manchester/Blackpool Road Relay in 1948.

With a wise eye to the future Sutton, at the AGM in September 1947, formed a special section for boys 14-16 years of age. Membership thereby increased and with this the numbers competing in the 1948 track season.

In 1949, therefore, there were successes for Sutton Harriers at various meetings in events other than the two mile team races. Joe Harrison showed his versatility by winning the 880 yards at Leigh and a number of one mile races, which earned him selection for the Lancashire team to compete at the Royal Ulster Constabulary Sports, Belfast. This meant travelling overnight by boat from Liverpool, competing, then typically after the meeting returning to Liverpool for work the next morning.

A sprinter from Cheshire, Ted Ashley, came to prominence by winning the 100 yards and 220 yards at Dunlop Sports, Speke, and continued to have success. Junior member John Orrell was successful over 880 yards and newcomer Eddie Balmer in the 220 yards. Mick Maleedy had another good season in one mile, two mile and three mile events.

The publicity following the cross-country successes and the civic recognition of the club in 1949 attracted new members from local schools, which had revived their annual schools sports, and young runners joined Sutton Harriers despite the club not having a regular training facility until a cinder track at Allanson Street School in Parr was made available in 1951 for summer use.

At the many meetings during 1950 Sutton athletes, notably Mick Maleedy, Tom Hackett, Austin Tipping, Ted Ashley, Joe Harrison, Les Lamb, John Orrell and Tom Mcintyre, were amongst the prizes, as were the juniors Eddie Balmer, Don Friar and Tommy Ryan. In the St Helens Youth Sports, Sutton Harriers' juniors, both boys and girls, were always prominent in track and field events, with Jimmy Doyle and Frank Carlton the best of the boys. The best of the girls, Barbara Billington,

Margaret King, Margaret Astell and Rose Wheeton, all showed promise of achieving success in open competition.

The Youth Sports were organised by the Education Department of the St Helens Council, under the directorship of Mr N F Newbury, for boys and girls between the ages of 15-19 to ensure that continuity was provided for youngsters who wished to participate in athletics. Winners and runners-up at these sports were selected to represent St Helens in the Inter-Town Sports promoted by the Liverpool and Cheshire Youth Activities Council.

Group Photograph at Ruskin Drive, St Helens in 1950

The 1950 Lancashire County Senior Championships were held in early June in Liverpool. Sutton were well represented in the track events and, although looked upon as a cross-country club they gave evidence of their growing track strength.

Tom Hackett provided the big surprise of the day by upsetting the favourite, E Holderness (Salford AC), the 1949 Northern Counties 440 yards champion. Not long out of the army, Tom certainly shook everyone present with his strong running to win in a time of 50.9 secs. Meanwhile, in the one mile Mick Maleedy, whose form had continued successfully during and since the cross-country season, ran a great race to finish second behind international Alan Parker, whilst Tom Fillingham showed flashes of his cross-country form in running 3rd in the three miles event. A surprise winner in the 220 yards was Austin Tipping, who later in the year joined Sutton. On the same afternoon Ted Ashley was only beaten by inches in both the 100 yards and 220 yards events at the Cheshire County Championships at Port Sunlight.

The following week, at the Lancashire Junior Championships, Ken Friar won the high jump. At the All-England Schools Championships, held at Port Sunlight, the under 15's 440 yards Championship was won by Jimmy Doyle.

The Chester Autumn Sports, held at the Roodee Racecourse each August Bank Holiday Monday, always attracted a large crowd because of the carnival atmosphere within the grounds and the two major events - the Chester Five Miles Championship, run over five laps of the racecourse, and the straight 220 yards. In 1950 Sutton athletes won both these events, Bill McMinnis the five miles and Tom Hackett the 220 yards. These, ironically, linked the cross-country and track sections of the club. There was in fact a Sutton clean sweep in the five miles because Bill was followed by his brother Fred and Tom Fillingham in 2nd and 3rd places respectively.

With training sessions under way at Allanson Street School, the beginning of the 1951 track season saw two Sutton athletes in the Lancashire team for the Inter-Counties Championships at the White City Stadium, London, over the Whitsun Bank Holiday. Austin Tipping was selected to run in the 220 yards and Tom Hackett the 440 yards, with Mick Maleedy reserve for the three miles. Alas, Tom Hackett had to withdraw through injury.

In the Lancashire County Championships at Salford Tom Hackett retained his 440 yards title and Austin Tipping (220 yards) and Bill Elliott (shot) both finished third in their respective events. Ted Ashley had an excellent sprint double in the Cheshire County Championships, winning the 100 yards

in a new championship record time of 10 secs as well as the 220 yards, and at Leigh Police Sports Sutton had their first-ever relay championship success when the team of Tom Hackett, Austin Tipping, Norman Vose and Eddie Balmer won the Lancashire County 4x440 yards relay Championship.

Austin Tipping won the Civil Service 220 yards for the second year in succession and was 2nd in the 100 yards, whilst in the RAF championships Bill McMinnis won the three miles event.

Fred McMinnis, Bill McMinnis and Tom Fillingham at Chester Sports in 1950

Ged Hughes started the 1951 season with a number of places in various one mile events. Ted Ashley, Austin Tipping, Tom Hackett, Don Friar and Phil Burrows were successful at various athletic meetings, as also were the junior members Alan Troilet, Jimmy Doyle and Keith Graville.

Following the tragic accident on Snowdon which took the life of John Orrell, a memorial meeting was held on Tuesday, 12th June 1951, in which the newly-instituted Memorial Mile for the John Orrell Cup was won by Jimmy Doyle.

At the Chester Autumn Sports, Fred McMinnis won the five miles race around the racecourse, having finished 2nd the previous year behind his brother Bill.

John Orrell

I first met John Orrell when we were both members of Whiston Youth Club, an excellently organised society which I look back on with great affection. This was during the war years. (1940s)

At this time I was playing football for the youth club, and Prescot Guild Hall. I already knew of John's prowess as an athlete. The youth club organised a road race (for members only) around the perimeter wall of Halsnead Park , a distance of approximately 3 ¼ miles. I was down to run, but on the day I was laid low by a heavy cold. The race was won easily by John Orrell. I would have been content with a minor place.

However the 'bug' had bitten, and from thereon John and I had long conversations on athletics. John invited me to go to Sutton. This had to be placed on hold due to my having to fulfil another more serious engagement, two and a half years' National Service in His Majesty King George VI's forces. Whilst serving, I met Bill

Tom McIntyre and John Orrell in walking gear

McMinnis when we were both competing at RAF Cardington. I introduced myself to Bill, and mentioned John Orrell. He, too, invited me to join Sutton Harriers which I eventually did in 1949.

My association with John grew, and we trained, ran, and talked for many a happy hour. John was a member of the YHA (Youth Hostels Association), and soon afterwards I also joined. We went on many wonderful hikes together,

sometimes with Frank Neal and John Murphy, two other Harriers. On one occasion, John and I were lost in heavy hill fog on Kinder Scout, Derbyshire. It was with the help of our faithful compass we found the solace of Edale. Sunday mornings were special, five to seven mile runs over the fields and roads of Rainhill and Whiston.

John Orrell (2nd) and Tom McIntyre (3rd) in the 880 yards at Ruskin Drive

John Orrell was a very generous, kindly, lovable person. After attending Whiston Central School (now demolished) he served his apprenticeship to become a cabinet maker. It was whilst working at Furlows at Huyton Quarry that he became friendly with Marjorie Huxley. Both loved the 'open air', and they did much walking together.

On 10th February 1951, John was a member of Sutton's team that won the West Lancashire Junior Cross-Country Championship at Wallasey. Six weeks later during the Easter weekend he was walking with Marjorie 3000 feet up on Snowdon when a blizzard started. They decided to start a descent when they encountered a patch of ice. They slipped and fell over 300 feet. John, who was carrying Marjorie's kit, was killed and Marjorie sustained a fractured skull. The fall was seen by scouts from Dublin and they went to the couple's assistance. The scout troop split into two groups, one to assist the walkers and one to get stretchers. Colin Hinton, leading the scout party, semaphored a message for help; Rover Scouts S Malloy and R King ran the two miles to Llanberis to get the rescue party; the others lifted Marjorie from an icy stream and kept her warm until help arrived.

In many of our conversations, John had touched on his athletic ambitions for his 21st year. He informed me that he intended to concentrate on the one mile, not the half mile. A few weeks later, after John's untimely death, I conveyed his thoughts to Mr and Mrs Orrell. They told me about their plans for a memorial race, to be competed for each year by members of Sutton Harriers.

Thus was instituted the John Orrell Memorial Mile Handicap, a one mile race to be held as near as possible to John's birthday, 11th June, and for which a trophy was presented to the club by Mr Frederick Orrell and Mr J H Orrell (John's father and uncle). Arrangements were made for a meeting at Allanson Street, Parr on Tuesday 12th June 1951 and also incorporated into the meeting were sprints for seniors, juniors and ladies. The first winner was Jimmy Doyle, a junior athlete who the previous year had won the All-England Schools 440 yards Championship, and for many years afterwards the other prizes at this event were generously provided by Mr and Mrs Orrell.

Ken Wilcock with the John Orrell Trophy in 1952 wearing the official Sutton Harriers blazer

Tom McIntyre

On Thursday May 1st 1952 evening training at Allanson Street School began again. Held between 7pm and 9pm each Tuesday and Thursday, it was well attended, with many juniors taking part in the organised sessions.

One of the early meetings was the Lancashire County Senior Championships at Stanley Stadium, Fairfield, Liverpool, but Sutton's only success was Austin Tipping's 2nd place in the 440 yards. Harry Johnson, who had joined from UGB, ran well in the 100 yards, winning his heat to reach the final but was unplaced. At this time Tom Hackett was attending Carnegie College and won four events at their sports. Another successful sprinter who hit the highlights was Chris Frodsham by winning the 100 yards in the Liverpool University Sports and then the 100 yards in the Christie Championships for Liverpool, Manchester and Leeds University students. Meanwhile, Ken Friar won the 120 yards hurdles at Fallowfield in the Northern Counties Schools Championships.

Austin Tipping was selected to run for Lancashire in both the 220 yards and 440 yards in the Inter-Counties Championships at the White City Stadium, London and a few weeks later finished fourth in the 440 yards when competing for Lancashire at the RUC Sports, Belfast. He and Tom Hackett continued to produce fine performances throughout the summer, picking up prizes at various sports, as did Bob Maleedy in the one mile events. Tom Hackett won the straight 220 yards at the Chester Sports again, having previously won it in 1950.

It was however the juniors who had a tremendous season, starting at Bradford Police Sports when Ken Wilcock, Frank Carlton, Harry Eden and Jimmy Doyle won the Junior 880 yards medley relay against some of the best teams in the north. Ken Wilcock and Jimmy Doyle dominated the junior 880 yards events at meetings throughout the district. Being placed in every race they formed a formidable pairing. In the final track meeting of the season at BICC Helsby, Ken Wilcock, although a junior, turned out in the Senior 880 yards which he won, and it was interesting to see the final of the Senior 440 yards handicap involving Tom Hackett, Austin Tipping and the junior Ken Wilcock. Ken finished 3rd, but Tom and Austin, the backmarkers, found their handicaps too much.

The young members had many successes on the track and in field events at the Youth Sports and Inter-town competitions at Fazakerley (Liverpool) and Widnes, both events being won by St Helens. Frank Carlton showed his all-round ability in sprints, hurdles, jumps and throwing events in the 15/16 years group and John Davies did likewise in the 17/20 years group in the 440 yards, high jump, shot and discus events. Later in the year Frank signed professional forms for St Helens Rugby League Club and had a very successful rugby career.

Sutton's success on the track and field gave encouragement for the future, with so many good youngsters within the club having benefited through training at Allanson Street.

A floodlit meeting at Bolton on Easter Monday opened the 1953 track season. The floodlights were like streetlights sited about thirty yards apart so the runners other than in the finishing straight were rather ghostlike, but nevertheless the spectators enjoyed an excellent meeting. Austin Tipping recorded a convincing win in the 100 yards invitation against good opposition in bad conditions. In the Junior 880 yards medley relay the Sutton team of Jimmy Doyle, Harry Eden, Adrian Johnson and Ken Wilcock ran well to finish a close second behind a very strong Bolton United Harriers team.

At the Lancashire County Athletic Championships, held at the Liverpool Passenger Transport Ground, Knotty Ash, in a half gale and on a waterlogged grass track, Sutton Harriers gave the opposition a lesson in team spirit and co-operation by winning the Senior 4x110 yards relay, the team being Tom Hackett, Phil Burrows, Chris Frodsham and Austin Tipping, and also, with Tom Hackett, Norman Vose, Keith Graville and Austin Tipping, the 4x440 yards relay, which they had won the previous year. In the individual events Fred McMinnis finished 2nd in the Senior six miles Championship. There were no winners in the Junior championship events, although Ken Wilcock was 2nd in the 440 yards and Jimmy Doyle 2nd in the 880 yards.

This series of caricatures of Sutton athletes and officilas was drawn in in 1953

The following week at Salford, Austin Tipping won the Senior 220 yards Championship and was 2nd in the Senior 100 yards event, whilst the Junior team of Jimmy Doyle, John Davies, Adrian Johnson and Ken Wilcock won the Junior 4x440 yards relay Championship.

The Northern Counties Junior Championships were held on Saturday, 4th July 1953 at Woodbank Park, Stockport, and the only Sutton entrant was Ken Wilcock who travelled by public transport unaccompanied and, having to race heat, semi-final and final, won the 440 yards in the fast time of 51.9 secs, which entailed having to avoid a shot that had rolled into his lane during the race. The Sutton Senior team, Tom Hackett, Phil Burrows, Chris Frodsham and Austin Tipping, finished 2nd in the Northern Counties AAA 4x110 yards relay, behind winners Lincoln Wellington.

Although Sutton had many runners competing during 1954 in the weekly athletic meetings, only eight members competed in the Senior and Junior Lancashire Championships at the White City Stadium, Manchester - a disappointing turnout since this meeting provided the best opportunity for all members, especially juniors, to gain valuable track experience.

Four did reach the finals of their events:- Austin Tipping was 3rd in the Senior 100 yards, Tom Hackett 3rd in the Senior 440 yards, ahead of Ken Wilcock, 4th, and in the Junior 220 yards Tony Howard gained 4th place. Two weeks later at the Northern Counties Senior Championship, Sutton's representatives performed well without obtaining any honours; the nearest being Austin Tipping who finished 4th in the 440 yards.

It was left to the relay teams to gain the honours that season, though in the Lancashire 4x440 yards

Relay Championship the Sutton team of Keith Graville, Tom Hackett, Ken Wilcock and Austin Tipping failed to retain their title and finished 3rd. However, at this same meeting the one mile medley team of Tom Hackett, Austin Tipping, Chris Frodsham and Ken Wilcock were the winners, marking the start of a successful period for Sutton in this event.

At the Northern Counties Junior Championships at Ruskin Drive, St Helens, the programme included the two Senior relay races. The first event was the one mile medley race but, as Phil Burrows had not realised that the event was to be held early in the meeting, Sutton only had three members of the team present prior to the start and they had to extract Dave Pointon from the crowd. He had only intended to watch but fortunately had brought his kit with him as he was included in the list of reserves. However, the team - Tom Hackett, Austin Tipping, Dave Pointon and Ken Wilcock - won the race for the first time in the club's history. Later that same afternoon Phil Burrows, Chris Frodsham, Tom Hackett and Austin Tipping won the 4x110 yards relay title in a new championship best time.

Northern Counties Senior One Mile Medley Relay Championship winners in 1955. Phil Burrows, Tom Hacket, Ken Wilcock and Austin Tipping with Jack Burke (Secretary)

The 1955 Lancashire County Championships saw Tony Howard win the Junior 100 yards in a very close finish at the White City, Manchester, but in the Senior 220 yards Austin Tipping was surprisingly beaten into 3rd place. Earlier, he had been 4th in the Senior 100 yards. Ken Wilcock, having moved up to the 880 yards event, as a result of good performances in the one mile medley races the year before, was placed 3rd in 1 min 56 secs, a time which beat the previous championship record. Tom Hackett, competing in the Senior 440 yards, won his heat convincingly with the fastest qualifying time, but he had to return to Liverpool to supervise a PT demonstration at his school, St Edward's College. He hoped to be back in time to compete in the final, scheduled for 5.30 pm, but failed to arrive and the event was won by Harry Connor (Liverpool Pembroke) in 50.8 secs a time well below Tom's best.

In the Northern Counties Senior Championships, Sutton's only success was Ken Wilcock's 3rd position in the 880 yards in 1 min 54.3 secs, in a race which broke the previous championship record. Austin Tipping was 5th in the 220 yards, but Tom Hackett did not qualify for the 440 yards final after only finishing 4th in his heat.

Sutton's hopes were high when they travelled to Staveley (Derbyshire) to compete in the Northern Counties Senior Relay Championships, both of which they had won the previous year. In the one mile medley relay Tom Hackett (440), Austin Tipping (220), Phil Burrows (220) and Ken Wilcock (880) won very convincingly, but unfortunately the sprint relay 4x110 yards team were disqualified due to a faulty baton exchange. However, the one mile medley team went on to win at three separate meetings, including at Widnes, when Tony Howard and Ted Ashley had to be drafted in to replace the unavailable Tom Hackett and Austin Tipping.

As a result of his performances in the 880 yards events Ken Wilcock was selected to run at Manchester Police Sports in an Invitation 880 yards race won by Tom Courtney (the USA athlete who the following year became Olympic 800 metres champion), with Ken finishing in 3rd position. He also was selected to run 880 yards against Czechoslovakia at the White City, Manchester, in October, and despite not having competed for six weeks, recorded a creditable time of 1 min 56.9 secs to finish 5th, behind established international athletes who all ran the following year in the Melbourne Olympics.

The 1956 season started with Ken Wilcock being selected by Lancashire for the 440 yards event in the Inter-Counties Championships at the White City, London, over the Whitsun Bank Holiday weekend, with Tom Hackett (440) and Austin Tipping (220) reserves. Ted Ashley was selected by Cheshire for the 100 yards event. Later, in the Lancashire Championships at Finch Lane, Liverpool, Austin Tipping was 2nd in the 220 yards and Ken Wilcock 3rd in the 880 yards. Tom Hackett failed to qualify for the 440 yards, being only 3rd in his heat.

The Northern Counties Championships at the White City, Manchester, saw Austin Tipping finish 2nd in the 220 yards behind the Great Britain international, and AAA champion, George Ellis. Ken Wilcock battled into 4th place in the 880 yards with a time of 1min 56.5secs but was unfortunate to be baulked in the finishing straight by an illegal runner who, although beaten in his heat by inches for the qualifying spot, thought himself good enough to run in the final and joined the race some distance after the start. Gordon Yale was 3rd in the Junior high jump and it was good to see a medal being gained in a field event.

In the Northern Counties Senior relay championships held at Port Sunlight, Sutton's one mile medley team could not make it three wins in a row, and finished 2nd after Austin Tipping injured a muscle during his run. A weakened team competed in the Lancashire 4x440 yards at Manchester and Roy Ashley, Mike Stafford, Phil Burrows and Ken Wilcock finished 2nd, only a yard behind the winners. A team entered in the AAA 4x440 yards relay for the very first time finished 5th in the final. After qualifying comfortably in the heats, Sutton then had the misfortune of Austin Tipping, running first, having a recurrence of a thigh injury he had suffered at the same Port Sunlight track three weeks earlier. It was as much as he could do to hang on to complete his relay leg. Ted Ashley and Phil Burrows fought hard to reduce the gap and Ken Wilcock just failed to catch Achilles and Belgrave Harriers who battled out 3rd place.

Austin Tipping and Ken Wilcock were in the Lancashire team against Yorkshire at Bradford and thanks to Austin, who won the 220 yards to gain the points in the last event, the match resulted in a draw. Ken also competed for Lancashire in an Inter-county match at Rugby and was selected by Northern Counties for the Inter-region match against Southern Counties and Midland Counties at Wolverhampton, which was televised by ITV in one of their first live outside Saturday afternoon broadcasts.

1957 was a rather flat year with Austin Tipping and Tom Hackett not competing and Ken Wilcock, although producing good 880 yards times, appearing to be more suited to 440 yards, a distance at which he was never beaten during the season, recording times that would have been good enough to win championships. Gordon Yale achieved the club's only success, finishing 3rd in the Lancashire Junior High Jump.

Up to this time, an athlete could usually attend around fifteen sports meetings from early May until September. However, by 1958 many of these had been replaced by scratch meetings and representative matches, because spectators were becoming used to seeing top athletics on television and wanted to watch live the best athletes in competition. This resulted in very few handicap meetings remaining, until they ceased to be held at all by 1960. To ensure competition was available, Club Captain, Ken Wilcock, arranged for a full range of early season inter-club track meetings to be held at regular intervals when Allanson Street track became available at the end of April. These meetings would involve Sutton and two other clubs and proved to be a great success. On one occasion the high jump took longer than anticipated and could only be completed by using the headlights of a car shining on the equipment and landing pit, thus enabling the athletes to jump safely.

Sutton's only championship success during the season was through Ken Wilcock winning the 440 yards in both the Lancashire County Championships at Blackburn, in record time, and the Northern Counties Championship at the White City, Manchester. He also competed in the 880 yards for the North against South and Midlands, finishing 6th in a fine time of 1min 51.6 secs, which convinced him to concentrate on the 440 yards event for the future. As a result of these performances Ken was awarded the Blair Trophy as Liverpool and District Outstanding Athlete for 1958, the first Sutton athlete to win the award.

A group of Sutton members at Ruskin Drive in 1960. Hubert Wilcox, seated second from right, returns after 50 years

Open graded meetings at Port Sunlight and Warrington formed the early competition for the 1959 season which saw Ken Wilcock (440 yards), Joe Harrison (20 miles) and Gordon Yale (high jump) selected for the Lancashire team for the Inter-Counties Championships at White City, London. Ken Wilcock again won the 440 yards in the Lancashire County Championships at Ruskin Drive, St Helens, but was only second in the Northern Counties 440 yards Championship when drawn in the outside lane. Austin Tipping and Tom Hackett resumed competition in inter-club matches but after a couple of seasons of not competing, together with the injuries they had sustained playing rugby for West Park, their racing edge was missing.

Peter Priestner had a very good 1960, running on the road. He won both the Cheshire 20 miles and Marathon titles. Over the Whitsun Bank Holiday weekend Ken Wilcock competed in Holland, twice winning the 400 metres - at Groningen, and on grass at Zwolle, the following day - each time creating a new track record. After this he won the Lancashire County 440 yards for the third consecutive year, in a new championship record time, and then the Northern Counties 440 yards Championship. He had an excellent run in the AAA Championship 440 yards, recording the fifth fastest time in the heats, but finished 3rd in his heat, with only two runners qualifying from each heat. A regular member of the Lancashire team during the summer, he finished the season with a terrific performance by being placed 2nd in the 440 yards at an international invitation meeting at the White City, Manchester, on 30th September, 1960. After leading the 400 metre Olympic champion Otis Davis (USA) and other internationals into the final straight, he was overtaken by Davis to be beaten by only five yards.

As a result of his performances during the 1960 season

Ken Wilcock winning the 440 yards for Lancashire in an inter-counties match at Cowley Girls School, St Helens in 1960

Ken Wilcock was rewarded by selection to represent AAA against Cambridge University in May 1961 in the 440 yards, which he won in 48.2 secs, equalling the track record held by the great Jamaican athlete Arthur Wint. This was followed by his winning the Lancashire County 440 yards Championship for the fourth successive year, and retaining his Northern Counties 440 yards title, both in new championship record times. In between these successes he was second in the Inter-Counties 440 yards Championship at the White City, London. A number of good performances for the Northern Counties and Lancashire followed, which set him up for the AAA championships, and despite an outside lane he finished third. As a result of this he was included in the list of runners for the 4x440 yards relay in the Great Britain v USA match the following weekend, and the Great Britain v Hungary match over the August Bank Holiday weekend, but did not run in either although placed fourth in the 440 yards rankings. However, he was selected for the Great Britain and Northern Ireland team to visit Germany and Poland in September 1961 and made his international debut against Poland in Warsaw in the 4x400 metres relay, running the second leg. Selection for the England team against Russia followed, but of the five selected for the 4 x 440 yards relay Ken was only the reserve on the night.

During the AGM on Thursday 21st September 1961 at the *Bull and Dog Hotel*, Sutton, a presentation by Sutton Harriers of a pair of starting blocks was made to Ken Wilcock to mark his selection to run for Great Britain against Poland in Warsaw. The fifth Sutton Harrier to be honoured since 1946, he was the fourteenth club member to gain international honours over cross-country, road or track since the club's formation in 1899, and only the second to represent Great Britain up to this time, the other having been Bill McMinnis in 1955.

Early in 1962, in the hall above at the Gas Showrooms, St Helens, Ken Wilcock was again presented with the Blair Trophy - this time as Liverpool and District Outstanding Athlete for 1961. The event was followed by the film *Athletic Highlights of 1961*.

After competing indoors at RAF Cosford where he won the 440 yards, Ken was invited to take part in the first indoor meeting at the new indoor track at Wembley Stadium. This was sponsored by the Daily Herald and incorporated the Great Britain v West Germany match. In the invitation 440 yards (there was no 440 yards in the match), Ken won a narrow victory.

Ken Wilcock being presented with the Blair Trophy from NCAAA President George Warburton surrounded by Sutton Harriers Officials

When the 1962 track season started three weeks later, Ken ran a couple of representative matches for the AAA and was selected for the Great Britain team to compete at the relay trials in Stanley Park, Blackpool, as preparation for the European Championships later in the year. For the fifth successive year he won the Lancashire County 440 yards and for the third consecutive year the Northern Counties 440 yards, both in new championship record times, but between these races he again finished second in the Inter-Counties 440 yards Championship, narrowly beaten when clear favourite. (Sadly, the winner David Brown (Middlesex), serving in the RAF, was killed when his plane crashed on the way to Aden five days later.) An hour after this race Ken won an international 440 yards in the outside lane in the considerably faster time of 47.6 secs. A magnificent double representing AAA in the 220 yards and the 440 yards at the RUC meeting, Belfast, and coming 2nd in 47.6 secs at the Inter-area match for the North in the 440 yards set him up for the AAA championships. Running in the outside lane, he finished 3rd in 47.2 secs behind Robbie Brightwell, who broke the UK all-comers, National, AAA and European records. The following week he finished 2nd to Adrian Metcalfe (Yorkshire) in the Inter-County match 440 yards in a personal best of 47.1 secs.

Selection for the Great Britain team against Poland at the White City, London, on the August Bank Holiday weekend followed and Ken ran the second leg, with the team winning the 4x440 yards relay. The following week Ken kept his place in the team in the relay trials for the European Championships. A good run at the British Games, (second in 47.8 secs) confirmed his fine form and he was selected for the Great Britain team to compete in the European Championships as a member of the 4 x 400 metres relay, and reserve for the 400 metres.

At the European Championships in Belgrade in their heat of the event, Ken, running second leg took over in fifth place and pulled the Great Britain team into first place for the other two members, Adrian Metcalfe and Robbie Brightwell, to finish the race as heat winners. The final saw the first runner Barry Jackson give the team the lead ahead of Germany, but as Ken Wilcock came to his handover to Metcalfe he lost the lead to the German runner. Unfortunately Ken had not noticed Metcalfe was not in the fifth lane, where Britain had been drawn, but on the inside. The German, Manfred Kindermann, attempted to hand over to Metcalfe who brushed him aside, seized the baton from Ken Wilcock and sprinted hard round the first bend, cutting inside the German third leg runner, and handed it on to Brightwell in second place who managed to come up to the German fourth leg runner, Manfred Kinder. Inches separated them at the finish in Germany's favour.

Two weeks later Ken ran for England against Finland at the White City, London in the 4x440 yards. This proved to be his last competitive race, as he was overlooked for the England team for the Empire Games in Perth, Australia, the selectors opting for a 880 yards runner to complete the 4x440 yards team together with the 440 yards selection. Ken was again awarded the Blair Trophy as the Liverpool and District Outstanding Athlete for 1962.

During this season Bob Meadows had a winning treble in the Royal Navy Championships in the one mile, three miles and six miles. It was also good to see that two youngsters, Maurice Rylett and John McLoughlin, were showing promise in various inter-club meetings after having had a successful cross-country season.

A Harrier looks back along the athletic track

For me, grammar school days were war days (1939-46) when the older teacher, who had not been called up to fight and who cared, struggled to provide some sporting opportunities for his pupils with little help or equipment, although one acknowledges that the provision for cricket was first rate for those of us who showed ability and enthusiasm. Athletics consisted of the annual Sports Day: running, of course, the hurdles over canes and the field events: throwing the cricket ball and the high jump (over a weighted rope). The running track was the pegged outfield of the rugby pitch, five laps of tufty grass.

So 'Athletics' had to take place outside school and we were fortunate that Pilkingtons Glassworks, which dominated St Helens' industry, provided extensive recreational facilities for bowls, tennis, football and cricket at Ruskin Drive, although only a small percentage of employees used them. The cricket field was beautifully manicured all over and its outfield gave us a running track which was a joy to feel beneath our feet and for the price of three (old) pence a visit we got the opportunity to use the palatial dressing rooms and showers.

Morever, it provided a forum for fitness seekers to meet: schoolboy runners, emergent club runners from Pilkington Recs AC, some of the Sutton Harriers in their off season and the odd 'Saints' rugby player doing a spot of fitness training in the summer. Importantly, it was here on notice boards that one could pick up information on what seemed like something new: athletic meetings which mentioned words like prizes and handicaps and secretaries to write to. I wrote to one or two, like Earlestown Viaduct and UGB and found myself designated as 'unattached' in the progamme, whereas others had the name of an athletic club beside their own.

I was away in a Teachers' Training College near London during 1946 - 48 but was a frequent visitor to Ruskin Drive in the vacations and it was during this time, about summer 1947, that I was approached by Harry Wilson who, though never in a pair of shorts, was a very enthusiastic Secretary of Sutton Harriers. He seemed to be trying to extend the scope of the nationally well-known club by adding an athletic section and asked me if I would like to join. Having been enormously impressed by the prodigious work rate of one of their members, Joe Harrison, who trained regularly at Pilkingtons, and having got to like his reserved and humorous manner, and being flattered by the invitation, of course I accepted it. Harry Wilson was employed by Mr Stubbs, a well-known estate agent with offices at the bottom of North Road and President of the club, who had in his London days run for London Polytechnic.

Among my earliest recollections of being a member of the club team was travelling by train to an athletics meeting at Perry Bar, Birmingham, with some of the Harriers of the club, for with the growth in number of such meetings they could extend their running season from winter cross-country events to track running where many of them ran in half-mile and one-mile handicap races as well as in two-mile team scratch events. This was the first time I met Bill McMinnis, very handsome with his sun-tanned face and in his RAF sergeant's uniform and I remember being embarrassed during the return journey when, in discussion, he referred to youngsters like me being 'the future of the club', perhaps because I had run second in the 440 yards that afternoon to Tom White, one of Britain's three representatives in the 1948 London Olympic 800 metres. A few weeks earlier in the London Inter-College meeting, I had run second to a student from Borough Road College, named Roberts, who was one of the three 400 metres' representatives - a poor second in both cases, I must add. Surely of all triumphs which the athletic section of Sutton ever achieved, Bill's victory in the AAA Marathon must rank as the greatest and with all his other achievements must make him the most distinguished member of Sutton Harriers in all its proud history. Indeed, with his other victories in marathons he could credibly claim to be St Helens' athlete of the century despite the 'men of steel' who have graced Knowsley Road.

Still, possibly because of Bill's RAF commitments which kept him from most of the meetings in which I competed, it was his brother Fred who impressed me most at that time: so forthright, strong, courageous he seemed (and most of the Harriers at that time seemed to share these qualities, so necessary in their chosen sport - give me the pain which lasts for a minute or two, not their seemingly masochistic torture which sometimes lasted for at least half an hour and up to three hours). I can remember Fred having to run his leg in the Manchester to Blackpool Road Relay Race (about six miles) suffering from a bout of stomach trouble and diarrhoea and clutching a toilet roll: such loyalty to his team, such courage, such inconvenience! But I am convinced any one of the Harriers would have done the same, such spirit did they have, and it was difficult to live up to them; although the youthful and talented Mick Maleedy was very successful over cross-country and track, one feels sorry for him having to meet their challenges! It is a real pleasure now to have my memories of acquaintance with cheerful Tom Fillingham, the dry-witted and generous Joe Harrison, the McMinnis brothers, Jack Chidlow and others, all well supported by the smiling and hardworking back-room boy, Jack Burke. A team they were and a proud club they represented wholeheartedly. They deserved their national success if only for their willingness not to let each other down.

A few weeks after leaving college I watched the whole of the athletic events of the 1948 Olympics at Wembley. Such a treat must have somehow been within the range of a student's pocket then and I camped out on the Thames bank (skinny dipping in the river at midnight) and in the cricket pavilion of the college I had just left, sharing the whole experience with Bob Toothill (whose younger brother Fred ran for Sutton Harriers) and another friend from college. They saw me off on the bus from Richmond about midnight on the last Friday: they stayed to watch the closing ceremony of the Games while I left to run in the Junior Rugby League Sprint Championship at Clock Face the next day. (I did have a Phelps Cup runners-up medal for playing for Pilkingtons' Juniors against Glovers' Ropery on the Saints' ground at Knowsley Road). It was the only meeting, to my knowledge, run at Clock Face but I am glad I missed the closing ceremony, for the Rotary watch I won lasted me for more than thirty years.

We would have rebelled against any taunt of 'pot-hunter' levelled against us and we certainly would have run for points or the honour and glory of Sutton Harriers, but there is no doubt that the prizes that were to be won in those days provided some measure of incentive for us. Every summer Saturday seemed to have its athletics meeting and there were even one or two in the evenings, so fiercely did promoters guard their Saturday dates, as well they might, for people came in their thousands to pay for admission to these events. I am not sure that the concept of PR was in vogue at that time but these events must have been of some such benefit to the organizations which promoted them. The Police were prominent sponsors and organizers of handicap meetings in Liverpool and Widnes as well as St Helens, all doing something for the youth of the community. Firms such as Pilkingtons, Liverpool Transport and Dunlop, Speke, also ran meetings, as did local councils especially in year of the Festival of Britain, 1951. The City of Chester held a particularly grand spectacle on the Roodee Racecourse, a very large area by the river Dee, which was preceded by a colourful and very long procession of city dignatories, entertainers, exhibitors and competitors in the many events which took place on August Bank Holiday

Monday every year. Thousands of people thronged the city, making it very difficult to pass from one end of the main thoroughfare to the other, watching the procession wend its way down to the Roodee.

It was possible to survey the whole field below from the elevated roadway on the City side of the field. Packed into one spacious corner of the vast arena were the competitors in morris dancing, horse jumping, character and fancy dress, side by side with exhibitions by body builders, weight lifters and model aircraft flyers, as well as brass bands, sideshows and roundabouts. And all that was before

Tom Hackett winning a straight 220 yards at Chester Sports in 1950

and during the athletic events. The finishing post for all running races was directly in front of the County stand and the Tattersall stand and both of them would be packed, although seats would cost up to 5 shillings, at a time when my teacher's take home pay was £21 something per month (20 shillings = £1). These Chester Autumn Sports had one unique feature (in my experience): because the running track was part of the horse racecourse it could easily accommodate a 220 yards race run in a straight line (the 'straight 220' as it was known). Winning it early in the l950s, I remember feeling very strange, as though it went on for ever.

To safeguard our amateur status (pause for hollow laughter), the value of 1st prizes could not exceed 7 guineas (£7.35), and the 2nd and 3rd prizes 4 and 2 guineas, respectively, although their value was less than this at some meetings. Again prizes at Chester were of the best: reputable makes of chiming clocks (one still guides me through a disturbed night), canteens of silver-plated cutlery, silver nutmeg dishes, good watches and the like, all no doubt supplied by the shops on the high street. Other promoters awarded similar prizes (slightly lesser value) along with cut glass bowls with silver rims, ornaments, and I remember once getting a gents' umbrella for a third place in an 880 yards handicap at Liverpool Police Sports - not quite the thing I would use at my age, with my friends, or in our street, at that time. Over the years many of us accumulated prizes galore although mine seemed to leak away to friends and relatives for wedding gifts or birthday and Christmas presents, a sign of the easy-going attitude of youth and the shortage of money which most of us suffered from in those days.

The supply of prizes was limited in a way by the handicap system: winning or being placed in a race meant that one's handicap (the start each runner received measured in yards in front of the starting line) would be diminished. For example, if a runner won a 100 yards race his starting position would be 'pulled' back one yard diminishing the handicap (yards start) he had, the next time he ran a similar race: if he ran second he was 'pulled' ½ yard and a ¼ for third place; in a mile race he would be 'pulled' 15 yards for gaining 1st place and each race had its own formula. The handicapper for the region was a small, neat, man with short, neat, sandy hair by the name of Charlie Rice. Before each meeting began there would be a queue in front of his table of runners wishing to dispute the handicap printed by their name in the programme. One might say: 'You've pulled me 12 yards for my win in the 880 yards at Liverpool Harriers whereas one usually loses only 8 yards' and receive an answer: 'I think you can win the race off the handicap you've been given.' Any protest against such a perceived injustice would be received with a bland smile on a smooth, cherubic face. Injustice it seemed to talented runners, for they knew that even though they could win this race they would soon be pulled so far back (giving others longer and longer starts) that their chances of gaining prizes would be curtailed, no matter how hard they trained.

But for such runners there were always prizes to be won in the relay and team races, which were never handicapped, and fortunately Sutton Harriers almost always had strong teams. For the sprinters and the middle distance athletes there was the popular mile medley relay in which the four runners ran 220, 220, 440 and 880 yards respectively and for the Harriers the two mile team race was a popular event at most meetings. After Austin Tipping joined the club some time around 1950 we seemed to come on apace, and with others, such as Phil Burrows and Chris Frodsham, our sprinting team was the best in the region for a few years, winning the Lancashire and Northern Counties Relay Championships more than once in the years 1951-54. Even in 1954, '55 and '56 with little change in the team which won Championship Relays in 1951 we won further championships in 4x110 yards, 4x440 yards and the mile medley relay.

I had known Austin Tipping at school as a far better natural sprinter than I was. He was strong with powerful shoulders and sturdy legs and his great determination and belief in his own sprinting ability brought him, and the club and relay teams, much success. He was a very good team member and I can not remember a cross word between us, though he could respond strongly if officialdom tried anything on us as a team. Austin remained involved with the club far longer than myself, marrying the Ladies Section's outstanding all-rounder Margaret King. He had come to us from Earlestown Viaduct AC, and a few weeks later Phil Burrows joined us from Pilkington Recs AC. Phil was a tall rangy runner, fast and dependable and took his running very seriously; perhaps too seriously for he worried for days about his Saturday performance, even to the extent of seeking advice from some columnist of the magazine Athletics Weekly. Chris Frodsham joined us straight from Liverpool University where he had won their sprint championship; living in Rainhill he practised as a dentist while his father led a prominent firm of solicitors in St Helens. Chris suffered from nerves, too, and had been known to put his fingers down his throat to make himself sick as the baton was on its way to him; he was a great specialist sprinter with a slight upper body but extremely sturdy, strong legs. The four of us made a great team, got on very well together and enjoyed a long period of success, which included the Northern Counties' 4x110 yards Championship and I have very pleasant memories of that part of my life - not least of which was acting as best man at Chris' wedding.

I remember that there were others who ran the longer distances in relays, particularly Norman Vose and Eddie Balmer and, of course, Ken Wilcock. Norman was tall, broad-shouldered and very handsome and also very pleasant to be with (wasn't everybody at Sutton?). He was a very good 440 runner who played a prominent part in our Lancashire 4x440 Relay Championships in 1951 and '53 as well as in many a medley relay. Eddie I remember not for his looks but for his dry wit and for his great help in Lancashire 4x440 wins and also for his half miles in the medley races. Ken was a brilliant junior at the beginning of this period but once he joined us to run the longer relays he was a great source of strength and played a big part in our Northern Counties' Mile Medley wins in 1954 and '55. Ken became one of the country's best 440 yards runners and, though placed a couple of times in the AAA 440 behind runners of great international calibre, narrowly missed gaining the Inter-Counties title.

We were very fortunate in having strong running reserves who could fill a relay place more than adequately whenever one of the team members had to drop out because of injury or personal commitment elsewhere. Even though it's almost fifty years since those days I can remember other names such as Peter Batterley, an early member who I think had an Oxford Blue, Ted Ashley, who was placed in Cheshire County Sprint Championships, Keith Gravelle, a good 440 deputy in Championship successes, and Jimmy Doyle, who came to us after he had won a National Schoolboys 440 yards Championship and gave much early promise as a half-miler. There was Dave Pointon, too, who turned up at Ruskin Drive to watch the 1954 Northern Counties Junior Championships and Senior Relays. However, as Phil Burrows had failed to arrive in time, and Dave, who had been entered in the list of reserves, conveniently had his kit with him, he found himself running the third leg in the Senior One-Mile Medley Championship race which Sutton won.

On one of my visits to Pilkingtons' field, Ruskin Drive, during my college vacation of Summer 1948 I think it was, I saw a most unusual sight: a girl training. She was dressed in black shorts and, again I think, a track suit top. She was obviously doing sprint training and very impressively too. I cannot remember whether I asked Harry Wilson who she was or whether he volunteered her name but one thing was sure. I would never forget the name Rita Almond again or the way she ran. She was quite small and almost frail looking but she had very firm shapely legs and when she ran flat out she showed a remarkable cadence. If her legs had been an inch or two longer, without any consequent loss in cadence, she would most assuredly have gained international status as a sprinter. As it was she inspired many young ladies to join Sutton Harriers and AC and led them to many victories in sprint relays, including the Northern Counties and Lancashire County Championships, as well as enjoying numerous successes for herself. She was very well supported by other talented sprinters, Margaret Astell, Rose Davin and Barbara Billington (who married Tom McIntyre, a real stalwart of the club on and off the track) and other ladies I should remember even fifty years later. Sadly, Rita died in 1999, more than fifty years since I first saw her, remembered by many even now for her running prowess, leaving Allan, who supported her in her athletic career, to mourn her loss deeply. I was proud to be best man at their wedding and to give an address at the Requiem Mass offered for the repose of her soul.

Playing rugby for West Park and then Liverpool, and as an 11 stone 2lb centre, led to quite a few injuries, and disappointments at not being able to accept two invitations to represent Lancashire in the early season Inter-Counties meeting at the White City, London, and to represent the AAA in season 1952. Rugby and married life in Liverpool probably led to me giving up the athletic scene round about 1956 but I am glad to say that I was able to run in Sutton colours much later in life. My son Michael had won a Lancashire Schools 440 Championship and hearing about Sutton's participation in League meetings (which had replaced the handicap meetings of my day) I got him to join the club, only to find that Austin Tipping (perhaps a year or two younger than I was) was running and that two of his children were participating as well. So it leaves me with a good memory of running in a relay race with my 17 year old son when I was 47, and gaining a few points for Sutton by taking part in the pole vault, shot and javelin and even gaining 1st place in a 'B' Hurdles when the leader fell at the last hurdle! I felt a mite sorry for the younger members of the team for they had never known the glory days of the great crowds of spectators and the award of prizes, but I am absolutely convinced that we would have run for points for the club just the same as they did.

I think that I could write more about the details of those days when Sutton Harriers and AC did really prove themselves an 'athletic club' but reaching back with a memory which I know has started to falter makes me wary of seeming even more boastful or sentimental. Here would be a good place to apologise for any sins of omission or commission which I have committed, particularly to those whose deeds I may have failed to mention. I am very grateful to the many members of the Club with whom I shared a part of my youth for the happy memories I have and hope that time has been kind to them all.

Tom Hackett

A small party of Sutton Harriers, Liverpool Pembroke and Liverpool Harriers made the journey together to the picturesque running track at Tibshelf, Derbyshire, in August 1954. There the Sports Meeting formed part of the Tibshelf and District Floral and Horticultural Show and pride of place that day went to Rita Almond who won both the Ladies' 100 yards and 220 yards handicap races, both from a back mark.

Chris Frodsham won the Gents' 100 yards. Ken Wilcock won the 440 yards, and Sutton Ladies and Gents both won their respctive 600 yards relays. The Ladies won quite easily but the Gents' victory involved a thrilling tussle. They were behind until the last changeover and then a tremendous run by Austin Tipping gave them an inches win over Notts AC and Birchfield Harriers.

Liverpool Pembroke had the winner of the one mile and occupied 1st, 2nd and 3rd places in the 880 yards, making a clean sweep for the party. Liverpool Harriers' athletes had to be content with a couple of second places.

There was a very happy atmosphere on the return journey which included a stop at a public house in Glossop for refreshment. Everyone was grateful that Lew Ludlow, the Sutton Harriers' trainer/masseur, had only won second prize in the raffle at the Tibshelf Show because the first prize, donated by the local farmers, was a live pig and the coach was already crowded due to our giving some Manchester athletes a lift, plus the many prizes scattered about the aisle.

It was whilst stopped at Glossop that everyone gathered around the radio in the bar. Over the air from half the world away came the commentary on the historic one mile race in the Empire Games at Vancouver, Canada, between Roger Bannister and John Landy. The result made a fitting ending to a truly great day.

The following year, August 1955, Sutton Harriers made their second visit to Tibshelf and once again had a resounding day. Ken Wilcock again won the 440 yards and was 2nd in the 220 yards. Roy Ashley won the 880 yards, Tom McIntyre won the one mile and Doreen Fitzgerald was 2nd in the Ladies' 220 yards. The Ladies' team finished 2nd in the Ladies' 600 yards Relay.

Trevor Simms, who suffered from alopecia and wore a skullcap when running, was the recipient of unkind comments from spectators near the starting area. He was running off scratch in the Boys' 100 yards handicap and won his heat very convincingly. In the final, he gave the winner 9 1/4 yards start and only just failed to catch him in 10.4 secs, earning him enthusiastic applause from the crowd. The Boys' team - Trevor Simms, G Smethurst, R Earps and K Platt - won the 600 yards Schoolboys' relay and received the King Edward VII Challenge Shield. That year, the organisers of the Sports had donated the Brookes-Waters Challenge Trophy to be awarded to the club gaining the most points in the individual events, which on this first occasion was Sutton Harriers.

In August 1956 Sutton again sent a party of athletes to Tibshelf and were rewarded by retaining the Brookes-Waters Challenge Trophy. Unfortunately details of the individual performances cannot be located.

Another raid on Tibshelf was made in August 1957 in an attempt to win the trophy for a consecutive third time. Jim Doyle, on leave from the forces, was 3rd in the 100 yards and 2nd in the 880 yards; Bert Tebb came 2nd in the mile, followed closely by Tom McIntyre 3rd; Ken Wilcock won the 440 yards yet again; Keith Platt was 3rd in the Junior 440 yards and the Ladies' team were 2nd in the Ladies' 600 yards relay.

Sutton Harriers did gain the most points and won the Brookes-Waters Challenge Trophy for the third year in succession, an achievement which meant it became the property of the club.

I always had a desire to run, even as a small boy; field days, chasing games, sports days, the reason being my great-uncle John was a mile runner of some distinction. For a time I lived over a mile away from the school which I attended. Few people possessed cars, and public transport was not as developed as it is today. Only about half a dozen children were allowed to have their lunch in school, because they lived three miles or more from school. The four miles that others and myself had to walk became the source of 'scratch' races. Lamp standards, trolley bus stops, and telegraph poles were our 'starts' and 'finishes' - the pavements our track.

The games we played were also instrumental in helping us to be fit, and healthy. One game was 'Rallyo' which involved two teams of equal numbers. One of them would run off, being given a certain length of time before the other team started to chase, and seek them. Counting was the order of the day. Very few boys or girls owned watches, and those that did could only wear them on Sundays. The way we counted was in a chant '5-10 15-20 25-30' and so on, up to 300, or 500. The idea was to 'catch' the opposition, and place them in a 'den'. If the team who were being chased could touch any of those in the 'den', and repeat the chosen code words such as '2-4-6-8-10' the captives were 'free' to run off again. When all had been caught, the other team ran off for their innings. 'Rallyo' was very popular, especially with the boys. This type of game made for sturdy legs, and sound lungs, and could go on for days. The children of today don't know what they have missed with this, and other street games. There is a parallel between this type of game, running, and the lack of available transport of yesteryear and the emergence of the athletes from the Horn of Africa, (Kenya - Eritrea - Somalia) who seemingly have had the foundations laid by the distances they travel from home to school, and back home again. This training, coupled with altitude, makes for a superb athlete.

When doing my National Service in the RAF, I played football at RAF Bridgnorth (Salop). Whilst there I was tempted to run in station sports, and won the 220 yards and 880 yards championships. I was chosen to represent Technical Training Command at RAF Cardington (Beds) in 220 yards, but was eliminated in the cross heats. It was there that I first met Sgt Bill McMinnis. He won the three miles, and lapped every runner in the field. Shortly after this I was asked to run in the cross-country team at Bridgnorth, but declined the invitation, an action I have often regretted. In fact it was a mistake, because there would have been numerous trips out to RAF stations elsewhere, along with other privileges.

This contribution of mine is a tribute to those who turned out for Sutton Harriers' ladies' and men's teams, and did not quite make the high spots - those who finished 4th - 5th - 6th and so on. These are people who ran cross-country, road, track and field events, who filled the minor positions. Nevertheless such athletes are the backbone of any club organisation. Without them there would be no competitions , and certainly there would be no champions, or trophies. Taking part is the action that really matters. Some of these people joined the club for a short while, while others stayed, and became the mainstay of the club.

For my part, I'm going to limit myself to a few highlights of my athletic career …

One was being a member of the winning teams in the Senior National Cross-Country Championships (9 miles) at Aylesbury (Bucks) in 1950, and at Richmond/Catterick (Yorks) in 1951. Aylesbury was largely flat, but there was quite a deep ford that had to be traversed three times. It was three metres wide and roughly 30 cm deep. The course at Richmond was hilly moorland, with a number of dry stone walls to negotiate.

In October 1951, I was selected for Sutton Harriers to represent the club in the first Lancashire County Road Relay Race (8 x 3 ¼ miles) which was held at Southport. Our team became the winners, and were proud owners of the trophy.

I ran several times in the Manchester to Blackpool Road Relay, a distance of approximately 55 miles. This race organised by the News of the World was run over eleven stages of different lengths, terrain, and duration. It started at Belle Vue, Manchester, and finished at Blackpool Town Hall. The race was limited to twelve competing teams, owing to traffic and police arrangements. One year I had the honour to be the first stage runner. My day was made memorable by the gentleman who set us on our way being Mr Frank Swift, the Manchester City and England goalkeeper. A wonderful person, and great entertainer on the football field, he was a giant of a man who made himself popular everywhere he went with his genial personality. On this occasion we eventually finished second to the great Midland club, Birchfield Harriers.

A race I have a special memory for was the first National Road Relay of Britain - the London to Brighton Race (distance 50-54 miles) again organised by the News of the World. It started at the News of the World sports ground at Mitcham, South London, and finished at the Esplanade on Brighton sea front. This was also over eleven stages of varying distance, time, and terrain. Twenty teams from all over Britain contested the event. We finished fourth, the first team out of the twenty who were not from the Southern Counties. I think the result was (1) Belgrave Harriers (2) Thames Valley (3) Reading AC (4) Sutton Harriers. Arguably, this was a race we could have won. (That's another story.)

Then there was my winning the John Orrell Mile when I was in my middle 40s. I had always tried my best in earlier races, but on each occasion had just not been good enough. The evening I won this race the handicapper (it was a handicap race) perhaps was quite generous. I had, however, trained exceptionally hard this time, and it paid off. It was a most pleasing feeling to have won the race, and I did feel it a great achievement eventually to win after my long-standing friendship with John Orrell.

Another pleasing venture was the formation of the Northern Veterans Athletic Club. I ran in one of their first Road Races in Manchester on Sunday 15th September 1968. I was then over 40 years of age. This was a 6½ mile race. I finished in 13th place out of approximately 40 competitors, which was most satisfying because I had not been training too often owing to having been injured.

During my athletic career I was invited to serve on the Sutton Harriers Committee which to me was a great honour. I was for three years Vice-Captain to Fred McMinnis, and was so proud of this promotion. Fred as captain led by example. He was seemingly a captain with great zeal and energy, and was straight when he told you anything, or disagreed with you. Fred trained very hard, and this following a day carrying on the family window-cleaning business which made him such a strong man. When Greenall's Brewers had the brewery in Hall Street, Fred cleaned their windows every Tuesday morning. After he had finished he was invited to draw himself a pint of beer of his choice, and enjoy it. There is no doubt in my mind that a great part of Sutton Harriers' success stemmed from the attitude, discipline, and personality of Fred McMinnis.

Tom Fillingham, one of the team at this time, was a genial man who thought out a number of plans to be carried out for the future success of the club. In committee he was fair, level-headed, and helpful. He had a most equable temperament, and athletes would always go to Tom for advice. Tom compiled the notes and results for the local paper. At that time, I think there was only one, The St Helens Reporter. He had chosen for himself the nom-de-plume of CLUBMAN after much careful thought, and it fitted him most perfectly. He was through and through a clubman, whom everyone could look up to with high regard. Tom asked me if I would assist him to send in the notes, and results. I was most willing to do so for such a kind and modest man. I became CLUBMAN II or TWO, a title I cherished. The notes had to be written by hand in those days, and to be ready by Sunday night. They were deposited at the Reporter office in Church Street, opposite the old Post Office, by the Parish Church. These were published on Tuesday's edition, which in those days was a broadsheet. The later edition on Friday, also a broadsheet, carried more news.

The unusual situation of these outstanding runners was that they hardly ever trained together. This Sutton team was one of rare athletic talents, each member having personal strengths and experiences always generously shared with other members who were willing to listen.

The driving force of the committee at this time was the 'engine room' where the strategy for success was planned. Coupled with their six or seven outstanding athletes this was the background for achievement which kept Sutton Harriers to the fore during this most successful period.

Tom McIntyre

Tom Hackett

Tom Hackett joined Sutton Harriers as a nineteen-year-old in the summer of 1947 when he was home on vacation from a Teachers' Training College near London. He was a very versatile athlete who ran 100 yards, 220 yards, 440 yards and 880 yards for Sutton, plus relays. In inter-club matches he took part in various field events such as long jump, high jump, shot, discus and javelin and, at least on one occasion, the pole vault.

A Rugby Union player of considerable ability, Tom was selected by Lancashire on many occasions during a period when the county had many notable international centres and wingers. It was on 9th October 1954 that he made his Rugby Union debut at centre for Lancashire against Ulster. Injuries acquired whilst playing rugby certainly stopped him achieving his full potential in athletics.

After National Service in the Army in 1948-9, he won the Lancashire County Senior 440 yards Championship in both 1950 and 1951, and represented the county in those years. He also won the straight 220 yards at Chester in 1950 and 1952, but did not compete in any championships in 1952 or 1953 other than relays, where his performance together with Austin Tipping played a significant part in the outcome.

In 1954 he returned to the championships and finished 3rd in the Lancashire Senior 440 yards. His excellent running on the 440 yards leg in the one mile medley relay in the Northern Counties Championship in 1954 and in 1955 gave the Sutton team a good lead on the first leg, enabling them to win on both occasions. His ill-luck in the Lancashire 440 yards Championships in 1955 is described elsewhere.

Rugby injuries sustained during 1956 affected Tom's athletics during the summer and in the Lancashire Championships he could only manage 3rd in his heat. He struggled through the season, after which he retired until he gave athletics a further chance as a veteran during the 1970s.

Austin Tipping

After coming out of the forces early in 1950 Austin was in outstanding form whilst running with Earlestown Viaduct AC. He was placed 1st in the 220 yards at both the Earlestown Sports and Upton (Birkenhead) Sports and 2nd at Pilkington's Sports in the 100 yards and 220 yards, before winning the 220 yards at the Lancashire County Senior Championships and the Civil Service Championships. It was later in 1950 that he joined Sutton Harriers.

During the years 1950-56 he won the Lancashire 220 yards Championships on two occasions, 1950 and 1953, was placed in 1954/55/56, but in 1952 chose to compete in the 440 yards in which he finished 2nd. In three consecutive years 1950/51/52 he won the Civil Service National Championship 220 yards, before leaving to study at St Mary's Teacher Training College, Twickenham. This restricted his 1953 athletic appearances. His only success in the Northern Counties Championships was a second place in the 220 yards in 1957.

A Lancashire representative on numerous occasions, he took part in the 1953 Inter-Counties Championships at the

Austin Tipping winning 220 yards race at Pilkington Recs in 1950

White City, London. However, he was beaten in his heat of the 440 yards by inches, thus not getting into the final; but on the next day, in the 220 yards, he won his heat only to meet the redoubtable McDonald-Bailey in the semi-final and thereby failed to make the final.

Austin was selected for various AAA Teams, ironically, on one occasion, in 1953 and whilst at college, to run against a Combined Universities team.

He was a very tenacious competitor, especially in relays and was a member of the Sutton teams which won the Lancashire 4x440 yards in 1951 and 1953, the Lancashire 4x110 yards in 1953, the NCAAA 4x110 yards in 1954 and the one mile medley in 1954 and 1955.

An injury during June/July 1956 finished his season early and Austin turned to playing Rugby Union before returning to athletics to compete in the Veterans' events for over 40 year-olds in the early 1970s.

BRIEF NOTES ON ATHLETICS CAREER

Date	Year	Event	Distance	Place	Location
23 & 24 June	1948		Army Athletics Championships		Aldershot
29 & 30 June	1948		Army Athletics Championships		Aldershot
3 June	1950	Lancashire Championships	220 yards	1st	Earlestown Viaduct
2 June	1951	Lancashire Championships	220 yards	3rd	Sutton Harriers
23 June	1951	Northern Counties	220 yards		Final rained off - track flooded!
7 July	1951	Civil Service Championships	220 yards	1st	
17 May	1952	Lancashire Championships	440 yards	2nd	
21 May	1953	Training Colleges Championships	100 yards	1st	
		Training Colleges Championships	200 yards	1st	
		Training Colleges Championships	440 yards	1st	
18 May	1954	Training Colleges Championships	100 yards	1st	
		Training Colleges Championships	200 yards	1st	
		Training Colleges Championships	440 yards	1st	
19 June	1954	Northern Counties	440 yards	Semi-final	
25 June	1955	Northern Counties	220 yards	5th	
4 June	1955	Lancashire Championships	220 yards	3rd	
2 June	1956	Lancashire Championships	220 yards	3rd	
23 June	1956	Northern Counties	220 yards	4th	
22 June	1957	Northern Counties	220 yards	2nd	

Ken Wilcock

Upon leaving Prescot Grammar School Ken started work at BICC in 1951 and having won the 880 yards and 1 mile handicap races in the work's annual sports meeting at the age of sixteen, it was suggested he join Sutton Harriers, which he did in September 1951.

In 1952 Ken's potential was noticed by club officials during training and junior trial races at Allanson Street, Parr. This resulted in his selection for the Harriers' Junior 880 yards Medley Relay team which in June 1952 won at Bradford. He then finished first in his initial individual event, the John Orrell Memorial Trophy, and was successful throughout the season in 220 yard, 440 yard and 880 yard events at the many open handicap meetings in the district.

A brilliant 440 yards in a junior relay at Bolton on Easter Monday 1953 set him up for another good season which saw him 2nd in the Lancashire Junior 440 yards Championship on a waterlogged grass track at Finch Lane, Knotty Ash, Liverpool and winning the Northern Counties Junior 440 yards at Stockport, as well as running the final leg in the Sutton team that won the Lancashire Junior 4x440 yards relay at Salford.

Although he was primarily a 440 yards runner the club needed someone to run the 880 yards leg in the mile Medley Relay and Ken was selected. The team became the most successful in the district over the next few years, coming 1st in the NCAAA one mile Medley Relay Championship in 1954 and 1955, gaining 2nd place in 1956, and winning many races at the open meetings.

Ken became quite proficient at 880 yards, finishing 3rd in the Lancashire County Championships in 1955 and 1956, and 3rd in the Northern Counties Championship in 1955, recording a personal best time of 1 min 54.3 secs, whilst in the years 1956 and 1957 he was just outside the medals. During 1955, in the Northern British Games, he was placed 3rd in the 880 yards behind Tom Courtney (USA), who fifteen months later became Olympic Champion in Melbourne. As a result of his season's performances Ken was selected for a Mancastrian Select team against Czechoslovakia at the White City, Manchester, in October 1955.

The early events of the 1958 season saw him running 220 yards, 440 yards and 880 yards with equal success and, despite setting a personal best 880 yards 1 min 53.4 sec at the Northern British Games at the White City, Manchester, which earned him selection for the north in the Inter-Area match, he entered the Lancashire County 440 yards at Blackburn. His winning time of 49.3 secs set a new record. The following week he was back to the 880 yards in the Inter-Area match, setting a personal best of 1 min 51.6 secs and finishing last of six runners to Brian Hewson, whose time of 1 min 47.8 secs was a European record. It was then that Ken decided to concentrate on 440 yards in championships.

Cariacture of Ken Wilcock drawn in Warsaw September 1961

This proved to be the correct decision because the next week he won the NCAAA 440 yards in 49.3 secs and followed this in the AAA championships with a personal best of 48.9 secs in the heat; but his 3rd position was no use as only the first two in each heat qualified for the semi-final. 1959 saw him retain the Lancashire County 440 yards but he could only finish 2nd in the NCAAA championships and reach the AAA championships' semi-final.

Most people at this time believed the national team selectors had been unfair by not selecting Ken for the Great Britain 'B' International with Holland at St Helens in July 1959, especially as he had victories over all those named among the provisional runners in the 4x440 yards. The team included a number of Northern athletes being introduced to international athletics.

A visit to Holland in May 1960 saw him set two ground records in the 400 metres, at Groningen and at Zwolle, which he followed by winning the Lancashire County 440 yards for the third consecutive year, in a new championship time, and the NCAAA 440 yards, plus maintaining consistent performances over this distance throughout the season. At the end of September, on a wet and blustery night and a heavy White City, Manchester, track, Ken finished 2nd to Olympic Champion Otis Davis, after leading the race until the home straight, when only the powerful Davis had the strength to pass him to win.

As a result of his performances Ken was invited in 1961 to run for AAA against Cambridge University, where he won the 440 yards in 48.2 secs, a new ground record. Later in the Inter-Counties at the White City, London, running for Lancashire, he finished 2nd in 48.2 secs and then won the Lancashire County 440 yards at Bolton for the fourth successive year, again in a new record time. Although he finished only 3rd in the inter-area match, closely behind two established Great Britain 440 yards runners, he officially ran the fastest leg in the 4x440 yards relay and it was thought the selectors must sit up and take notice.

In June 1961 Ken won the NCAAA 440 yards for the second year in succession in a new championship time 48.1 secs and in the AAA championships finished 3rd in 48.2 secs after a terrific thunder shower had flooded the track. As a result of this performance he was invited to join the Great Britain teams to compete against USA and Hungary, as one of eight to be considered for the 4x440 yards relay, but was not selected in the final four, although he had the pleasure of being 2nd in the Invitation 400 metres during the Hungary match.

The next meeting was the Lever Trophy at Port Sunlight where he won the 440 yards in a ground record 47.8 secs, a qualifying time for the European championships to be held in 1962.

Selection as a member of the Great Britain party for matches against Germany in Dortmund and Poland in Warsaw was the reward for consistent performances throughout the year. After finishing 2nd in the Invitation 400 metres in Warsaw on 6th September 1961 he was selected to run the second leg of the 4x400 metres relay which GB duly won, but the overall match was lost by one point. The 1961 National rankings showed him in 7th place with only 3/10ths of a second covering the third to seventh places.

1962 saw him selected for the Great Britain team in the relay trials at Blackpool in May. He won the Lancashire County 440 yards for the fifth consecutive year, the Northern Counties 440 yards for the third successive year (fourth time in five years), came 2nd in the Inter-Counties, where he was expected to win but was beaten over the last few yards by David Brown, who died in a 'plane crash five days later. In the AAA championships he again finished 3rd and was selected for Great Britain against Poland, running second leg in the 4x440 yards relay.

Ken was confirmed as a member of the Great Britain team for the European Championships in Belgrade in September 1962 where he won a silver medal in the 4x440 metres relay. Upon returning home, he ran for England in the 4x440 yards relay against Finland and, following his omission from the England team for the Empire Games in Perth, Australia, decided to retire from international athletics. However, illness in April 1963 caused him to miss any competition that year and he acted as assistant team manager to the Lancashire team.

Over the eleven years' competition he had the ability to run all distances on track, road and cross-country. On the track his best times were:

100 yards	10.0 secs
220 yards	21.6 secs
440 yards	47.1 secs
880 yards	1 min 51.6 secs
1 mile	4 mins 19.2 secs

Off the track, his best individual cross-country performance was to come 4th in the West Lancashire Championships in 1959. He ran in the Lancashire Road Relay at Southport on five occasions between 1956 and 1961, missing 1957 due to Asian Flu, and twice ran the three mile 8th leg in the Manchester-Blackpool Road Relay, breaking the record in the 1957 race.

Chapter 5

THE LADIES' SECTION TAKES OFF

Though none served on the Club Committee nor were listed as attending any AGM, there were certainly women Harriers around in the 1920s. Most well-known was Albert Worrall's sister, Edna - later Mrs Duckworth and a long-time resident of Burtonwood. In her late eighties in 2001, she was proud to recall being the club's first lady member.

'The lady runner, Miss N Linden' was described by E J Stubbs, then Club Secretary, as 'one of our best performers on the track' in his report on the 1930 season. Thereafter the ladies get no mention. Did they move to other clubs with better facilities and opportunities for competition, such as UGB which then had a large Ladies'section trained by Ted Highcock, and set an example to their young successors of the 1980s? Certainly Edna Worrall joined Liverpool Harriers. Had her brother realised the situation when he seconded a proposal at the 1929 AGM 'that the ladies' section be left over'. It was.

Almost two decades later, the men's successes in the 1947 cross-country championships brought many recruits to the club. Amongst these was the young sixteen-year old schoolgirl Rita Almond.

In 1948 Rita was the only female member of Sutton Harriers and though still at Cowley Girls' Grammar School was winning open ladies' races. Early in 1949 a Ladies' Section was formed by the club, and coached by Horace Green. Its initial members - Rita, Jean Simpson, Betty Houghton, Rose

Rita Almond

Davin and Alma Ashton - competed with moderate success at the various Merseyside meetings. This encouraged more girls to join, including 15 year-old Barbara Billington who, in May 1950, finished 2nd in her first competitive race in the Ladies' 100 yards at Earlestown, behind Rose Davin. The following week Barbara won her first race at Crewe LMR Sports with Rose Davin in second place. Later in the year Barbara won the Lancashire Schoolgirls' 100 yards Championship at Preston, then went to the All-England Schools' Championships at Port Sunlight and was a member of the Lancashire relay 4x110 yards team, which came 3rd. In recognition of her early season running Rita Almond, who had finished 3rd in the Lancashire Women's AAA 100 yards Championship, was selected by Northern Counties Women's AAA to compete in Northern Ireland on 17th June 1950. The Ladies' relay team ran very well for the club, winning at Birkenhead and at St Helens Police Sports, and being placed on a number of occasions. Their best result was to win the Northern Counties WAAA Relay. In the St Helens Youth Sports these young Harriers produced good performances - Barbara Billington and Margaret King in sprints, hurdles and long jump and the younger girls, Margaret Astell and Rosemary Whetton, in sprints and long jump respectively. All showed promise of future success in open competition.

During the cross-country season attempts were made to establish a ladies' team and a number of members participated. A team entered the Ladies' Northern Cross-country Championship at Royton in February 1951 where they had a rough time, but completed the course, with Jean Huxley the best placed, despite an injured ankle, in seventeenth position.

The 1951 track season showed the ladies becoming stronger as a section, and they had a number of successes during May, especially with the relay team of Rita Almond, Barbara Billington, Doreen Fitzgerald and Rose Davin. In the Northern Counties Women's AAA 100 yards Championships Rita Almond reached the final, only to have the disappointment of being disqualified for making two false starts; whilst Margaret King in her first full season in senior ladies' athletics won the Northern Counties Ladies' Long Jump Championship at Ashington. During the rest of the season the relay team featured regularly in the prizes and Margaret King showed herself to be ready to challenge for honours in the sprints, in addition to the long jump.

Margaret King (left) and Rita Almond (right) at the finish of 100 yards race at Ruskin Drive, St Helens

At the Blackburn Centenary Sports on 22nd September 1951 the Sutton Harriers' great tradition was kept alive by four young schoolgirls competing in the Northern Counties Women's 4x110 yards Relay for juniors under 15 years of age. They had to run three times, heat, semi-final and final, and on each occasion they won by a large margin. Margaret Astell gained the initial lead on the first leg each time, and Rosemary Whetton, M Jones and Cecilia Lawrenson ran brilliantly, each of them increasing the lead. A feature of the final was the expert baton change between Whetton and Jones which gained the team an extra three to four yards.

The 1952 season opened with Rita Almond finishing 2nd in the WAAA 100 yards Championships. The St Helens Youth Sports again highlighted how far the ladies' section had progressed in such a short time by the number of girls competing not only on the track but also in field events. The St Helens team won the Inter-Town competition promoted by the Liverpool and Cheshire Youth Activities Council and by the Widnes Further Education Council.

Margaret Astell and Rosemary Whetton were consistent throughout the season, whilst Barbara Billington, Rita Almond and Margaret King won prizes at various meetings. The 4x110 yards relay team were successful yet again and in the Northern Counties WAAA 660 yards Relay finished 2nd.

Northern Counties 4 x 110 yards Ldies relay champions in 1952.
M King, R Almond, B Billington and M Astell

Field events were now looking good with Margaret King in the long jump and discus, and the youngsters Jennie Welding and Sheila McCauley producing good performances in high jump and discus respectively.

1953 proved to be a very successful season with both individual and team performances in the various championships. Margaret Astell won the WAAA Junior 100 yards Championship, Rosemary Whetton the NC WAAA Junior

Long Jump and Jenny Welding the NC WAAA Junior High Jump whilst Rita Almond reached the final of the NC WAAA 100 yards, finishing 4th. In the relay championships Sutton won the NC WAAA 660 yards Relay and the 4x110 yards Relay as well as finishing 2nd in the Lancashire WAAA 4x110 yards Relay.

The track season started quite well in 1954 with Rose Davin (440 yards) and Rita Almond (220 yards and relay) both being selected for the Lancashire Ladies' team at Stockport on 14th May. The relay teams were again successful, once more winning the NC WAA 660 yards Relay through Rita Almond, Margaret Astell, Barbara Billington and Rose Davin, and finishing 3rd in the NCWAAA 4x110 yards Relay. The ladies' relay team were then invited to compete in the WAAA meeting in London and finished a creditable 4th in the final. Barbara Billington also competed in the 80 metres hurdles at this meeting and was placed 2nd. The relay team's success continued throughout the season, except for one week in July when their closest rivals, Liverpool Harriers, beat them into second place on three occasions - at the St Helens Police, the Widnes Police and Pilkington Recs Annual Sports Meetings.

In 1955 the team, Barbara Billington, Rita Almond, Margaret Astell and Doreen Fitzgerald, won the NC WAAA 4x110 yards Relay, equalling the championship record time, at Liverpool Police Sports.

Barbara Billington (right) in hurdles race at Widnes

Margaret King was third in the NC WAAA Discus Championship. Barbara Billington had a very good season, winning prizes at various sports meetings in 100 yards, 220 yards and 80 metres hurdles and relay events, as well as representing Lancashire in the 220 yards at the Inter-county meeting. New members attracted to the Ladies' Section were successful. Pam Thompson was 2nd in 100 yards and 220 yards ladies' events, whilst young Beryl Elliott won the schoolgirls' 100 yards at the St Helens Police Sports.

During May 1956 Barbara Billington again ran for Lancashire in the 220 yards at Earlestown. A new member, Brenda Nunley, won her first open competition race at Helsby, the 220 yards, and then went on to assist the 4x110 yards relay team to victory. The same team, Barbara Billington, Brenda Nunley, Doreen Fitzgerald and Pam Thompson, won at the Widnes Police Sports and finished 2nd at St Helens Police Sports, and also second in the NC WAAA 4x110 yards Relay at Moston, Manchester. Margaret Astell again won the British Rail 220 yards Championship, whilst fifteen-year-old Beryl Elliott won the Lancashire Schoolgirls' 100 yards Championship and competed in the All-England Schools' Championships. In addition to sprints, Beryl was a very useful high jumper. Another schoolgirl, Maureen Earps, won the Junior Ladies' 100 yards at open meetings on three consecutive weekends during July 1956.

That autumn, when Sutton had no permanent home, the ladies rapidly took advantage of the Saturday afternoon training facilities made available for the club at Allanson Street to add netball to their keep-fit routine. Selected for their first fixture, with Fairfield, Widnes, were:- Maureen Earps, Pat Padmore, Barbara Billington, Pam Thompson, Barbara Livesey, Beryl Elliot and their coach Margaret Ashley (Roy's wife).

Brenda Nunley married fellow-Harrier Alan Skeath in the autumn of 1956, and during May 1957, in only her second competitive season, was chosen to run the 440 yards for Lancashire in the Inter-Counties match, finishing 3rd. The ladies' team, Barbara Billington, Pam Thompson, Brenda Skeath and Margaret Astell finished 2nd in the 4x110 yards Relay to Liverpool Harriers at Winton, again at Helsby, and in the Lancashire WAAA Relay at Pilkington Recs sports. Maureen Earps once more had a good season in schoolgirl sprint races.

Things went less well in 1958. The older ladies were by then pre-occupied with marriage and raising families, whilst with the demise of the handicap meetings the schoolgirls were failing to continue to compete successfully. Pat King (Margaret's sister) did win the Lancashire Schools' Girls' Discus event in 1959, but otherwise Sutton's ladies' section barely existed competitively until the introduction of the Leagues, in the late 1960s, and other events brought about a resurgence.

Happy Memories

My interest in athletics started at an early age. I took part in all Sports Days at school, all Whitsun Walks and all Sunday School Field Days.

When I was eleven years old I began to take a serious interest in all kinds of sport, so much so that when I was thirteen my father paid £1 per season for me to go and train at Ruskin Drive twice a week. It was here that I was trained and coached by a Mr J Gornall, who had a draper's shop in Duke Street, St Helens. He made it very interesting, and I used to look forward to my training. He also knew my Aunt Ida Jones, who had represented England in the Empire Games in 1934 in the 880 yards. She was a member of Liverpool Harriers at that time, whilst she was studying at Liverpool University to become a teacher. She trained at Liverpool University's Grounds at Wyncote.

In 1950, I joined Sutton Harriers. I entered my first race in May 1950, at Earlestown Viaduct Sports, in the 100 yards Handicap Race, and finished 2nd; I was now being trained by a Mr Horace Green at Sutton Harriers. At the end of May 1950, I ran and won my first-ever 100 yards Ladies' Handicap at Crewe, and I received a ladies' brush and comb set on a floral tray.

In July 1950, while I was still at school, my father entered me individually (we got permission from the Local Education Authority), to take part in the Lancashire Schools' Qualifying Heats at Preston. So I was the only girl from school representing St Helens. My mother travelled with me on two trains, and two buses, as the ground was quite a distance away from the town of Preston. It took a long time getting there, but it was worthwhile. I ran off scratch in the 100 yards sprint, to win by 2½ yards in 12 seconds.

After this success I went on to represent Lancashire Schools at Port Sunlight, Cheshire. A Mr William Garner (Headmaster of Rivington Road School) was the teacher in charge of me - as well as Alec Davies and Frank Carlton who were also representing Lancashire Schools at the All-England Schools' Championships at Port Sunlight. Incidentally, both these boys later played Rugby League. The first played for the Saints, and the second for Wigan. I ran in the 100 yards, and finished 2nd in my heat to a Miss June Foulds, who then went on eventually to win the 100 yards race. She was also to achieve international fame later, and represented Great Britain in the Olympic Games. However, I was also picked for the 4x110 yards Relay team, in which event Lancashire finished with a creditable 3rd position. I remember it well, as we had the outside lane, and had to keep in front all the way, and then, on the last change-over of the relay, the final 110 yards was a very, very close race. We were all thrilled to gain a much desired medal, but so very tired. We were told that we had given our 'All' for Lancashire.

In all the years competing, I had many successes, and enjoyed every moment. I met some very kind, good, solid friends in the Harriers. They were real genuine people, very loyal, supportive, and caring. We had a very successful Ladies' Section, under the captaincy of Rita Almond, whom I was to be with on many occasions. Our successes were great, especially the relay teams'. We all enjoyed it so much. Rita was a great captain, both on and off the track. She looked after us all, and advised us on many occasions whenever it was needed, both socially and competitively. We went on many coaching weekends - Lilleshall, with Mr Len Ward (Women's AAA Coach). Rita's mum would send us off with some lovely home cooked foods, such as cooked ham with a fresh pineapple, and my mother would make us some Lancashire parkin.

In July 1954, Sutton Ladies travelled down to London by train. Southgate Harriers were holding the Women's AAA's 660 yards Relay Championships. In these, of each competing team , two ran 220 yards, and two ran 110 yards. We finished in 4th position. After travelling all morning, and then having to run our heat, the semi-final and final in the same day we were all quite tired. However, especially enjoyable for me, after the relay was finished, was being invited to compete in the 80 yards hurdles, against Miss Iris Pond - who was an international athlete. I finished in 2nd position, and was awarded a shield from Beverley Baxter, Tory MP for Southgate.

On this occasion, Rita and I stayed overnight at the Salvation Army Hostel, in London. We had a good laugh at our bunk beds, as we had to climb up to get into them. We had a huge dormitory to ourselves.We were awakened next day, Sunday, by the Salvation Army sisters, who had cooked us a breakfast of bacon and eggs, toast and coffee. It was lovely. And the cost of the overnight stay was seven shillings and sixpence (37½ p), including the breakfast. It was very enjoyable. We boarded our train home at Euston and were met at Rainhill Station by our current boy-friends who later became our husbands (Tom McIntyre and Alan Watkin).

Our winter activities included netball, and in the 1950s we had a successful team under the guidance of Mrs Roy Ashley, an outstanding PE teacher. Sadly she is now crippled with arthritis. We trained at a primary school in Mill Lane, Sutton, mostly on Saturday mornings.

Joining Sutton Harriers was a very important step in my life. I learnt how to mix with people of all ages. It was a pleasure to be with them all. We were a happy-go-lucky group, caring for and helping each other, and taking valuable advice from our elders. It all helped me gain confidence, very necessary when I became first of all Ladies' Vice-Captain, then Captain, and then in 1956-7 Ladies' Secretary.

The last time I ran (age 40) in an inter-club event was in Manchester. Sutton Harriers had a chance to keep this cup if we won, so we all entered in whatever races and field events we could, just to gain points. I remember Margaret Tipping (nee King) coaching me for about two hours to throw the discus, and put the shot, which were Margaret's field events. So the time came for me to throw and do my best, I just plucked up courage and threw with all my might, had a good laugh, then collapsed on the floor, laughing yet again. We did manage to gain some points. I remember my son crying (he was only four) when I attempted to run the 100 yards - I finished last - but there were only four runners, so I did gain 1 point for 4th. Yes, and we did win the cup! Next day we were very, very stiff.

After having my children, I used to take them with me. I still played rounders, hockey and netball with UGB for hockey and rounders - though Sutton Harriers at one time had a rounders team too - plus playing for BICC as well. I played hockey and rounders up until my 49th birthday. Great times we had in those days.

Yes, those were happy days indeed, which I shall treasure always. Penning these notes has been a joy to me, as it has brought back many, many happy memories.

Barbara Billington

'Why not enter the Northern Counties Long Jump Championship?' This suggestion I thought preposterous! Only into Senior Athletics for 12 months, surely this wasn't for me. At that time, at major sporting meetings there would be one Northern Counties Ladies' Championship event to act as a crowd puller. Today all Championships are held during a two-day period.

In 1951 Ashington (Northumberland) was the Ladies' Long Jump Championship venue. What a long way to travel! (I recall my mother gave me her wages - hard earned then - to pay for my transport to go to the Championships.) Tickets were booked and I had the Club Captain, Rita Almond, to accompany me. It was a long coach journey, as there was a rail strike, and our accommodation was with the Secretary of the meeting and his wife. Obviously Rita's fame had gone before her. I can honestly say that I hardly understood a word of what people said to us, and I'm sure the reverse was so. I even had to point to six teaspoons to take back home for my mother in the window of a gift shop!

In the haze of competition, little of which I even remembered, I was awarded the Winner's Medal for jumping 16 feet 4½ inches by none other than Jackie Milburn, Newcastle FC Captain. That was amazing! I really had the boys at work green with envy. I also picked up a place in the 100 yards handicap, which Rita won along with the 200 yards. Rita also competed in the high jump and we left the stadium weighed down with not just Rita's Northern Counties medal, but also an array of bedding, as prizes. What a shame the rest of the relay team hadn't been with us!

After a tour of Ashington to be shown where the footballing Charltons lived, we were on our travels, weighed down by sandwiches which contained a bright orange goo. Needless to say we arrived home hungry. Well, we did say we liked eggs and tomatoes. How were we to know that in Ashington they blended them together? My whole concern was whether I would be in time to go to the parish Sunday night dance, as I knew my father would want to know the finer details of the competition which, sadly now I recall, he didn't get until the following day.

I worked at Pilkington's Head Office in Grove Street in 1951. You only got one Saturday morning off in three. At 12 noon I had to run to the car park on which Century House is now built, where the smell of the hops from Greenall's brewery floated over, to get a seat on the coach to go to an athletics match. Often it was three to a seat and some half-standing, half-sitting in the aisle. At the sight of a police car Harry Wilson used to shout, 'Police! Get down', and you had to practically lie in the aisle until the danger passed.

A ten-minute world record

I had been shot putting and discus throwing quite well. So I decided to compete at the National Veterans Indoor Championships at Cosford. The first shot flew - and when you don't feel it off the fingertips, you know it's a good one.

There was much activity amongst the officials when measuring the distance. 'Oh no', I thought, 'I must have fouled the front of the circle'. The chief Field Judge arrived - more measuring. Then he came over to me, told me I had broken the world record for my age group. I was ecstatic. Well, for ten minutes. Then who no less than Rosemary Payne, ex-European Champion, came along and set a new world record. Ah well, better 10 minutes to reign than not at all.

Margaret Tipping (nee King)

Margaret Tipping on rostrum in third position

Ladies Captains as listed in Club Records	
Rita Almond	1951-1954
Doreen Fitzgerald	1955
Barbara Billington	1956
Margaret Astell	1957
Pam Thompson	1958-1959
Elaine Porter	1962

Chapter 6

CELEBRATIONS AND CIVIC HONOURS

Both Dr Baker Bates (seen in photo on page 10 with 'Ham' Finney and Charles Rigby, then Club Secretary, awaiting the start of the Paris race in 1907) and Joe Hughes, a novice in 1913 and Vice-Captain in 1920, were to become mayors of St Helens. Each was to lead a war-torn borough, Dr Bates 1913-18 and Joe, by then Cllr Hughes, in 1941.

Less than two years after World War II ended, and exactly a fortnight after Sutton Harriers' victory in the National Cross-Country Championship another mayor, according to the *St Helens Newspaper* of March 25th, played his part in the club's history.

'ST.HELENS honours its champion (Sutton) HARRIERS

St.Helens through its Mayor and Mayoress (Counc. and Mrs.R.O.Robertson) honoured its England cross-country champion Harriers from Sutton on Saturday 22nd March 1947 at a celebration tea and trophy presentation which was held in East Sutton Labour Club. In presenting the individual awards to Sutton's successful runners, the Mayor said he spoke for the whole town. St.Helens was proud of them having brought the national trophy to the district. He hoped Sutton had the will to win again next year; the goodwill of the town would be behind them.

Sutton Harriers have done a great service to the North of England in winning this trophy again. The last time it visited the North was in 1927 when Hallamshire won. Sutton Harriers were last successful in 1906 and the only other Lancashire clubs to win were Salford Harriers in 1898 and Liverpool in 1895. It is small wonder then, that Sutton organised a special celebration and they were also commemorating the winning of the Northern Counties Cross-Country Championships.

SUTTON WORTHY OF MORE SUPPORT

Alderman J.Hughes, himself an old stalwart of the club, added his congratulations, and said it was a staggering performance on the part of a small club like Sutton, who ran under adverse conditions. The runners were a credit to the club, the district and the North.

When Sutton lost the old pavilion in Helena Road, he said, it was expected the club would die a natural death. But the old hands and the young blood rose to the occasion and worked hard to put Sutton back in the top flight of athletics.

The club was worthy of more support. They were grateful to East Sutton for keeping the club alive through hard times but they had to plan for the future. They were going to be housed in a better pavilion and he wanted them to build up a membership of young and enthusiastic runners so that lads could graduate naturally from the novice, through junior to championship form.

STRENGTH FROM THE OLD "UNS"

Mr.Fred.Ireland, Northern Counties Cross-Country Secretary, brought the congratulations of the North of England to Sutton. They were all thrilled to have the trophies in the north. Sutton's performance was the more meritorious because they competed against teams which had rested overnight while Sutton had been travelling through the bitter conditions which prevailed. He thought that if Sutton had the same advantages as other teams they would have three runners in the England team.

Ex-Secretary of the club, Mr.E.Stubbs, spoke in appreciation of the club's old members, some of whom were present that evening. The strength of the club was from the interest of its old runners. It was a strange thing that a town of the size of St.Helens did not provide bigger membership than Sutton had. It could do and it was up to the club to build up its membership.'

The Mayor then presented the medals to the six Harriers who had won both the Northern and the National Cross-Country Championships :- Tom Fillingham, Alf Tyrer, Joe Harrison, Fred McMinnis,

Bill McMinnis and Ernie Henderson. Tom Fillingham was presented with the H J Taylor Cup for the best individual performance, and then the 'good young 'uns' (to quote the Mayor) Dennis Wilson, Bob Maleedy, Mick Maleedy, Frank Tootal, Gratton Pursell, Alan Burrows, Denis Saunders and Roy Carr were given the prizes they'd won in that afternoon's handicap race. Despite food rationing an excellent tea completed the celebration.

Cllr Robertson's immediate successor, Mayor W Marshall, not only paid Sutton Harriers the honour of travelling to Sheffield to watch the senior team compete in the National Cross-Country Championships, in which victory just eluded them, he also accorded them the honour of the first civic reception in their long history.

Gathered for the occasion at the Town Hall 'Sutton Harriers' (in the words of St Helens Newspaper and Advertiser) 'were told by the Mayor (Counc.W.Marshall) at the Town Hall "you bring prestige to St.Helens and it is only right that you should be recognised in the proper way". The Mayor, whose idea the reception was, also told them "I notice you have been consistently in the front rank for almost fifty years - if that does not warrant public recognition I don't know what does".

Then the Harriers' junior and senior members heard the Deputy Mayor (Counc.R..O.Robertson) who is one of the representatives of East Sutton Ward of the Town Council, say that after all those years they were to have presented to them King George's Field on which to train. So now they may have a clubhouse built - stripping wherever they could they have hitherto been the finest team in England considering they have no headquarters.

Counc.Robertson, who as a public representative, thanked the Mayor, added "King George's Field has been granted by the Parks Committee. The delay in the Secretary, Mr.Harry Wilson, not getting word is due to the fact that certain formalities have had to be gone through. The grounds are now at your disposal".

Mr.N.F.Newbury (Director of Education) was also present with Alderman J.O'Brien, Counc.Griffiths, Mr.E.J.Stubbs (President of Sutton Harriers) and Mr.Fred Ireland (Northern Counties Cross-Country Association Secretary) with his wife. "It is wonderful for any corporation to entertain any harriers club" said Mr.Ireland who then left to catch a train to Manchester.

Thanking the Mayor and Corporation on behalf of the Club, the President said "We, as a club, have had hopes that there may have been Olympic cross-country racing at which one or more of Sutton's men may have been selected to take part. We are definitely attempting to engage more and more members in the athletic side of the track".

The Mayor who had expressed keen delight at being the first in office civically to welcome a sporting organisation so well known for its magnificent achievements had said "Why you have not been recognised in the town I do not know but anyway you have won many great battles on the field and now you have been able to break down this barrier of the civic authority. The members present included the senior runners who won the English National Cross-Country Championship in 1947 and the evening concluded by entertainment with mind-reading and conjuring acts.'

Sadly, the promised clubhouse and facilities did not materialise.

Almost a year later, and by then fifty years old, Sutton Harriers held their Jubilee Celebration Dinner at the *Fleece Hotel* in Church Street, on May 12th 1949. Among their guests were Mr N F Newbury, the borough's Director of Education, and a good friend of the club, and Mr Fred Ireland, a vice-president of the AAA and secretary and past president of the Northern Counties Cross-Country Association.

A review of the Jubilee year revealed it as one of the most successful in the club's history *'For the third time',* readers of the *St Helens Newspaper and Advertiser* were told, *'since it was formed in 1899 the club won the National Cross-Country Championship with the greatest winning margin over the second team ever recorded in this race. Sutton won the West Lancashire Senior and Junior Cross-Country Championships with Fred McMinnis and Mick Maleedy retaining their respective titles, and came second in the Youths' championship.*

In the Northern Counties Cross-Country Championship which they won, Sutton had six men in the first twelve finishers. Further honour came when Mick Maleedy ran for the England team in the International Cross-Country Championship.

In track running they also had great success, winning many relay races. Sutton won the Stalybridge and Bradford Road Relay Races and came third in the Manchester to Blackpool Road Relay organised by the News of the World.

Three members of the club were in the winning Lancashire team which ran in the Inter-Counties Cross-Country Championship and earlier in the season six members were in the winning team which represented the Northern Counties in the Triangular cross-country fixture against Midland Counties and Universities Athletic Union at Birmingham.'

Members, officials and dignatories at the Jubilee Celebration Dinner 1949

Following the presentation by Mr Newbury of an England International track suit to Mick Maleedy, the Senior Club Championship Cup to Tom Fillingham and the Youth Club Championship Cup to Dennis Wilson, the toast *'Sutton Harriers'* was proposed by Mr Ireland.

All present, including three very senior members, Charles Rigby, Billy Brough and F J Whittle, would have agreed with Mr Ireland that *'fifty years of club life were magnificent and although there had been ups and downs Sutton Harriers was a name that was looked to'.*

Responding to the toast the Club President, Mr E J Stubbs, mentioned the advisability of building up the track strength, saying that cross-country running was the Cinderella side of athletics and did not get the publicity of track running. *'Last year we broke new ground with the mile medley team,'* he said, and added, *'At the Helsinki Games there would be much interest to see Sutton Harriers going round the track, and it is possible to have one or two representatives'.*

Mr Stubbs continued, *'Last year we had a sole lady member, Rita Almond, but this year it is hoped to form a ladies' section'.* He said that with Mr Newbury taking a great personal interest and with the help of local headmasters there should be more men coming from the schools.

When Sutton Harriers once more dined at the *Fleece Hotel*, in May 1950, their guests included the Mayor (Cllr E Price) and Mayoress, and Mr Ireland.

Again proposing the club's health Fred Ireland commented that a glance at Sutton Harriers' feats over the years showed a great deal of work had been put in by officials, and he expressed the hope that in future Sutton's name was going to be engraved on the Championship Cup as Birchfield's used to be in years gone by. He added, *'Sutton is a famous club and I do not think any club has won both the National Senior and National Youths Championship in the same year before. I hope you will be a force in athletics.'*

Applause greeted the Club Chairman, Mr Myles Morris, when during his response to the toast he announced that club member Ted Ashley had been selected to represent Cheshire in the forthcoming Inter-Counties Championships.

In responding to the toast to *'The County Borough of St Helens'* which had been proposed by the Club President, Mr E J Stubbs, the Mayor spoke of St Helens appreciating the fame Sutton Harriers had brought the borough, putting it on the map by their efforts. He congratulated the club on its outstanding achievements in the sporting world and then, confessing it was the first time he had had the honour of presenting a runner's cup, went on to present Mick Maleedy, Senior Club Champion for the second year in succession, with his trophy, and Ivan Williams with the Club Youth's Championship Cup.

Following these presentations Mr W Heyes, the club trainer, in discussing the club's notable successes, wondered whether people in St Helens realised how highly esteemed and popular Sutton Harriers were throughout the athletic world. They had friends nationwide.

Then Cllr R S Ellison echoed a reference made by Mr Heyes to the Mayor's recent comment on hoped-for improvements to the club's astoundingly poor training facilities. Calling Sutton Harriers *'a great club with a grand national reputation of which we in St Helens are very proud'* he added, *'We hope you will soon have headquarters worthy of such a fine club'*. Next to speak was Mr W Wild, a vice-president of the AAA and Northern Counties AAA Secretary, who regretted that Sutton, the finest runners in England, had not received an adequate share of publicity in the national papers following their successes. *'We are the cinderellas of sport'* he declared. *'The fellows turn out week after week doing their five and ten miles, with nothing to show for it but froth around their mouths and dirty water to wash in, but they are well satisfied.'*

Next Mr Charles Rigby, a Sutton Harrier since 1900 and former Club Secretary, Treasurer and President, paid his tribute to the club's successes and congratulated its staunch body of officials.

The singing of *'For He's a Jolly Good Fellow'* greeted the Club Secretary, Mr Harry Wilson, who said *'We have in Sutton Harriers a club team - I do not mean a team brought from all corners of the country - a team made up of local runners, the majority of whom were born within two miles of the club headquarters. I defy any club in the world to bring a team collected within ten miles of their headquarters who will run with Sutton over ten miles of cross-country. It has been an inspiration for me to work for the Harriers. In St Helens we have not had the facilities a club of our standing should have. This is being remedied by our friends - we all know who they are. Up to now we have travelled the length and breadth of the country and held our own with people who have not only their own tracks and headquarters, but money behind them which would make Arsenal FC look as though they needed to go to the poor house. Within five years with the material we have - and I say that because the facilities we need will not be ready for 12 months - we will have a reputation on the track like that our cross-country runners have gained.'*

Entertainment by the Gillespie Brothers, Liverpool, followed Mr Wilson's confident conclusion that the club was going from triumph to triumph. Successes there certainly were, but disappointment too, as the improvements hinted at failed to take shape.

On Friday 16th March, 1951, only six days after the club's senior team had returned from Richmond, Yorkshire, National Cross-Country Champions for the third successive time, Sutton Harriers were once again at the Fleece Hotel, ready to enjoy their Annual Dinner and Social Evening.

After the meal the Club President, Mr E J Stubbs, reviewed the club's successes in the past season before calling upon Mr N F Newbury, the Director of Education, to present trophies to the Senior, Junior and Youth Club Champions - Bill McMinnis, Ged Burke and Jock Hendry respectively.

Then followed a varied programme of dances old and new, and of entertainment provided by club members. Duly thanked were Frank Cunliffe for his witty monologues, Mick Maleedy for his Irish melodies and Jock Hendry for his singing of popular songs.

Not quite a fortnight later, on Thursday 29th March, Sutton Harriers, as winners of the National and the Northern Cross-Country Championships, were accorded the club's second civic reception. Held at the Town Hall, with the National Championship trophy displayed on one of the tables, the event included an excellent meal.

Following this, the Mayor (Alderman Mrs E McCormack) proposed the loyal toast, and then referred to John Orrell's tragic death on Snowdon the previous weekend. A minute's silence was observed.

Going on to propose the toast *'Sutton Harriers'* Mrs McCormack (as readers of the *St Helens Reporter* were told) *'said she considered herself a very fortunate Mayor of St.Helens in that twice during her year of office it had been her privilege to offer a civic reception to townspeople of the borough on an outstanding event in which they were personally associated.*

Members and officials with the Mayor of St Helens, Alderman Mrs E McCormack, on the steps of of the Town Hall at the civic reception

"No-one who has lived in St.Helens for even a short time can be unaware of the existence of Sutton Harriers," she said. *"Their success in the athletic world is such as has made them internationally as well as nationally famous, and I thus count it as my own particular privilege to welcome them."*

The Mayor said she could not claim to be a harrier, but, like the rest of her sex, she was well used to running. In modern times a housewife must be what they called "well in training" to cope with modern conditions, and that perhaps had something to do with the success of those of her own sex who were members of Sutton Harriers.

The Mayor added: "All honour to you. May your long and sustained run of success carry you on for many years to come and enable my successors in office, from time to time, to preside over such a gathering and offer, as I am doing, a very sincere and an equally hearty welcome to Sutton Harriers."

In response Mr Myles Morris, Sutton Harriers' Club Chairman, expressed the club's pride at having the honour of civic recognition added to that of winning championships. Expressing the club's thanks to the Corporation, Mr Morris felt their best way of showing their appreciation would be to try to bring additional honour to the town by achieving further successes.

Alderman N Birch listed the club's many successes before proposing the toast *'Sutton Harriers and their achievements'*. He wished the club continuing success, emphasising the crucial role played by their team spirit.

Responding in his turn Mr E J Stubbs, the Club President, dwelt on the achievements of individual members. Six of the club's National Cross-Country Championship team had run for Lancashire, five had represented Northern Counties, and three had run for their country, whilst on the track successful members included Rita Almond, Barbara Billington, J Doyle, T Hackett, K Fryer, J Chidlow, M Maleedy, D Fryer, I Williams, T Fillingham and E Ashley. Applause followed Mr Stubb's mention that Bill McMinnis, the recent winner of the RAF Championship, had been selected to captain the Combined Services team at Sheffield on April 14th 1951.

Having referred to Tom Fillingham's captaincy of the winning Lancashire team at the Inter-Counties Cross-Country Championship, and described the Harriers as the West Lancashire champions Mr Stubbs added that *'with modesty, he could sincerely claim that Sutton Harriers was probably the most popular club in the country at the moment.*

Stating that the club's correct title for the past 18 months had been Sutton Harriers and Athletic Club, St.Helens, Mr Stubbs observed that they were proud of being citizens of St Helens and thought they should identify themselves more closely with the town. They were grateful to the Corporation for the many kindnesses shown them in the past and the many facilities they had granted.

"Running", said Mr Stubbs, "is as clean a sport as you can get. We, as a club would like to encourage as many of the younger people in the town as possible to take an interest in what is a healthy recreation."'

Two Sutton Harriers of very long-standing, Charles Rigby and Hubert Wilcox, were among the guests invited to the club's Annual Dinner, held at the *Fleece Hotel* on Tuesday, 28th October, 1952.

Mr Rigby joined the club four months after it was formed in 1899. He had been a member ever since and served as treasurer, secretary and president. Mr Wilcox was a member of the 1906 National winning team and of the club's successful team in Paris in 1907.

The dinner, attended by 92 members and friends of the club, was honoured by the presence of the Mayor and Mayoress, Cllr and Mrs Percy Griffiths. The toast to the guests was proposed by Mr E J Stubbs, the Club President.

Mr N F Newbury, Director of Education, in responding for the guests, referred to the splendid work being done in the schools for young athletes, and said he was pleased to see the talent being further developed by Sutton Harriers. The Mayor spoke of his long association with the club and pledged his support for the future before he then distributed the club championship cups.

Miss Margaret Astell, Ladies Champion, was undoubtedly one of the most popular winners, and the Club Secretary, Mr Jack Burke, mentioned that she was then a double English champion, being the title holder for the 60 yards and 100 yards Junior races. The Senior Track Champion was Austin Tipping, and the Cross-Country Championship winners were Les Laithwaite (boys' section) Ken Mather (youths' section) and Bill McMinnis (senior section). In addition, Bill was presented with the track suit awarded him for being first reserve in the English Cross-Country team.

Years later, when the receptions and dinners that spanned Sutton Harriers' glory years as National Cross-Country Champions were becoming rather distant memories, one of that distinguished band of champions, Bill McMinnis, achieved a double dose of civic recognition.

Unique among Sutton Harriers, Bill had a road named after him - McMinnis Avenue in Parr. Then, following his return from the first World Masters Athletics Championships in Toronto with three gold medals (for the 5000 metres, 10000 metres and cross-country events) came a very special Mayoral reception. Feeling honour was indeed due to the veteran Harrier, the Mayor (Cllr Mulcrow) welcomed Bill and specially invited guests to the Mayor's Parlour at the Town Hall. Here scones especially baked by the Mayor featured amongst the refreshments!

Chapter 7

ON THE TARMAC

Road Relays

Road relays have been a feature of the athletics calendar for many years. They are usually held in September/October between the end of the track season and the start of the cross-country season and again in March/April between the end of the cross-country season and the forthcoming track season. However, these races are so popular that they have been held in various parts of the country throughout the year.

It is impossible to mention all these events. Here then is a selection, including those Sutton Harriers have taken part in. The most exciting ones for both runners and spectators were those sponsored by the News of the World, each involving twenty teams, all by invitation, with eleven stages of varying distances in each race.

(i)	London to Brighton	for Southern, South Western and Welsh Clubs
(ii)	Manchester to Blackpool	for Northern and Midland Clubs
(iii)	Edinburgh to Glasgow	for Scottish Clubs
(iv)	Northern Ireland	limited to teams from Northern Ireland

Inaugurated in April 1951 the *News of the World* National Road Relay Championship took place annually over the London to Brighton course, starting from the *News of the World* Sports Ground at Mitcham, and ending on Brighton promenade at the Esplanade, a distance of approximately 55 miles. To qualify for this event, teams from the Northern and Midland clubs had to finish in the first six in the Manchester to Blackpool relay, and Sutton Harriers duly received an invitation in 1951. Their finishing positions in the National Relay were:- 1951 - 4th, 1952 - 10th, 1953 - 15th and 1954 - 20th.

Bill McMinnis finishing the last leg of the London to Brighton Road Relay at Brighton

In 1951, at a meeting held by the Sutton Harriers' commitee, it was decided that in the *News of the World* London to Brighton National Road Relay Championship, each of the club's runners would wear a black rosette, provided by the club, as a mark of respect for John Orrell who had recently lost his life on Mount Snowdon.

An interesting feature about these events was the sportsmanship and friendly rivalry they engendered. Harry Wilson, then Sutton Harriers' Club Secretary, would 'cadge' lifts from any coach, car, motor cycle (in those days riding pillion without a helmet) or even bicycle to urge on Sutton runners. One of his really encouraging actions was to say to a runner, *'The next time you see me it will be one mile to where you finish, and the next after that you'll be a half mile from the finish'.* That he was usually correct in his calculations stemmed from Harry's vast background knowledge about runners and teams the length and breadth of the British Isles. His breakdown in health in the mid 1950s was to deprive the club of a very valuable member of its backroom team. Harry's enthusiasm, coupled with his wide knowledge and organising skills had also earned him membership of the West Lancs', Northern Counties' and English Cross-Country Union's committees.

Runners at the start of Manchester to Blackpool Road Relay at Belle Vue

NEWS OF THE WORLD

Manchester — Blackpool Relay Race

(Under A.A.A. Rules—By Permission of N.C.A.A.)

MAY 11th, 1957   START 11.0 a.m.
From BELLE VUE, MANCHESTER

FIRST RELAY.
(4m. 880yds.)
Approx. Time of
Arrival.—11.20 a.m.

Starting in Belle Vue Sports Arena, opposite Firework Island (dressing-room adjoins), turn left at the green coloured Lion and Tiger House, under arch, bearing left and right to Main Gate, out into Hyde Road. Turning left, straight on to Devonshire Street North, turn right, under railway arch, left into Pin Mill Brow (1¾ miles), under railway arch, bearing left into Great Ancoats Street, turning right at Oldham Road Corner into Oldham Road, then second turning on the left, Addington Street, left into Rochdale Road, down Shudehill into Withy Grove, crossing Corporation Street into Fennell Street, passing Manchester Cathedral on left; "S" bend now, right and left Exchange Street and Chapel Street, under railway arch, round The Crescent to the Fire Station opposite Salford Technical School.—First Take-over. Distance: 4¼ miles.

SECOND RELAY.
(4m. 440yds.)
11.40 a.m.

Straight along Windsor Bridge to the junction of roads, taking right hand, Pendleton Road, now Broad Street, passing Pendleton Church (right) at "Woolpack" junction of roads, again right hand, Bolton Road, and right hand again at "Pack Horse Hotel" junction of roads, still Bolton Road, and on to Clifton Memorial.—Second Take-over. Distance: 8¾ miles.

THIRD RELAY.
(4m. 1,056yds.)
12.5 p.m.

Main Manchester-Bolton Road, Kearsley, Farnworth, Higher Market Street, passing Farnworth Post Office, Moses Gate Station to Bolton Wanderers' Football Ground.—Third Take-over. Distance: 13 miles, 616 yards.

FOURTH RELAY.
(5m. 792yds.)
12.30 p.m.

Main Road for some 500 yds., abrupt turn left, Orlando Street, left again Orlando Bridge, sharp right into Moncrieffe Street, abrupt left into Crook Street, under railway arch, over Cross Roads, Flash Street, left into Deane Road, right into Mayor Street, Park Road, Gilnow Road, right into Tudor Avenue, left into Chorley New Road to "Green Wood Hotel," Horwich.—Fourth Take-over. Distance: 18 miles, 1,408 yards.

FIFTH RELAY.
(5m. 264yds.)
1.0 p.m.

Main Chorley Road, Horwich, passing signpost "Chorley," bearing left to "Squirrel Hotel," Rivington Reservoirs, Adlington, Chorley Golf Club. "Yarrow Bridge Hotel."—Fifth Take-over. Distance: 23 miles, 1,672 yards.

SIXTH RELAY.
(4m. 880yds.)
1.25 p.m.

Main Chorley Road, passing Chorley Town Hall on left, Memorial Park, Whittle le Wood, Clayton le Woods, "Half Way House Hotel."—Sixth Take-over. Distance: 28 miles, 792 yards.

SEVENTH RELAY.
(5m. 1,408yds.)
1.50 p.m.

Main Preston Road, passing Clayton Green Post Office, Bamber Bridge (level crossing or subway), Walton le Dale, abrupt turn left at Walton le Dale Garage, passing "White Bull Hotel," Main Preston Road abrupt right turn passing "Harp Inn" and the Prison, abrupt left turn, Deepdale Road, to Preston North End Football Ground.—Seventh Take-over. Distance: 34 miles, 440 yards.

EIGHTH RELAY.
(3m. 440yds.)
2.10 p.m.

Abrupt left turn at traffic lights, Moor Park, over railway bridge, passing Tuiketh Cotton Mills, Main Road, Ashton, Blackpool Road, to Quinney's Restaurant, Lea.—Eighth Take-over. Distance: 37 miles, 880 yards.

NINTH RELAY.
(5m. 1,312yds.)
2.35 p.m.

Main Blackpool Road to "Lea Gate Hotel," then continuing for 500 yards, to large signpost on left, Lytham St. Annes, turning here for Freckleton and Warton, passing "Clifton Arms Hotel," to Warton Boundary Post, 520 yards West of Hotel.—Ninth Take-over. Distance: 43 miles, 432 yards.

TENTH RELAY.
(4m. 360yds.)
3.0 p.m.

Main Road to Lytham Sea Front. Take-over opposite Baziey Road, 200 yards before reaching "Fairhaven Hotel."—Tenth Take-over. Distance: 47 miles, 792 yards.

ELEVENTH RELAY.
(6m. 1,256yds.)
3.35 p.m.

Main Road, passing King Edward and Queen Mary Schools, Hotel Majestic, and Sand Dunes, to the Blackpool signpost, then taking the left-hand road past Starr Gate, under the "Welcome" arch, and continue along the carriage-drive, under "News of the World" banner opposite the Tower, and turn right to finish at the Town Hall. Distance: 54 miles, 288 yards.

TWENTY TEAMS OF ELEVEN TO COMPETE.

All competitors MUST travel in the official coaches. To avoid congestion, coach drivers are asked to make sure that no coach is parked within 100 yards of each Take-Over.
A letter from the Lord Mayor of Manchester, addressed to the Mayor of Blackpool, will be handed to the first representative of Sheffield United H. & A.C. at the start and delivered to the Mayor of Blackpool at the Winning Post.
ALL teams will carry a baton throughout the race. Competitors in each relay will be taken to their respective exchange stations by coach, Mr. A. Spicer being in charge.
Coaches are numbered as per relays 1—11.
All competitors except those running in the first relay must be in their respective coaches, ready to start at 10.30 a.m. NO COMPETITOR WILL BE WAITED FOR. Coaches will await competitors at the end of each relay. A steward will be in charge of each coach and relay.

only competitors and officials with coach tickets will be allowed in these coaches.
All competitors must keep to the left-hand side of the road throughout the course. Any competitor attempting to leave the course, to cut corners, or to cross to the right-hand side of the road for any purpose, will render his team liable to disqualification.
Competitors are asked not to trust their clothes or valuables to anybody other than the transport officials who cannot otherwise be responsible for their safe custody.
Competitors must wear letter numbers back and front, corresponding with the number in the programme.
Dressing—(Start) Belle Vue, Manchester. (Finish) Corporation Baths, Cocker-street, Blackpool.
Immediately after the race competitors and officials with tea tickets should go to the Winter Gardens, Blackpool, where High Tea will be served and the Trophy and Medals will be presented.

Printed by permission of News of the World

The Manchester to Blackpool Road Relay, which began in 1932, was initially held over a distance of 51 miles and comprised ten stages of varying distance, starting from Belle Vue, Manchester, and ending at the Blackpool Town Hall. A tradition of the race was that it be started at 11 am by the Mayor of Manchester who passed to the previous winning team's 1st stage runner a baton containing a message. This was to be handed to the Mayor of Blackpool at the finish of the race by the leading runner. The expenses of all twenty teams were covered by the *News of the World*, who also provided competitors and officials with high tea at the Winter Gardens after the race.

From 1939-46 no relays took place. When they resumed in 1947 the distance had been increased to 54 miles, comprising the eleven stages shown in the extract from the 1957 programme.

The runners on these eleven stages were transported by eleven single-decker North Western buses which displayed in their front windows *News of the World*, whilst stuck in each back window was a card with a stage number eg 'Stage 6'. Whichever stage you ran, you 'changed' on the appropriately numbered bus. Having deposited you where your stage started, your bus then travelled to the end of the stage to wait for the twenty runners to finish.

As Ron Hill wrote in *The Long Road*, recalling the Manchester Blackpool relay: *'This race had an atmosphere which can never be realised in* relays round a set circuit. Each leg had its own mystique, and the distance of the race taxed every club to its limit, 11 good distance or near distance runners having to be found. On the "long" legs went the best runners in the club, with perhaps the best being reserved for the last leg, from St.Annes to Talbot Square, in the shadow of Blackpool Tower. Half-milers were often shanghaied into running the shortest leg, but it was an event in which club members, who would not normally get on the first team, suddenly had an extremely important part to play, and some runners trained all year for no other purpose than to get into the "Blackpool" team. Part of the excitement was that it was a point to point race, with a definite goal: getting to Blackpool as quickly as possible, and many dramas were played along that road.'

Though Sutton Harriers competed in the 1930s, their achievements then are unknown, other than in 1934 when they finished 8th, and twelve minutes after the winners, Birchfield. Post World War II their positions were:-

> 1947-5th, 1948-4th, 1949-3rd, 1950-2nd, 1951-3rd, 1952-2nd,
> 1953-6th, 1954-8th, 1955-6th, 1956-14th, 1957-16th, 1958-19th, 1959-20th

Increasingly congested roads led to this type of point to point relay becoming replaced by events run on traffic-free circuits, usually in park areas, and the final Manchester-Blackpool Road Relay took place in 1963.

Manchester to Blackpool Relay Race Winners and Times

51 miles

1932
Salford H.	*4:30:25
Birchfield H.	4:30:40
Hallamshire H.	4:37:10

1933
Birchfield H.	4:30:32
Hallamshire H.	4:36:15
Salford H.	4:36:20

51 miles, 200 yards

1934
Birchfield H.	*4:32:54
Salford H.	4:33:04
Hallamshire H.	4:35:16

1935
Birchfield H.	4:35:10
Hallamshire H.	4:35:46
Salford H.	4:37:40

50 miles, 1256 yards

1936
Birchfield H.	*4:32:14
Hallamshire H.	4:36:36
Salford H.	4:36:49

1937
Birchfield H.	4:34:57
Salford H.	4:38:54
Hallamshire H.	4:40:54

50 miles, 1376 yards

1938
Birchfield H.	*4:32:00
Salford H.	4:34:15
Liverpool Pembroke	4:36:25

54 miles, 288 yards

1947
Birchfield H.	4:55:20
Bellahouston H.	4:56:31
Coventry Godiva	4:56:67

1948
Birchfield H.	4:58:54
Tipton H.	4:59:05
Coventry Godiva	5:03:20

1949
Birchfield H.	4:53:25
Tipton H.	4:54:48
Sutton H.	4:56:02

1950
Birchfield H.	4:50:48
Sutton H.	4:53:10
E. Cheshire H. & AC.	4:54:28

1951
Birchfield H.	4:45:08
E. Cheshire H. & AC.	4:47:27
Sutton H.	4:47:53

1952
Birchfield H.	4:45:28
Sutton H.	4:47:21
Manchester A. & CC	4:50:38

1953
Birchfield H.	4:49:02
Bolton Utd H. & AC	4:50:38
Tipton H.	4:52:51

1954
Sheffield Utd H. & AC	4:39:15
Birchfield H.	4:41:16
Coventry Godiva	4:43:52

1955
Sheffield Utd H. & AC	4:44:17
Birchfield H.	4:44:33
Bolton Utd H. & AC	4:45:07

1956
Sheffield Utd H. & AC	4:51:24
Birchfield H.	4:53:22
Derby & Co. AC	4:53:45

1957
Sheffield Utd H. & AC	4:37:18
Derby & Co. AC	4:40:13
Pembroke A. & CC	4:41:38

1958
Derby & Co. AC	4:35:16
Sheffield Utd H. & AC	4:37:35
Birchfield H.	4:38:35

1959
Derby & Co. AC	4:43:04
Coventry Godiva	4:44:33
Birchfield H.	4:44:58

1960
Derby & Co. AC	*4:32:16
Bristol AC	4:38:09
Coventry Godiva	4:38:11

1961
Derby & Co. AC	4:35:34
Coventry Godiva	4:36:49
Blackpool & Fylde A.C.	4:38:36

1962
Coventry Godiva	4:33:51
Bristol AC	4:33:42
Bolton Utd H & AC	4:35:43

1963
Coventry Godiva	4:39:12
Derby & Co. AC	4:42:14
Bristol AC	4:42:28

* Full course records for the distances stated

Intermediate Course Records

Stage No.							
1	P. Hedley	Sheffield Utd H. & AC	22:04 (1958)	6	W. Berry	Bolton Utd H. & AC	22:53 (1962)
2	G.D. Ibbotson	Longwood H. & AC	20:34 (1961)	7	V. Bateman	Pembroke A. & CC	22:53 (1957)
3	E. Strong	Bristol AC	22:21 (1960)	8	B.B. Heatley	Coventry Godiva	26:38 (1962)
	G.D. Ibbotson	Longwood H. & AC	22:21 (1960)	9	S. Smith	Pembroke A. & CC	16:15 (1957)
4	R. Hill	Bolton Utd H. & AC	26:40 (1962)		E. F. Strong	Bristol AC	26:53 (1962)
5	E. Matley	Derby & Co. AC	24:37 (1960)	10	B. Jackson	Bolton Utd H & AC	20:51 (1962)
				11	F. Norris	Bolton Utd H & AC	32:39 (1960)

Thanks to Horwich RMI's attempt in 1989 to re-introduce the relay on a more informal basis, the following table, detailing winners and times for all twenty-four relays held between 1932 and 1963 was provided in their programme. (fig y) In 1989 each stage was started as a separate race with a cut-off time, after which the next stage was started. This enabled a team to continue in case a runner did not make the change over on time, went off course or pulled up injured en-route. In these circumstances the cut-off time plus five minutes was added to a team's cumulative time.

Decades later, for Sutton Harriers, the *News of the World* road relays still trigger warm recollections such as these:

It's a few years ago since the Manchester to Blackpool Road Relay was a very popular fixture with the leading road racing clubs. The race started at Belle Vue in the centre of Manchester, then travelled along the main highway through Salford, Pendleton, Bolton, towards Preston, in eleven stages, passing through Bamber Bridge where there was a railway crossing. The start of the race was timed for most of the teams to have crossed the railway lines before a local train was due but if your team was not performing very well, you could, and it did happen, arrive at the crossing with the barrier down and a train blocking your path. In such circumstances you had no alternative but to go down 13 steps, take the underpass, and climb the other 13 steps to resume your run - not an ideal way to road race.

One year, my stage in the Manchester/Blackpool relay was from Fairhaven to Blackpool Town Hall (approximately 7 miles), the last stage. A friend of mine at RAF Weeton was very interested and said he would enjoy seeing me run, so I suggested that he could be riding his cycle somewhere along the stretch of road at about 2.30 pm on this certain Saturday. The race developed, and Sutton were running second behind Birchfield Harriers and doing a very good time. I left my wife, Doreen, and baby daughter playing on the sands at St Anne's, and I took over my part of the successful Sutton team's run and we finished second to Birchfield.

I collected my tracksuit top at Blackpool Town Hall and proceeded to jog back to Doreen at St Anne's. Halfway along the road I met this friend of mine on his bike looking for me, and I appeared in the opposite direction. He would not believe that I had raced 7 miles to Blackpool, turned round and was jogging back along the same distance.

Bill McMinnis

By a supporter

The Manchester to Blackpool race was another event in which Sutton took part in the late 40s and early 50s. Although they never won it, I think they came second on two occasions. The race started at Belle Vue and finished at Blackpool Town Hall, just off the front. The total distance was around 54 miles and consisted of eleven legs varying in length from approximately 3 miles to over 7 and took about five hours to complete. So it was a long but very exciting day for us spectators.

Athletes and supporters before travelling to the Manchester to Blackpool Road Race

Our supporters' coach would take us to Salford Fire Station which was the first changeover. Often Billy McMinnis would run the first leg and be up with the leaders. After cheering Billy in and seeing our next man off we would run back to the coach, catch our lad up, cheering like mad as we passed him. The coach would then stop further along the route so that we could give him more encouragement; then on to the next changeover. This went on all the way to Blackpool via Bolton, Preston and Lytham St Anne's. The best moment was when a Sutton runner passed the leader and took the baton from him.

Birchfield Harriers, a Midlands club with a large membership and first class facilities, were the team to beat. Sutton being such a small club would be stretched to field eleven top class runners. Nevertheless they would be up there with the leaders. Fred McMinnis used to run the last leg, which was the longest. It was run along the sea front from Lytham St Anne's and I remember that on one occasion he started off leading the race but unfortunately he could only finish second.

One very exciting finish was when two leading runners were racing neck and neck with barely a hundred yards to the finishing line, not bad after 54 miles. I also seem to remember a young David Coleman of television fame running for Manchester Athletic Club. We usually spent the evening in the Winter Gardens at Blackpool before returning home to St Helens tired but very happy.

Allan Morris

By the President's daughter

Thinking back to the London to Brighton Road Relay Race, to the best of my knowledge Billy McMinnis and Mick Maleedy both ran in that. My youthful memories are of a day of fun and excitement following "our team". The family travelled down to London, staying overnight with my uncle (my father's brother) in Ealing. They then joined with us to follow the race by car. There were the various supporters' club coaches all supporting their teams. We would stop at intervals on the various legs and pile out of the cars and cheer on our Sutton Harriers's Man, together with the Sutton Harrier's supporters in their coach, picnicking on the way! In those days Sutton Harriers had a leading reputation. I wonder if the football supporters of today have as much innocent fun as we had then. Then the arrival at Brighton to see the team come in!

Then there was the Manchester to Blackpool Road Relay Race. My father was a great supporter of that also, taking his family along with him whenever possible. One memory I have of that race, is when my father thought "our" man on one of the legs needed some help and encouragement. He then leapt out of his car (or was he in the Supporter's Coach then? I cannot quite remember!) and proceeded to run the whole of the leg behind the Sutton Harrier's Man, fully clothed in a suit, nattering at him all the way! Unfortunately I cannot remember if the Harrier won his leg, but at the end he turned and said to my father that he should have run that leg instead and probably would have done better than him. My father would have been well into his forties, if not his fifties, and had not done any running for many years, though still active in badminton. As always he was a great active supporter of the Sutton Harriers, and not just a figurehead President.

Lynn Lawton nee Stubbs

Well before escalating road traffic finally drove such events to the safety of park paths, the Lancashire County Road Relay was inaugurated in October 1951 at Southport, on which occasion, having completed its eight legs, each of 3¼ miles, starting and finishing outside the Floral Hall on the promenade, in 2 hrs 11 mins 54 secs, Sutton were the winning team.

Over the years there were many popular relays, one being the Sefton Park Road Relay, held in September, with its six stages, each of 3¾ miles and attracting many Sutton Harrier entries. The Waterloo Road Relay, in which Sutton's six-man team were placed 3rd in 1965 and again in 1967, was unusual - being run in November, at night and under street lights.

Then there were the Egerton Road Relay staged on the outskirts of Bolton, the Salford Relay, and those at Blackpool, Longdendale and Wallasey. The Wallasey Relay, over two miles, with four men per team, started and finished on the promenade and was won by Sutton in 1969 and again in 1970, when Peter Roberts ran the fastest time of all the competitors with 9 mins 45 secs.

But without doubt the most picturesque was the Hollingworth Relay, involving a four-man team with each runner covering approximately 4¼ miles around the path that encircled Hollingworth Lake. Sutton's best performance here came in 1971 when they finished 3rd, thanks to Ron Barlow, Colin Johnson, Brian Renshall and Peter Roberts.

Sutton Harriers also helped organise the National Dairy Festival Road Relay in June 1964 which started outside St Helens Town Hall. The team of John McLoughlin, Brian Renshall, Trevor Prescott and Tom McIntyre finished in 7th place, with McLoughlin and Renshall having the satisfaction of being among the day's ten fastest runners, with times of 13 mins 10 secs and 13 mins 8 secs respectively for the

2½ mile distance. The race was won by the powerful Bolton Harriers, who included internationals Ron Hill and Mike Freary in their team.

In July 1968, a century since the growing town had become a borough, St Helens was in festive mood, and one of the many celebratory events was an evening relay race organised by Sutton Harriers. Held in Sherdley Park, the race was for teams consisting of four runners, each of whom would cover a distance of approximately 2¼ miles around the footpath perimeter of the park. The runners started at the park gates on Marshalls Cross Road and ran down to the Score. Here they turned left on to the path that skirted 'Pets' Corner', went on past the football pitches, along Eltonhead Road, and then turned left down to Marshalls Cross Road (thus passing where the Sports Centre is now situated) and so back into the park.

A report of the race in the following week's St Helens Newspaper recorded that Brian Renshall took the Sutton team from 11th place to 3rd on the second 'leg' and achieved the fastest time of the day, 11 mins 8 secs. There is no mention of the other three runners in the team, which maintained its third position to the end of the race.

The following day Renshall travelled to Leverhulme Park, Bolton to run in a three-mile invitation race. Despite his efforts of the previous day he ran a personal best time of 13 mins 44 secs, finishing just behind Ron Barlow (13 mins 43 secs) in a race won by Altrincham's Alan Blinston, who later that year represented Great Britain at the Mexico Olympics.

When, in 1964, the H S Finney cross-country races for West Lancs clubs were changed to relays, Sutton were placed third (Prescott, Renshall, Griffiths, McLoughlin) but were second in 1967 (Walsh, Roberts, Renshall, McLoughlin) before being triumphant in 1968 (James, Renshall, McLoughlin, Roberts). They won again in December 1969 (James, Renshall, Barlow, Roberts), having also won the Liverpool and District Road Relay Championship that October.

In the regional relays during this period Sutton struggled to make any significant impact in the twelve-man Northern Relay or the eight-man Lancashire event, largely owing to a lack of depth compared to the likes of the Bolton and Manchester clubs who boasted internationals amongst their teams. Sutton's third place in the 1970 Lancashire Relay, was due in no small measure to their being able to include Ron Barlow and steeplechase international John Jackson (a previous winner of the Sutton Road Race) in their squad. Barlow had recently joined from Wallasey AC. Jackson, although a first claim member of North Staffs AC, was living in the area whilst working at Pilkington's laboratory in Lathom, and had joined Sutton as a 'second claim' member, and as such was able to compete, having satisfied the necessary residential requirements. The other members of the team that day were Bernard Lloyd, Renshall, Frank Rimmer, Colin Johnson, Roberts and McLoughlin. Also in 1970 Sutton finished runners-up to Bolton in the six-man Northern Road Relay Championships at Blackpool. Just ten seconds separated the two teams. Sutton's six that day were Lloyd, Renshall, Barlow, Roberts, James and McLoughlin.

Sadly, in an era in which traffic congestion has driven almost all of the club relays out of existence, and regional and national events to the safety of large parks, Sutton Harriers have not achieved the successes of those teams of the 60s and earlier decades, though the club has continued to have representation in the district relays. With a far larger catchment area Liverpool Harriers and Liverpool Pembroke Sefton AC have come to dominate all aspects of athletics, making it very difficult for Sutton to compete effectively, particularly at senior level.

The Sutton Road Race

When Sutton Harriers' committee decided to stage an inter-club road race in April 1959 as the official opening function for the club's new headquarters in Chester Lane, they were in fact inaugurating a popular annual athletic event, initially intended for senior men only.

The proximity of the Green Dragon in Gartons Lane to Sutton Manor Colliery (and its invaluable changing accommodation) often made it the starting and finishing point for this seven-mile race with its three 2-mile laps and one of 1 mile. However, Harriers who participated also recall the event beginning and ending in the clubhouse in Chester Lane, particularly after the improvements there were completed.

A three-mile Boys' Race, for the 14-16s, was added to the programme in 1965 and a two-mile Colts' Race, for the under 14s, in 1976. 1977 brought metrication and 7, 3 and 2 miles became 12, 5 and 3 km respectively. Lack of support led the Boys' and Colts' Races to be discontinued after 1983, the year in which the Senior Race become open to both sexes. The final road race took place in 1992, the distance having been reduced to 10 km in 1991.

Brian Renshall leading in the Sutton Road Race ahead of No 38, Ron Hill

Over the years there were a number of famous winners of the Senior Men's Race: Olympian Ron Hill must head the roll of honour with three wins, whilst the former European Indoor 3000 metres gold medallist Ricky Wilde, and local athletes Neil Smart and Steve Anders each won twice. John McLoughlin is the only Sutton Harrier to have won, back in 1965. Far the most successful contestant in the Ladies' Race was Sutton Harriers' Sue Crehan who, from its inception in 1983, triumphed on five successive occasions.

Marathon

When, in 490 BC, an invading Persian army was encamped at Marathon, barely 25 miles from Athens, a long-distance runner, Pheidippides, was despatched to seek help from Sparta, 150 miles away. He is said to have accomplished this in two days, and remains famous for such an incredible run.

Indeed his fame has confused his name with that of an unknown Greek who, after the Athenians (unaided by the Spartans) had defeated the Persians, took tidings of the victory back to Athens from the battlefield at Marathon.

Appropriately, it was in Athens that the first of the modem Olympic Games were held in 1896 and included in the events was a 26 mile long-distance race - the marathon. When in 1908 it was London's turn to host the Olympics the length of the race was increased by 385 yards so that, having started in Windsor, the runners would finish in front of the Royal Box at the White City Stadium, Shepherds Bush, London.

The marathon was usually run by athletes who were extending their careers having lost speed, getting older, but retaining stamina through regular training, and enthusiastic to continue running on a competitive basis. It was not until the 1970s that fun runs were introduced, following media emphasis on jogging for a better and healthier lifestyle. They became the accepted thing, resulting in the numbers in a race increasing from around a hundred runners to the many thousands now seen in marathons like the London, New York, Chicago and other city runs throughout the world.

In Sutton the club committee, having at their January 1909 meeting acepted Manchester Chronicle AC's invitation to compete in a marathon race, in February decided to stage a trial half marathon that April and invited other local clubs to take part. The 16½ mile road race consisted of three equal laps from School Lane to Junction Lane and Bold Road continuing alongside the wall of the Bold Estate to Clock Face, Marshalls Cross, Eaves Lane and New Street.

Among the 19 entrants were runners from St Austins, St Helens Recs and Newton and all were photographed before the race, together with Mr Bell, the Sutton Harriers' President, who acted as starter and kneels at the right.

In the 'Chronicle' Marathon itself the club did well. Their five runners were the first team to finish, with two of them coming in amongst the first twelve. One Harrier came fourth in the Great Northern Marathon. There were successes, too, in the Ormskirk and Widnes marathons, whilst F J Whittle won the club's own marathon, thereby winning a trophy presented by Oxo.

Athletes before Sutton Harriers Marathon in 1909

The following season the club's team came second in the 'Hackenschmidt Marathon Race', whilst W H Begg, who came in second on that occasion, won the Manchester event in 1911, thus winning the Manchester Wheeler Cup.

During the 1920s and 30s there were quite a number of marathons held in the North West, for example in Manchester, Bolton, Blackpool, Liverpool and Sheffield. Sponsors included the Sporting Chronicle and Daily Dispatch. The earliest mention of a Sutton Harrier successfully competing in one of these marathon races was of Billy Maleedy winning the Bolton Marathon in 1929. He had previously finished 2nd in the Sporting Chronicle Marathon when running for Sacred Heart AC. When Billy competed in the 1929 Liverpool City Marathon he led at one stage by a half mile but was caught with five miles to go to the finish and was placed 6th, with Jimmy Morris's son, Sutton's Club Captain, E J (Teddy) Morris, in 8th position.

Peter Priestner in the 1960 Liverpool Pembroke 20 miles being encouraged by Eddie Edwards on his bike

During the late 1930s, Sutton Harriers' Gordon Edgar, a postman from Liverpool and an Eire international, ran a number of marathons. His philosophy was that after the training and competition throughout the cross-country season a runner was strong enough to run twenty miles and the remaining six miles were a matter of willpower and mental toughness.

In 1946, when competitive athletics resumed after World War II, Alf Tyrer ran in the Doncaster-Sheffield Marathon and finished 2nd, to win the Northern Counties' Championship, a feat he repeated in 1947 in the same race. Bill McMinnis's record-breaking winning run in the 1953 event also won him the Northern Counties' title, and two years later he finished 3rd in this race. Peter Priestner competed in the 1960 race with considerable credit, and it was a successful year for him as he won the Cheshire Marathon title and 20 miles championship.

The Liverpool City Marathon brought Sutton Harriers many successes during the 1950s, mainly through Bill McMinnis, who won the 1951 race in his first attempt at the distance, repeating the feat

Bill McMinnis entering Anfield when winning the 1962 Liverpool Marathon

in 1952 and 1953. He also finished 6th in 1954, 3rd in 1955 and 2nd in 1956. With three contestants Sutton might well have won the team race in 1954, with Joe Harrison finishing 7th, just behind Bill, but unfortunately Fred McMinnis was forced to drop out in the later stages of the race. All went well a year later when Fred McMinnis, Bill McMinnis and Jack Chidlow were the winning team, and Sutton's second success in the team race came in 1959 with Peter Priestner 2nd, Joe Harrison 3rd and Trevor Prescott 19th. Peter and Joe, not realising the team position, were in the showers when Trevor walked in with the team prizes and trophy, much to the surprise of the showering pair.

The Polytechnic Marathon, run over a course from Windsor to Chiswick, was a popular event for Bill McMinnis and Joe Harrison. Both competed in the 1952, 53 and 54 races. It was in 1955 that Bill reached the pinnacle of his marathon career. After finishing 3rd in the Doncaster to Sheffield Marathon in April, he six weeks later won the Polytechnic Marathon, and four weeks after that race won the AAA Marathon at Reading.

Writing in *Athlete's World* in May 1981, Mitcham AC Veteran Jack Fitzgerald in his *Where are they now?* column recalled the 1955 AAA marahon and Bill McMinnis's role in the race:-

'The scene of the 1955 race is a hot July in Reading, where the stage was set for the AAA Marathon. The other two AAA Championships to be staged on that day were the 4 x 100 and 4 x 440 yards relays.

Bill McMinnis in RAF uniform with trophy for the Polytechnice Marathon

Happily my own club were to be successful in the latter of these two, with a team comprising of Dave Durham, Dick Boyce, Lofty Lloyd and Brian Hewson. Unfortunately, I wasn't to have the pleasure of witnessing this, as by the time of this race, I was sharing three hours of agony with the rest of the Marathon Field.

Pre-race favourites were Bill McMinnis, who had won the Poly Marathon earlier in the year; Geoff Iden, who had lived in the shadows of Peters and Cox for so long, that, with their retirement from Marathons after Vancouver, a large section of the road running fraternity were willing him to win at least one major championship, and Jackie Meckler, the South African who had been placed in the sweltering conditions of the Vancouver Marathon.

Even as early in the year as July, we had already experienced a long hot summer, ideal for lethargic holiday sun worshippers, but not so good for those of us dedicated to churning out long distances on the road each weekend. Nonetheless, there was really no excuse for non acclimatisation, although in the last analysis it was the Veterans of the day who proved to be by far the fittest men.

The race was originally scheduled to be commenced at midday, but the organisers delayed it for an hour in the hopes that the weather would cool down a little. If anything, it got warmer, as we started in temperatures approaching the nineties.

In a recent discussion with Bill on the race conditions, we both held similar memories of the course; of narrow country lanes with high hedges which had a definite claustrophobic atmosphere. We also agreed that there were very few feeding stations on the course.

Something like 70 starters were decimated to less than 30 after one lap. After my usual steady start, I was amazed to discover that at that point, the only runners ahead of me were Bill, Geoff and Bill Kelly as I caught Jack Meckler. Here I was imprudent enough to accept an orange drink from Jack's attendants, the one and only time I have ever taken a fruit drink in a long distance race. It would be too simple to say that this single action converted me from a reasonably fit athlete in to the shambling hunk I deteriorated into over the second half of the race, obviously there was more to it than that.

The dangers of fruit drinks on a normally sensitive stomach on an exceptionally hot day became more than apparent for the rest of that fateful journey, although I won't upset anybody's sensibilities with lurid details. The elder statesmen of the day had much more sense, and it was an object lession for the advantages of experience.

Bill McMinnis was in fact a Veteran at the time, as he had just reached his 40th birthday. After a long career as a Cross Country runner, in which he had assisted Sutton Harriers to win many ECCU National team races, he made his marathon debut in 1951. A regular serviceman, Bill spent a lot of his service career developing talent as it entered the RAF at Padgate. Among these were Peter and Gordon Pirie, Andy Ferguson and John Stone.

Sutton were based at St Helens, and were distinctive among athletic clubs, as they won the National year after year with an active membership of seven. It used to be said that it was easier to make the Lancashire team than the Sutton team, but I think that this was an extravagant statement by that other great Sutton Cross Country International, Norman Ashcroft.

Unlike many of his contemporaries, Bill is still in World Class in his age group, winning M65 Gold Medals at both World Veteran Championships at Palmerstone North and Christchuch. When Bill won the Poly, Rex Alstone in a memorably abysmal broadcast, proved that he could neither recognise club performers or read competitors numbers by announcing the winner as Geoff Iden.

Bill confused nobody in this race as he finished in 2.39.35, wearing his RAF Singlet and over 12 minutes in front of Geoff who was nearly caught on the track by Jack Meckler. If only I could have stayed with him! Dear old Bill Kelly, who died recently after courageously continuing to run long after he contracted throat cancer, was an easy fourth, while yet another Veteran, Bill Parr, of the local Club, Reading AC, was the next to cross the line, having passed me halfway through the last lap.

Within sight of the stadium, I still held on to sixth place, but then in rapid succession I was passed by Mick Porter, later to be the first treasurer of Northern Vets AC, Ted Hefford, and my mature clubmate Larry Scott. As I staggered round the final lap of the track and over the line I was conscious of two stretchers, one occupied and one vacant. It transpired that the first of these contained the carcass of Geoff Iden who had collapsed with heat exhaustion on finishing, and I was guided on to the other by a gentleman who years later I was to discover was John Martell, the present Administrative Officer of the AAA's.

Next to appear on the track was my other clubmate, Ray Bott. Ray never one to be upstaged, occupied the stretcher vacated by Geoff as he was loaded unceremoniously into the ambulance. Even in my comatose condition, I couldn't help *reflecting that if there had been a team race in the AAA's, we would have won it for the second time in four years, as in 1951, we were the only Club to finish three runners.*

Eventually, Ray and I were transported off to the "Battle Hospital", appropriately named on this occasion. There we were fed with endless bottles of saline and water. Peter Scott of Cheltenham and Bill Watts of Herne Hill were already convalescing there, which brought the casualty list up to five out of only sixteen finishers. Poor Bill, the gentlest of men was unable to keep the concoction down, which necessitated his overnight stay while they injected it into his veins. Luckily Geoff had a couple of loyal Victoria Park Harrier officials who had waited with a car to transport us back to London.

So the curtain descended on a fantastic championship in which the first eight runners included four vets and one near vet. Could it happen today in similar conditions? Possibly, rather than probably. Younger runners are putting in more miles in training, but I still like to think that experience is almost as valuable as form in the circumstances.'

Three weeks after his triumph at Reading it was undoubtedly through tiredness resulting from the exertions of the earlier marathons that Bill was beaten into 3rd place in the Liverpool City Marathon. However, in October 1955 he was selected to represent Great Britain in the Kosice Marathon in Prague, Czechoslovakia, did so, and finished 12th. Bill was the first-ever Sutton Harrier to be selected by Great Britain since the Club was founded in 1899.

It was during the mid-fifties that Joe Harrison decided to test his endurance beyond the 26 miles marathon distance by entering the 1956 London to Brighton individual road race - a distance of 50 miles, starting at 7 am outside the Houses of Parliament on Westminster Bridge and finishing at the Brighton Aquarium. After completing his shift at Pilkington Brothers, St Helens, on the Friday evening, he travelled from Liverpool on the midnight train to London and made his way from Euston Station to the start of the race. He ran the distance in 6

St Helens Charity Half Marathon 1983

hours 22 mins 33 secs, returning to London for an evening's dancing before catching the midnight train to Liverpool and reporting for work on the Sunday morning. He also competed in 1958 when he finished 2nd in 5 hours 51 mins 23 secs, and again in 1959, on both occasions with the same travel arrangements. A similar race from Liverpool St George's Hall to Blackpool Town Hall, a mere 48 miles, was introduced in 1959 and Joe was amongst the starters and finishers, as he also was in 1961 and 1962 when he finished 5th and 4th respectively.

In 1983 Jim and Sue Crehan competed in the New York Marathon and Hugh Dixon was 3rd in the Mersey Marathon in a time of 2 hours 26 mins 30 secs, a club best time for the event. The following year he finished in 6th position.

By this time charity-based marathons were becoming popular, with participants attracted by the challenge of simply completing the distance and making money for charity. Thus Sutton Harriers and St Helens Lions joined forces to organise the first St Helens Charity Half Marathon, which took place on 27th March 1983.

Patrons of the event, Lord and Lady Pilkington, started the 1,026 entrants on the gruelling 13 mile

192½ yard course - which began and ended in Sherdley Park. Kevin Jacques, of St Helens AC, winner of the Newton Half Marathon in 1982, was first to finish, completing the course in 1 hour 7 mins and 44 secs.

Kevin received the Nancy Kershaw Shield, to retain for one year, and a portable television set when the Mayor of St Helens, Cllr Nancy Kershaw, presented prizes and trophies at Sutton Sports Centre after the event.

A special award, a voucher donated by Lady Pilkington, was made to 72 year-old Sutton Harrier, Ted Johnson, the oldest competitor in the event, who was among the almost 900 entrants who completed the course. Disappointed with his time of 1 hour 51 mins 2 secs, Ted nevertheless finished well ahead of many participants half his age.

Excluding money due in from sponsors the event had already raised £1500 for charity by 31st March.

An Expert Reflects on Marathon Running

There are two ways of completing those 26 miles.

Running - when time does not really matter

Almost anyone who is fairly young and active and reasonably fit, possesses two legs, a pair of lungs, and a heart that works OK can do this.

If the early pace is slow enough, the 26 miles can be completed in around 4 to 4½ hours, ie at 6 miles per hour approximately - a mixture of trotting and walking. The runner will obviously be very tired at the end, but otherwise OK. But there are one or two points to remember :-

Do not attempt your first mile in 5 minutes or your last mile will take 25 minutes, and you will be lucky to be still on two feet.

If your first few miles seem to be slow, that is all right! You will probably finish OK.

Try to find someone of equal ability as company, or you may become lonely and dispirited, even though surrounded by hundreds of other performers.

Keep in mind that you will start running at breakfast time, and you will still be running at lunchtime, and that this can be a frightening thought.

Never stop moving forward. Time goes very quickly, even if the miles do not.

After the first TWO or THREE hours if you do stop, you will probably not start again.

If you are 'lucky enough', or 'stupid enough', to complete the full distance, still keep moving and expect that the next day will be awfully painful. Your whole body will ache. Most probably you will temporarily have lost your appetite, and you will most likely utter the time-honoured phrase 'NEVER AGAIN'!

Racing - when time is very, very important

Racing 26 miles is totally different from just running 26 miles.

The only people or athletes who race this distance have prepared for it by training hard, often daily, by running approximately 80 to 100 miles a week, perhaps 15 to 20 miles per day. Anything less than this means you are only playing with the marathon.

If your objective is to complete the full distance in 2 to 2½ hours, you will definitely need to train so intensively, and this intensity of preparation must continue for years, depending on your physical capacity to take this level of punishment.

Racing itself is simply a relentless grinding of other competitors into submission until they or you have had enough - usually with the thought 'What am I doing here?'. When you reach this stage of exhaustion, winning or doing well is out of the question. In other words, you just give up. The element of competition is gone, and you must be content just to finish the distance.

'Hitting the wall' No knowledge or experience can help. When you have gone you have gone!

If you are lucky, and it's your day the last few miles of a marathon can be really interesting. It is very often a cat and mouse situation as you watch each other for signs - too disguised or too numerous to mention..Nearing the finish To find yourself running away from your nearest competitors (your friends, the ENEMY) as the finish gets nearer, is indeed a great thrill. You seem to find extra energy from somewhere, but it is usually the case of the one who wins the most races is the one who has trained the hardest.

There's no secret formula - just plain hard work or grind, obviously at the expense of many of the pleasures in life.

Snippets overheard

'Keep going, mate. We have passed half way. Only another 13 miles to go!'

Q. 'What do you think about when you run for so long ?'
A. 'If you are in front you are worried about all those athletes behind you, or if you are not in front you are concerned about those who are in front.'

'When I passed you just before the finish mate, your legs were all over the road.'
'Look pal, you had more control over my legs than I had, at that time.'

Second and third remarks to the winner:
'What do they feed you on - birdseed?' 'You were flying at the finish.'

Remark by the winner: "Can't understand my form. I haven't trained all week because of this, that or the other.'
Retort by 2nd and 3rd 'Tell us another.' 'We've heard that one before.'

Q. 'Do you have a diet for runners?'
A. 'Yes, as much as possible, as often as possible.'

Q. 'Is it monotonous running laps, rather than a straight course?'
A. 'No. If you are interested in the countryside, you are not interested in the race.'

Question by a novice: 'Whom should I consult if I want to run a marathon, a doctor or a psychiatrist?'
Answer: 'BOTH.'

Footnote

In 1936 the exploits of Ernie Harper, in running second in the Berlin Olympic marathon, fired my ambition and I decided to give up football, rugby, cricket, cycling, etc. and concentrate on the marathon. Little did I expect that many years later, in 1951, on winning the Northern Marathon, Doncaster to Sheffield, in record time, the person who wrapped a blanket round my shoulders would be, YES, Ernie Harper.

Bill McMinnis

Saturday 6th - Sunday 7th July 1974

'The idea for the relay was put forward one evening after training, over a pint in the Glassmakers Arms in Sutton. Four main benefits were seen to come from such an occasion: to mark the anniversary with a special athletic event; to involve the whole club, young and old; to raise money for the recently started rebuilding project, (which was to replace the wooden hut erected in the 1950s); and to present a petition at 10 Downing Street asking the Government to provide more money for sports facilities in line with the 'Sport for All' campaign of 1974.

Once the committee had approved the proposal, much work had to be put into the organisation of such an ambitious event. It was important to encourage as many people as possible to take part. In fact nearly 40 athletes were involved in the relay, including 17 youngsters. As a fund-raising event it was decided to hold a raffle in which people were asked to guess how long it would take to run the full distance of 199 miles.

The main concern was how to get each athlete to and from his or her particular leg of the relay. Tom Byrne, a local businessman, who had become involved in the club's redevelopment project and who gave much valuable advice and financial assistance, solved that problem. He arranged to provide a coach and two cars, which would accompany the runners and provide some protection from the traffic. The two cars would also be used to guide the night-shift runners. The coach would be used to carry the main body of runners, waiting at each take-over point so that the in-coming and out-going runners would receive

encouragement and vocal support. It would also enable the majority of runners, especially the younger athletes, to have a rest during the night.

The weather was fine and dry that weekend and athletes and supporters gathered outside St Helens Town Hall at 10am on the Saturday morning. The MP for St Helens, Mr Leslie Spriggs, started the relay and the Club President, Ted Johnson, also the oldest runner, began the first leg. The relay proceeded along a route provided by the RAC for Club Treasurer, Tony Walsh, who had travelled along it the previous weekend with Paul Byrne, one of the drivers, to fix the take-over points and check it for safety. It passed through Warrington, Holmes Chapel, Newcastle under Lyme, Lichfield, Coventry, Towcester, Dunstable, St Albans and Mill Hill. The stages were of varying distances up to 10 miles, to match age and fitness and also to give everyone an opportunity to take part.

Ted Johnson leaving St Helens Town Hall

At each stopping point there was an opportunity to get more signatures for the 'Sport for All' petition and tell local people about the relay. From midnight until the early hours of the morning the coach parked outside a transport café on the A5 near Dunstable, whilst the night shift runners, Peter Langley, Frank Rimmer, Jim Crehan, Alan McGauley, Dave Bate and Dave Burton did their 10 mile stages.

The route through London in the early hours of Sunday morning took in Oxford Street, Piccadilly, Trafalgar Square and Whitehall. Club Captain Jim Crehan ran the final stage through London and into Downing Street. The entire relay took 20 hours 29 minutes to complete, somewhat less than expected. As it was earlier than had been announced to the authorities, everyone returned later to present

Outside No 10 Downing Street

the petition at 10 Downing Street and pose for photographs by the club's official relay photographer, Roger McCall.

In between there was some time for relaxation in Hyde Park, church attendance at Westminster Cathedral or Abbey and a spruce-up and meal at the YMCA centre. The party's very obliging coach driver then took them all on a mini-sightseeing tour of London before a rather tired and sleepy group of athletes began the long journey home, albeit with much satisfaction that the relay had been successfully completed. The only setback occurred when the coach broke down due to a snapped fan belt on the M6 near Haydock. A temporary repair was carried out thanks to a donated pair of tights, and the coach arrived back in St Helens early on Sunday evening.

The event was a great success and was talked about for years after. A letter was received from the Prime Minister's office thanking the club for the petition. Prizes, including a television set, were duly distributed to those who guessed the nearest times, the new building project got a healthy financial boost, and the Sutton Harriers's 75th Anniversary was truly marked.'

Tony Walsh

Norman Ashcroft and the 'Vets'

Norman first came to prominence as a member of the Manchester Athletic Club in the mid-1940s, towards the end of World War II. He quickly made his impact on local distance running, winning cross-country and road races, and went on to represent England at cross-country in Paris in 1947. Although not quite so successful on the track he did take home a number of awards, both team and individual, in two-mile events. Later he made excursions into the longer road runs, including the marathon, and enjoyed a fair degree of success.

Eventually his occupation took him away from Manchester into the St.Helens area, and he joined Sutton Harriers. Here he served as Club Secretary for almost a decade, giving much of his spare time to official duties, including timekeeping, receiving many a soaking as he waited to give the last runner his time.

Norman, who still enjoyed training and the occasional race when well past 50, realised he was not unique, and consequently played a major role in the formation in 1968 of the Northern Veterans Athletic Club - designed for athletes aged 40-plus. When three years later sixteen Northern Veterans travelled to Czechoslovakia in four car loads to compete in a world veterans' championship it was Norman who had organised this trip.

One of the result sheets has survived from 1975, when the Northern Veterans Athletics Club held its sixth annual Track and Field Championships, and amongst the competitors listed were Sutton Harriers' Austin Tipping and Norman Ashcroft. Ten contestants were Northern Veterans AC members and all in all thirty-one clubs were named - largely northern, but including Highgate and Clyde Valley, whilst there was also a guest runner from Hilden, Germany.

That the 'Northern Vets' have gone from strength to strength must in large part be due to the ever-cheerful and enthusiastic Lancastrian who was their Club's first secretary.

Norman's Joggers

It was towards the end of May in 1976 that Mr Norman Ashcroft, a stalwart of Sutton Harriers, advertised in the local newspaper that he was to start a 'jogging class'. The project was aimed at people who wanted to get fit, and those who were fit and wanted to remain so. The first meeting was to be in Sherdley Park, and would include an initial 'run'.

On the appointed day several people arrived to join his class, their ages being in the 30's, 40's and 50's. They were all completely unfit, and after a slow jog around the inside boundary of the park, they were reduced to lying on the grass, flat on their backs, their chests heaving uncontrollably as their lungs gasped for air.

However, with Norman as their trainer, after a few weeks they had progressed in fitness, and could jog more quickly around the paths on the outside of the park, and without the distress with their breathing. From that stage of their training, their progress was such that soon they could leave the park, and jog along *Peasley Cross Lane*, past the hospital, then left and along the full length of *Sherdley Road*, in those days a long uninterrupted uphill run, with a wide grass verge between the pavement and the traffic. Then came a left turn into *Eltonhead Road* and back to the clubhouse of *Sutton Harriers*, in *Chester Lane*, of which by this time they had become members.

A few weeks of this training led to some of this group increasing the distance of their jogging sessions, and in what seemed a very short time, their route was increased to a seven mile circular which passed through *Rainhill* and back, an exercise that was undertaken three times per week. This then led to this group becoming members of *The Northern Veterans*, whose badge, an 'Infinity Symbol', was stitched onto their vests or track suits. As members of 'The Vets' they were able to enter the organised road races, usually on a Sunday, and of 10,000 m. in length, held in various towns of the surrounding area. This was just one year from their first meeting in the park. Although they never won any of these races, because they were competing against real veteran athletes, they gained great pleasure and satisfaction from the fact that they were never the last to cross the finishing line. At about this time also, one or two of these joggers volunteered to take a course which would qualify them to take on the task of supervising and training the younger members amongst the junior runners. Amongst the rest, such was the fitness and eagerness of some of this group of 'Norman's joggers', that by the year 1982 some had entered to run the 'Daffodil Marathon', which was held in April at *Stockport*. This turned out to be a new and exhilarating experience for them. And, surprisingly, it proved emotional too, caused by the cheers and encouraging shouts from complete strangers who lined the route, some of whom had picked out the number on a runner's vest in order to shout a better encouragement. At the end of the race there was the medal, the first one ever, and then the satisfaction of watching the scores of runners, most of them much younger, but not as fit, who were still arriving to cross the line.

Eventually with the passing of years, and the increase in age, the jogging had to end. The fitness however, that had been gained, has carried the joggers on into old age, enabling them to enjoy a much more fulfilling lifestyle, with memories to be savoured. There are also the medals, for although there are many thousands of people who have completed the marathon, as a percentage of the population, they are very few indeed, and to be amongst that number is in itself an achievement. For the joggers, all of this is thanks to *Norman Ashcroft* and the *Sutton Harriers Athletic Club*.

Jack Twist

Miscellany

One evening a certain harrier forgot one of the basics of long distance running - 'Go to the toilet before training or racing'. He was about 30 or 40 minutes into his training run when he was taken short and he knew that 'when you've got to go, you have to go'. It was just about 8 pm on Prescot Road, near Toll Bar, and he spotted a Petrol Station open, with all lights on - so he entered the shop and explained his urgency. The kind hearted attendant obliged by allowing the now panic-stricken runner to use the station toilet - so in he went. He attended to his troubles, and got blessed relief. He then re-entered the shop to find it in complete darkness, empty, with the door locked. His situation had altered from one of acute physical urgency to one of embarrassing urgency: Getting a wee bit panicky, he noticed a phone. He rang the police to explain his predicament.

They suggested he stayed there and they would arrive. They did just that. So the position then was - a runner in a vest and shorts trying to leave a darkened shop, and two policemen trying to get in. To end the story, the police contacted the owners of the petrol station, who in turn contacted the manager, who in turn arrived back at his shop to allow a very cold, embarrassed long-distance runner to carry on his long-distance run. SO, DON'T FORGET THE BASICS.

Chapter 8

THE NOMAD YEARS

When after the 1937 season had ended and Sutton Harriers senior cross-country team were photographed outside the Morris Pavilion no-one could have guessed how soon their sturdy wooden HQ would be doomed.

A draft letter, intended for Pilkington Brothers, survives in a minute book. Written by the Club Secretary, Bill Glover, it explains the club's sudden predicament.

'As you are perhaps aware, at the present time we have our headquarters or pavilion on ground which belonged to Pilkington Bros. up to a short time ago, situated on left of Helena Rd., St.Helens Junction looking from the Railway. Messrs.Pilkington Bros. sold some land to Mr.W.Hardy for him to build a mission Hall, and unfortunately for us, this piece included the site of our pavilion. At the time of the transaction everything appeared to be plain sailing as Mr.Hardy told us we would have no need to worry as he didn't object to us having our headquarters next to his intended church.

I believe at the time, your agent sent for Mr.Morris, our Treasurer, and asked him did he think we could agree with Mr.Hardy, and Mr.Morris stated that he saw no reason why we shouldn't. Everything went well for a time, and Mr.Hardy regularly had the use of our headquarters for various functions for his church, until a few weeks ago he decided that he would build a gardener's cottage for the caretaker of the church, and he gave us notice to quit by Nov.30th. I got in touch with him and finally got him to extend our notice to March 31st. 1939 so that we could fulfil our season's fixtures.

Now we will have to build new headquarters and one of the suggested sites was a piece of ground situated directly behind our present building and extending to Normans Lane. We would be very pleased if you could give us an estimate of your price per acre or fraction of an acre for plots of ground on this site.

Knowing how keen Messrs.Pilkingtons Bros are on anything appertaining to "Keep Fit" I am sure you will assist our club by letting me have the details as soon as possible. Our meeting is being held on Oct 19th at 7-30 and I would be very much obliged if you can.'

This and other enquiries about possible sites continued throughout the cross-country season, with no real success, and on 21st March 1939 readers of the *St Helens Reporter* learnt that :

'On Sunday members of the Sutton Harriers club met in the partly demolished headquarters in Helena Road, Sutton to discuss the prospects of a new club meeting place and training centre.

The club is forced to leave the present place because of its having been acquired by another body which requires the land. The meeting was well attended, Mr.W.Worsley, National Cross Country president, being in the chair.

It was decided that a sub-committee be appointed to deal with the raising of schemes for the building fund, and various members of the club gave donations of 10 shillings and £1 each. As all members are only working lads, this giving of such substantial donations means a big sacrifice to them and proves the club will make every effort to get new headquarters. The subscription list is open to all and donations will be gratefully received by the secretary Mr.W.F.Glover, 119 Mill Lane.'

On April 14th it was further reported that:

'the sub-committee appointed to consider the provision of a new headquarters have gone very thoroughly into the matter and now have to await the result of the appeal to decide definitely on the type of building that can be acquired.

Any sportsman reading these notes, who feels he would like to help the Sutton Harriers by giving a donation will be very warmly welcomed, and should get in touch with the club secretary … All donations, however small, will be gratefully received, and acknowledged by receipt from the Secretary.'

Sadly, at the club's AGM on August 24th 1939, it was proposed *'that all firewood dealers be approached to send in quotations to committee for hut'.*

More positively, the Secretary was to approach East Sutton Labour Club to see if their premises could be used for training and as a base for Saturday events. However the outbreak of war on September 3rd effectively halted the club's activities for the duration. Many members were called up, or were working flat out in industry and in the pits. No major championships were held, though events did take place involving some clubs and teams from conveniently located armed forces. Athletes away from home and wanting a run would temporarily attach themselves to any groups functioning in their new neighbourhoods. Inevitably there were casualties - amongst whom was Bill Glover, killed on active service.

Still homeless when hostilities ended, the Harriers gladly made use of the cramped tobacco-impregnated rooms made available to them at East Sutton Labour Club. The club committee met there regularly. Hosting the 1948 Northern Cross-Country Championship at Sherdley Park was planned there. AGMs were held there too, and in March 1947, following Sutton Harriers' victory in the National Cross-Country Championship, it was the venue for a celebration tea and trophy presentation graced by the Mayor, Cllr Robertson.

Occasionally, as when the 1950 General Election was held and the Labour Club was bursting with activity, the Harriers' committee met in St Helens at the estate agents Grayson and Burrows, the business premises of their president, Mr Eddie Stubbs.

Alert to the club's needs, and advising on any suggested location for an HQ, Mr Stubbs was instrumental in obtaining the lease of the ramshackle premises off Norman's Lane, where the club's AGM was held in November 1950.

Part of the Old Powder Works - a former Safety Fuse manufactory, whose motley collection of ancient brick buildings and tall chimney had long been disused - it became the club's headquarters for nearly six years.

To gain entry to the buildings at the Powder Yard, one had to leave the main roads, Helena Road and Reginald Road, where they met, and then turn right on to a wide rutted pathway with many potholes, Normans Lane. Here there were at this time four or five terraced houses still occupied by families. The path then veered left into a fairly wide rough yard enclosed by crumbling structures and including the two rooms Sutton Harriers made their HQ. These were wooden-floored and felt truly spacious since, bereft of ceilings, their bare brick walls were visible right up to the rafters.

Initially conditions were spartan. Faced with no electricity and only a cold tap and bucket, runners frequently preferred to let their mud dry on, then dust off what they could and clean up at home. However, thanks principally to the Club Captain and Chairman, Fred McMinnis, and members Tom Fillingham, Jack Chidlow and Eddie Edwards, the Powder Yard premises were transformed into a place of comparative comfort. Tom Fillingham's great experience, knowledge, and training as a joiner and in building construction proved invaluable. The walls in the changing rooms were lined with wooden panels to a height of around seven feet. They were then painted with wood stain, and varnished. The bare walls above had already been covered with whitewash, or emulsion paint. The upper limits were left for the freedom of the birds and other wildlife.

Tom, who worked for MANWEB at this time, negotiated with Mr Stubbs and the Electricity Board to re-wire the two rooms, and heating panels were installed. In the 1950s these were rather a new way to heat a room or buildings, which made them costly both to install and in their consumption of electricity. However, there appeared to be little choice, and their big advantage was that they were clean. All members were urged to economise in the use of these panels, and constantly reminded about their being switched off when leaving the building.

Later, many photographs of members past and present were framed and attached to the wooden panelling. A few mirrors were acquired, and placed in the two rooms.

Jack Chidlow, who had served his apprenticeship in the plumbing trade, now devoted his expertise to building a bath. Although not in the class of the Romans it was an amenity that was to become much appreciated and well used. A pit was dug which had piped running water. Measuring some two yards square, and one yard deep, it was not exceptional by today's standards. The sides were lined with concrete, as was its base. Tiling was too much of a luxury and expense. However, along the top of each side were fixed smooth pieces of wood on which the runners could sit. These had been screwed into the surrounding floor. Jack supervised the cutting out of the bricks for the pipe to take the water outside. The water itself was heated by a gas geyser just above the bath. This improvement was really a huge move forward, because now several people at a time could clean themselves before going home. It wasn't a bath that anybody could linger in for any length of time, or for that matter was ever meant to be.

Many club members had assisted as labourers on a rota system to make these changes, but the four men mentioned were truly the main architects of the great transformation.

Other embellishments were gradually added - coathangers, pieces of carpet, lampshades and a selection of catering items, cups and saucers, tea pots and kettles. These all made the old building more welcoming, comfortable and, it must be said, cosier - not a description that could be applied to the WCs some 50 metres from the main building. These lines by Alma Peers and Carole Green quoted by Ron Freethy in *Lancashire Privies* may best suggest the scene at the Powder Yard:

'To reach it one must leave one's hearth,
go fifty yards down garden path,
By thorn, and bramble, nettle fringes
to find the door perhaps unhinged,
And when inside to sit in state
to ponder and to meditate,
The solitude 'neath clear blue skies
closeted from prying eyes,
Except for cracks, and knot holes wide,
and odd boards fallen off the side,
So Sanctuary is found at last,
and peaceful interludes are passed.'

One great advantage of the new HQ was its proximity to the Farmers' Arms, a popular watering-hole for club members, and another was that, like the Morris Pavilion, it was close to the start of the cross-country course in Reginald Road. Their run to the start was a useful warm-up for the Harriers and their visitors, all having stripped off at the Powder Works.

However, being well over eighty years old, it was far from ideal, and despite improvements made by the club, such as the gas water heater, electric heaters and boiler they installed, proved increasingly impossible to maintain.

Staging events elsewhere could pose problems - as when the Welfare Hall of the Ministry of Supply Establishment at Sutton Oak was available - but without lights, water or heating. Requests were made to use other premises as an HQ, including an offer to repair the pavilion in Sutton Park if the club could use it. Other letters sought permission to use the King George V playing field in Jubits Lane and part of the pavilion. Nothing positive materialised, but even so in May 1956 the Club Committee decided their tenancy at Normans Lane should be terminated that July.

It had cost the club £9 15s (£9 75p) a quarter to rent their deteriorating Powder Yard premises - where their tangible assets in 1955-6 were the gas water heater, the electric boiler and four 12 ft electric heaters.

Now what was to happen? A request for winter use of the facilities at Allanson Street was turned down by the Education Committee, though stopping the use of the running track there during summer months was not their intention *'since it has always been understood that you co-operate fully in training members of youth clubs and in helping in youth club sports'.*

Extensions then in progress at both East Sutton Labour Club and Clock Face Recreation Club prevented their use by the Harriers. Fortunately, however, the landlord of the *Farmers Arms* agreed to provide accommodation each weekend. Thus in December 1956 this was the venue for the Christmas Handicap.

Monies paid to Thatto Heath Rugby Club and Grange Park Youth Centre show that the Harriers, though still in Sutton, had temporarily moved their bases to the west, whilst from September 1957 to March 1958 the committee were meeting in the Neighbours' Club in Thatto Heath.

These changes meant that some club runs had to be re-routed. Cross-country runners could, having set off from Thatto Heath Park, find themselves crossing a vast uneven tract where infilled clay holes had been reclaimed, and all awaited the house builders. The route for road race trials began in Broadway. From here a series of left turns took runners into Freckleton Road, on to Prescot Road as far as the *Wellington Hotel*, into St James Road and up to Scotchbarn Lane, along this and then down Portico Lane. Bearing right at the little roundabout and heading towards *The Grapes*, a final right turn led runners into Scholes Lane and the finishing point, the entrance to the British Legion Club - in all a distance of some four miles.

Meanwhile a site for a new HQ was urgently being sought, and by April 1957 the Town Hall had been approached regarding derelict land on Chester Lane, close to its junction with Clock Face Road.

Negotiations slowly went ahead. Expenditure of £5.11s.5d (£5.57) on building materials for the new HQ was noted in the accounts, and October 1958 brought the despatch of the following letter, accompanied by a list of Sutton Harriers' impressive athletic achievements:

Dear Sirs,

HEADQUARTERS' APPEAL FUND

As has been publicly announced, the Town Council has generously provided our club with a site for a heaquarters and we are at last in sight of a home of a permanent character for probably the first time in our history.

It is our hope that we may celebrate 1959, our Jubilee year, with our headquarters an established fact, but much will have to be done to achieve this.

The provision of a building and the preparation of the training area is rightly the responsibility of the club. All the labour is being freely provided by the club members and supporters, but the high cost of materials and the provision of services is our main problem. To meet this the committee have decided to launch a public appeal fund with a target of £1,000. The club's own fund raising efforts have already raised £200 towards this amount and such efforts will be continued, but without public support they will, of course, be limited.

The details of our club's achievements, both team and individual, which accompany this appeal, give you an indication of the application and effort which go into our athletic performances. The club's record can indeed only be equalled by those clubs, small in number, who represent the great cities of our land, and it is a generally accepted fact in athletic circles that the leadership our club gave in the immediate post war years set the standards which resulted in the wonderful achievements of British athletes in the world competitions of the 1950's.

A word about the social character of our sport. Modern Athletics demand a high degree of self-discipline and moral application. Throughout the years, the many hundreds of young people who have passed through our hands have not all been champions but we are quite sure that contact with us has made them fit, not only in body, but in character and citizenship. In these days when juvenile delinquency is unfortunately a word too often heard, the stabilizing influence of our activities will surely be appreciated.

This appeal has the support of many public figures and the undersigned are convinced that you will also feel that it is a cause worthy of support.

Your donation may be forwarded to any of the above addresses or to the St. Helens Branch, Westminster Bank Ltd., Hardshaw Street. It will be gratefully received and publicly acknowledged.

(Signed)

E.J. Stubbs - President   H. Shacklady, M.B.E. - Vice President
T. Fillingham - Honorary Treasurer   P.J. Burrows - Chairman
J. Burke- Honorary Secretary'

By the time the Club Committee met on December 4th the appeal had raised over £50. Present that evening were the Chairman, Treasurer and Secretary, together with the Assistant Treasurer, John Carbery, and the past and present Club Captains, Fred McMinnis and Ken Wilcock. The occasion was historic - their first meeting at the Chester Lane headquarters (the 'Green Hut'). Albeit scantily equipped within (work on preparing a kitchen space to double as a ladies' dressing room was only authorised the following February), and with tipping, levelling and fencing still needed outside, the building's existence proved that Sutton Harriers' twenty nomadic years since demolition of the Morris pavilion had come to an end.

Chapter 9

A TIME OF TRANSITION

The beginning of the 1960s was a time when Sutton Harriers recognised that new blood would be needed particularly at senior level if they were to compete successfully even locally. However, it was only towards the end of the decade that this was achieved. Those runners responsible for the tremendous successes of the 1940s and 1950s had retired and whilst stalwarts such as Trevor Prescott, Roy Ashley, Joe Harrison and Norman Ashcroft remained, the senior men's team did not have the strength in depth required to match the all-conquering teams of Wirral AC and Wallasey AC.

On a brighter note, there was future potential amongst the juniors where Tony Walsh, Maurice Rylatt, Dave Costello and Geoff Allen were putting in promising performances. The same applied to the youths, through John McLoughlin Mike Griffiths, Ged Walsh, John Moffatt and Frank Costello.

Then, in the autumn of 1962, two new members arrived who were to figure prominently in the success that was to be achieved later. First Brian Renshall then Peter Roberts joined and although new to athletics they quickly established themselves as the two leading seniors. Both were successful in local events in a comparatively short space of time. For example, Renshall's first competitive cross-country race was in a Liverpool and District League race in January 1963 where he was placed 97th. The following year he finished 14th, and by 1967 was winning when the race was held at Woolton Woods. Roberts was similarly successful and in 1968 won the Liverpool and District Senior Cross-Country Championship from Ron Barlow of Wallasey AC (more of him later).

Brian Renshall behind M Freary (Bolton) in the Northern Cross-Country Championship at Sherdley Park in 1969

The senior men's team was further enhanced in 1964 by the arrival of Steve James and Colin Johnson, who, along with Roberts, Renshall, Prescott, Walsh and Dave Costello, helped the team push for top three places in the cross-country championships in Merseyside and south-west Lancashire. When eventually John McLoughlin and Mike Griffiths became old enough to run in senior competitions the team's strength made winning such events a distinct possibility. The top spot, however, continued to prove elusive.

Then, in the 1968 season, Ron Barlow and Brian Woolford, both formerly of Wallasey AC, moved from their Wirral homes to this side of the Mersey. Although the moves were coincidental it proved to be lucky for Sutton Harriers. Both decided to opt for a club nearer to their new homes, and as they had become friendly with Roberts and Renshall chose Sutton Harriers.

They had to serve a nine months' suspension period, throughout which time they could run as individuals for the club, but not count in any team events before January 1969. After that the team had the strength in depth that it had been looking for, and during that cross-country season won the Liverpool and District Cross-Country Championship, the West Lancs Championship and then, in February, was placed third in the Northern Cross-Country Championship behind the powerful Bolton AC and Manchester and District Club. Their strength can be judged from the fact that Sutton had their six counters home in the Northern before Bolton and Manchester, but those clubs had their first three runners in higher positions and so scored lower points. The counting team that day, in a race held in deep snow and blizzard conditions, was James, Barlow, Renshall, Roberts, Johnson and Woolford. In January 1970, and at Sherdley Park, Sutton, again took the West Lancashire title, their winning team being James 2nd, Renshall 4th, Roberts 5th, Johnson 9th, McLoughlin 10th and Woolford 12th.

The following season the team continued to be successful in the local cross-country league, despite a serious back injury having kept Brian Renshall out of action. A year later both he and Peter Roberts left Sutton to join Liverpool Pembroke AC, thus ending their almost-a-decade as Harriers. (Eleven years later they were back again as veterans.)

Throughout the 1960s and into the early 70s, when track leagues began to be established, track meetings revolved around inter-club competitions, open events, such as the Widnes Police Sports, Pilkington's Gala at Ruskin Drive and county championships. Often the circuit of a football pitch, and usually measuring 440 yards, the tracks were either grass or cinders. All-weather surfaces just didn't exist, and some clubs had no track at all on which to train. Locally, Sutton Harriers were fortunate in that they still had the use of the Allanson Street School track in Parr, whilst Pilkington AC used Ruskin Drive and Warrington AC took advantage of the facilities at Victoria Park. The track at Allanson Street was unusual in that its circuit was 352 yards, as opposed to the standard 440. Therefore, to run one mile, one ran 5 laps.

Owing to the lack of training facilities and equipment, field events were somewhat of a rarity, and although Sutton did have one or two people who contested the long and high jump when they could, nearly all their athletes concentrated their efforts on track running. Competition usually started in the spring, when hopefully the weather was improving. An entry in Brian Renshall's diary from March 1963 records him placed 7th in his first ever track race, being timed at 10 mins 17 secs for the two mile event.

A popular competition was still the Liverpool Parks and Gardens open meeting, held by then at Wavertree Park, which had a cinder track. Started in the mid-fifties the meetings had been held on grass at various parks in Liverpool, with the finals at Clubmoor. They provided Sutton athletes, both male and female, with good competition, and many were placed first, second or third in the finals. The races took place mid-week, usually on Tuesday evenings throughout June. The first meeting was devoted to inter-club competition, whilst on each successive Tuesday individual championship heats were held, with the finals taking place on the first Tuesday in July. One of Sutton's many successful runners at this event was Bob Meadows. On two occasions in 1963 he led the club to win the two mile team race for the first time for many years. Bob was the individual runner on both occasions, the other team members being Renshall, Trevor Prescott and Tony Walsh.

In the early 1960s Sutton occasionally hosted inter-club matches at Allanson Street. Unfortunately, although the track was enclosed within the school grounds, the local youngsters could always find a way in, which meant that before the track could be used it had to be clear of debris, mainly in the form of half bricks! At one of these inter-club events John McLoughlin demonstrated what great talent he had by winning the two mile race in 9 mins 28 secs when just 18 years old. This was a remarkable time, especially on a cinder five-laps-to-the-mile track, which meant he had to contend with lapped runners.

Locally, there were inter-club matches at Warrington, Ruskin Drive and at the C F Mott College track in Prescot, where the organising club was Liverpool Pembroke AC. Further afield, Sutton teams travelled to events in places like Blackpool, Leigh and Oldham.

Although few in number some meetings still featured handicap races, a very popular one being the Widnes Police Sports, held each July. One of its features was the one-mile handicap race, in which, in 1964, fate favoured Brian Renshall. Prior to these sports he had already run under two minutes for 880 yards and 4 mins 20 secs for the mile distance. He arrived at the meeting to learn that somehow he had been given a very generous handicap of 180 yards. This meant, of course, that if he ran to form the scratch man would have had to run close to four minutes to catch him. There was lots of good-natured banter, and some not so good, as to how he had been given 180 yards start, but Brian wasn't complaining, and proceeded to win the race by a handsome margin in 3 mins 57 secs.

Later that year Brian and John McLoughlin decided to enter the one-mile handicap race at the London Fire Brigade Open Championships held at the White City Stadium in London Although Brian was again given a good handicap, this time of 165 yards, he failed by one hundredth of a second to win and finished runner-up to Mike Stafford, (who had been a member of Sutton Harriers during the 1950s but was then running for one of the Southern clubs). With a time of 3 mins 54 secs Brian just managed to hold off John who had been given the same handicap. Both Harriers won very attractive dinner services which survive to this day.

Inter-club meetings were very popular and Sutton were usually well represented. At one such meeting in May 1964 an article in the *St Helens Reporter* recorded that club captain, Roy Ashley, had competed in almost everything including the 880 yards, long jump and 220 yards events. Mike Griffiths won the 1500 metres steeplechase, in 4 mins 34 secs, and Sutton won the two mile team race, thanks to Renshall, Tony Walsh and Peter Priestner. Another interestingly surnamed competitor was David McMinnis, nephew of the famous Fred and Bill McMinnis, who ran 5 mins 42 secs in the Youths' one mile race. The club had also sent a girls' team to Warrington that day and, although not mentioned by name, they finished second of the six competing clubs.

An unusual event was included in an open meeting in Radcliffe in July 1965. It was a 4x1 mile relay which was won by Sutton whose team that day was Renshall, Peter Roberts, Ged Walsh and McLoughlin.

Many meetings concluded with two-mile races which continued to be very popular with Sutton, particularly as with runners of the calibre of McLoughlin, Roberts, Steve James, Renshall and, later, Ron Barlow a team win was usually guaranteed. On one occasion, in 1969, Sutton turned up at an evening meeting in Chester to contest the two-mile race with a team that included Barlow, Renshall and Roberts. This didn't go down well with the lads from Wirral AC who, it appeared, had been running in this event for several years, had always won it and didn't take kindly to 'outsiders' muscling in on 'their' race. Their concern proved well founded when Barlow won, with Renshall second and

Roberts third, meaning that as well as winning the team prize they won the individual ones as well. To make matters worse, the same team went back the following year and won again. This time Roberts was the winner with Renshall runner-up and Barlow third. By then distances had become metricated and the two miles had become 3000 metres. The times on that very undulating grass track are worthy of mention; Roberts recorded 8 mins 21 secs, Renshall 8 mins 24 secs and Barlow 8 mins 25 secs - or, in 'old money', around 9 minutes for two miles.

In 1969 Sutton were once again represented at the County Championships when Peter Roberts, having won the 10,000 metres at the Lancashire Track Championships held at Kirkby Stadium, was selected to represent the county in that event at the Inter-Counties Championships at the White City Stadium, London. Already by then the structure of athletics was changing with the introduction of the track leagues. Although inter-club and open meetings did continue, many were to disappear as the league competitions expanded into what was then becoming a crowded track and field calendar.

John McLoughlin

John joined Sutton Harriers in the autumn of 1960 thanks to the encouragement of Joe Ludden and Dave Costello. John was 15 years old at the time and a pupil at St Austin's School in Thatto Heath when Joe, who was then team manager for St Helens Schoolboys' cross-country team, spotted him competing in an inter-schools cross-country match. Dave, also a St.Austin's pupil, had already joined the club.

Success was not long in arriving and just over twelve months later, in 1962, John won the boys' race in the Liverpool and District Cross-Country Championships, the Lancashire Boys' Cross-Country Championship and finished third in the Northern Cross-Country Boys' Championships. Tom McIntyre recalls that about this time Sutton Harriers travelled to an inter-club event organised by Widnes Harriers only to be told that John could compete in the boys' race but couldn't count for the club team as he was too good. This was reluctantly agreed to. John ran and duly won. On another occasion Sutton Harriers were having a time trial in order to select the best team to run in the forthcoming Lancashire Road Relay Championships at Southport a week later. Only sixteen at the time, John was too young to run at Southport, being under the qualifying age of eighteen, but ran in and won the trial! As Tom Fillingham, the club's press officer, told readers of the St Helens Reporter, even though Sutton were not the force they had been it was still a remarkable achievement for a sixteen-year-old to beat the seniors in such convincing fashion.

John continued to progress, winning both the Liverpool and District and West Lancs Cross-Country Championships at youth and junior level. He was a member of the Lancashire team that won the Junior Inter-counties Cross-Country Championship in 1966, being placed sixth in the race. His success was not confined to cross-country running, for he represented both Lancashire and the North of England on the track at junior level. He also remains justifiably proud of the fact that he is the only Sutton Harrier to have won the club's road race, which he achieved in 1965 when just twenty years of age.

'Undoubtedly', writes Brian Renshall, recalling the 1960s, 'apart from Ian Edwards during the 1990s, John was the most talented athlete I saw during my time with Sutton Harriers. Never one to clock up big mileages (although we used to do long Saturday runs together) his training sessions, be it on road or track, were usually of high quality and very quick. This, coupled with an abundance of natural ability made him a redoubtable competitor and he was never afraid to mix it with the "big boys". I distinctly recall him giving Bolton Harriers' international, Mike Freary, a really hard race at Salford over seven miles, when Freary had to call on all his experience and talent to get the better of him. John was one of those athletes who had so much natural ability that even when not fully fit he was still capable of running well and beating others perhaps not so talented. It was a pleasure to run both with and against him.'

Sadly, however, John was never to progress to the international level that many thought him capable of. Family commitments and unsocial working hours meant that training and racing became somewhat restricted, whilst there was also the serious knee injury he suffered, caused by tripping over the family dog.

Brian Renshall

One of those infusing new blood into the club at this time was Brian Renshall, who, having joined as a raw recruit in 1962 had become Club Captain (Track) five years later.

Recalling those and earlier days he writes:

'Fairly soon after I started at Grange Park School, I became aware that I might have some talent for athletics. On arrival at the school aged eleven we were put into houses, mine being Hanover. The others were Stuart, Windsor and Tudor. Our housemaster, Mr Watts, was picking the first year team for the inter-house cross-country race. Somehow I was selected, although I remember being sixth choice out of six! It wasn't really cross-country. We ran from the gates of Taylor Park on St Helens Road at Toll Bar, through the park, past the Sanitorium and up past "Red Rocks" to the finish at West Park Rugby Club - a distance of approximately one mile. To my surprise, I won easily, and in doing so ran 5 mins 20 secs, breaking the school record.

From then on I never lost a race during my time there, although on one occasion I was told that I had to lose the 880 yards at the school's sports day by another housemaster whose house was doing badly and needed points. He had a lad running, who he thought might win provided he could get past me. As my mother had come to watch me there was no way I wasn't going to try and win that race, added to which Mr Watts had instructed me to ignore what I had been told. So I won, and shortly after the other teacher came over and said I would regret it. Nothing happened for a couple of weeks, but one day, while on the sports field, he came and instructed me to go into the cricket nets where he proceeded to bowl "bouncers" at about 90 miles an hour!

Unfortunately, Grange Park in the 1950s didn't compete in local schools' cross-country races and there were no teachers there sufficiently interested in athletics to direct me to a club. So I left school at fifteen and didn't run seriously again until I was twenty-one. I did think about joining Sutton Harriers but I couldn't find out where their headquarters were. Had I gone to a school where the likes of Tom McIntyre or Roy Ashley were teaching it would probably have been different.

However, in 1962 I ran in a cross-country race organised by my local youth club, won it by miles, and set about trying to find Sutton Harriers again. I hadn't been having any success and was considering contacting the St Helens Reporter which each week ran an article written by "Clubman" (Tom Fillingham) that reported on the activities of Sutton Harriers. Then one Thursday evening I was returning from watching a friend of mind, Dave Lynch, training with St Helens Town FC and as we came up Mill Lane and into Chester Lane Dave spotted the Sutton Harriers' notice board outside the club-house. I told him to stop the car and I went in, interrupting a committee meeting that was taking place, where Jack Burke told me to go into the changing rooms. Here I met Maurice Rylatt and Trevor Prescott and my introduction to Sutton Harriers and athletics began.

My first training session, the following Monday, was an eye-opener. About eight of us went out on a run which took in Chester Lane, Gartons Lane, Leach Lane, Mill Lane and back into Chester Lane and the clubhouse. As we were going up Mill Lane we had just reached the top when Trevor Prescott said, "If you've got anything left Brian, now's the time to put it in". So putting my head down I ran as hard as I could to the clubhouse. When I got there I turned round to see the rest of the group about 40 metres behind, giving me an immense feeling of satisfaction at having beaten runners who I knew must be fitter than me. Imagine my surprise then when the group sailed past the clubhouse and disappeared up Chester Lane. "Where are they going?" I asked someone who was standing close by. "Oh, they are doing three laps," he informed me. Trevor, of course, knew that I could never have managed three laps (a total of about seven miles) it being my first-ever training session. Talk about having your ego deflated !

Another memorable but more painful incident took place during the Lancashire Road Relay (at Southport) in 1963. As I was finishing my leg and handing over to Peter Roberts, I tripped over his outstretched foot and went base over apex. I suffered cuts and bruises but put my track suit on and warmed down. However, as the afternoon wore on my right knee started to swell up alarmingly. After the race had finished Trevor Prescott took me to a nearby hospital, but it proved to be a children's hospital and they couldn't/wouldn't treat me.

We decided the best thing to do was to get home so that I could go to the A & E at Whiston Hospital. Normally I would have been able to lie on the back seat of Trevor's car with my left leg outstretched but unfortunately his mode of transport in those days was a Messerschmitt Bubble-car - a two-seater where the passenger sat alongside the driver with knees tucked up under the chin! Southport to Whiston had never previously seemed to take so long and I ended up with my leg in a splint for three weeks.

A more amusing incident occurred after I had won my first Liverpool and District Cross-Country League race in 1967 at Woolton Woods. After a titanic struggle with Steve James and Leo Carroll of Wirral AC I just managed to win the sprint finish up Camp Hill. A week earlier I had got married and my wife Nita and I had spent a week at Bournemouth. "Bloody hell!" commented Ronnie Williams (Liverpool Pembroke AC). "What were you doing on your honeymoon?"

Among my other Sutton Harrier memories looms an elusive Lancashire Cross-Country vest. I first ran in the Lancashire Cross-Country Championships just a few months after taking up athletics and joining Sutton Harriers. The date was the 5th January 1963, the venue Sherdley Park and I finished 70th out of 112 runners. Others who ran from Sutton that day were Peter Roberts (53rd) Maurice Rylatt (68th) and Roy Ashley (82nd). To ensure being one of the nine runners selected to represent Lancashire in the inter-county championships you had to be one of the first six to finish. A placing in the top nine would usually mean selection but was not guaranteed. For instance, someone who would normally be expected on current form to finish inside the first six but for some reason was not able to compete in the Lancashire Championship would usually be selected to be one of the county team (a change innovated by the selectors in 1953 with adverse consequences for Bill McMinnis).

Even though I had not been involved in athletics for long, one look at the first nine to finish that day told me just how strong competition for a place in the team would be for anyone who fancied his chance. Bolton's Ron Hill won, followed by Colin Robinson, Dave Swarbrick, Peter Hall, Mike Turner, Gerry North, Roger Carter, Brian Gill and Brian Craig. At least five of these were internationals and another contender and international, Mike Freary, also from Bolton, had not run! Not that I then entertained any ideas of reaching such lofty heights. I was a total novice just about managing to hold my own among the ranks of Sutton Harriers. The following year, 1964, saw little improvement in terms of position when I finished 64th. However, I was only 5 minutes behind the winner (Ron Hill again) compared to 8 minutes the previous year. I didn't compete in 1965 for some reason but in 1966, at Witton Park, Blackburn, I was placed 20th and had narrowed the gap behind the winner (yes, you've guessed - it was Ron Hill!) to 3 minutes. Also running in Sutton's colours that day were John McLoughlin (29th) Tony Walsh (46th) Colin Johnson (68th) and Trevor Prescott (71st).

Injury prevented me from competing in 1967 but in 1968 I was confident that I had a good chance of making the Lancashire team for the Inter-Counties Championships, particularly as a week earlier I had finished 5th in the Liverpool and District Cross-Country Championships held in Sherdley Park. The winner that day was fellow Sutton Harrier and good friend Peter Roberts. So he too was looking to do well in the Lancashire Cross-Country Championships.

Once again, the venue was Witton Park. The ground was very heavy following overnight rain. It was also very hilly. I remember little of the race, but I know that Peter Roberts and I ran stride for stride for almost the entire distance. We were still neck and neck as we got to the finish at which point, being the gentleman that I am, I let Peter go down the finishing funnel ahead of me with the result he was 9th and I was 10th, although we were both given the same time 35 mins 42 secs - just 1 min 53 secs behind the winner for the umpteenth time - Ron Hill. We were just outside the team count. However, a runner named Andy Holden from Preston who had finished ahead of us in the senior race but was still young enough to run in the Junior event at the Inter-Counties had told me earlier that he'd be running in the Junior Championship. This gave Peter and me a chance of county selection. John McLoughlin had also had a fine run, being placed 14th, whilst Tony Walsh came 42nd.

However, imagine our disappointment when the selection committee announced that the decision on the team to represent the county at the Inter-County Championships was to be held over and would be made after the result of the Northern Counties Championships a couple of months later, when the first nine Lancashire runners to finish would be selected. The reason for this? Well, there had been an outbreak of foot and mouth disease a few months earlier which meant that many of the farm fields sometimes used as part of the traditional cross-country races were out of bounds, particularly those in the agricultural areas of North East Lancashire. As a result not as many races had taken place, so some runners were perhaps not as "race fit" as they might have been.

"Oh well", I thought, "providing I stay fit I will just have to justify my selection by running well in the Northern." In the weeks running up to that race I was in good form, finishing 5th in the West Lancs Cross-Country Championships at Sherdley Park, one place behind Peter Roberts. Then a week later Peter was second and I was third in an inter-club match behind the aforementioned Holden. Unfortunately, the week prior to the Northern Championship at Groves Park, Sheffield, I contracted a chest infection and sore throat. I wasn't really fit enough to run, but did so and finished a very disappointing 65th.

Peter had a "blinder" in 16th place and made the Lancashire team to compete in the Inter-Counties race. Unfortunately it was not to be for him either, as a subsequent injury forced him out.

I only ran on two more occasions in the Lancashire Cross-Country Championships. In 1969 I was just outside the team count again, when finishing 13th at Clarke's Gardens, Liverpool and in my last championships, held at Allerton, I came 16th. A recurrent back injury which also affected the top of my left thigh meant that eventually I had to give up cross-country running, although I was able to continue track running and road races (provided they were not too hilly) without any problem. One interesting point, of the six Lancashire Cross-Country Championships I ran in, Ron Hill won five. The runner who broke the sequence was Ricky Wilde of Manchester, who was the winner at Allerton.

So, I never did achieve my ambition to win that County Cross-Country vest but I feel proud that I came within touching distance on several occasions. Had I been born in any other county it wouldn't have been a problem. But at that point the strength in depth of the Lancashire county teams was truly awesome. From 1960 through to 1972 they won the Inter-Counties Cross-Country Senior Championship on ten occasions and finished runners up three times. This included winning each consecutive year from 1960 through to 1966.

Boundary changes in 1974 and subsequently mean that the old county of Lancashire has been subdivided and no longer exists as far as athletics goes. Thus, for instance, a runner born in St Helens (or with a residential qualification) would now compete for Merseyside at the Inter-Counties Championships; one from Rochdale would compete for North-East Lancashire, whilst Boltonians would compete for Greater Manchester. No disrespect should accrue to the runners who compete, but these events are nowhere near the same standard as the old "Lancashire" event. In effect, the county races have been watered down. The success of those Lancashire teams of the sixties and early seventies will never be repeated.'

Chapter 10

SUTTON HARRIERS BECOME LEAGUE ATHLETES

League athletics was introduced in Great Britain on a national basis in the late 1960s, and quickly became established as the main form of competition in track and field events. Thus re-structured, athletics could move away from handicapping - a system which had not always brought athletes from around the country into competition. In theory, with a league system any club, whatever its size, would be able to progress up the divisions towards the National League. The resulting high level of competition would thereby produce better athletes.

National leagues were started for senior athletes (men and women) and these were soon followed by regional leagues, such as the Northern Men's and Women's Leagues, which offered a stepping stone to the National Leagues via a qualifying match. The Men's Leagues were always for senior athletes and a Boys' and Youths' League soon followed. This was organised on a national basis but with localised fixtures to cut down on travelling. The Women's Leagues initially catered for all age groups, but a Young Athletes League for Girls was introduced later, following the same structure as the Boys' and Youths' League. So successful has league athletics proved that at the higher levels it has overtaken county championships and now rivals regional championships for the quality of the competition.

The success of league competition led to the introduction of local leagues and Sutton Harriers joined the Cheshire League, one of the many country-wide. Offering competition for men and women of all age groups at the same meeting this has always provided a pleasant afternoon's athletics without the intensity of the Northern Leagues' events.

Sutton Harriers became involved with the Northern Leagues from an early date and during the 1970s made steady progress through the divisions in both the Men's and Women's Leagues, even fielding two men's teams in the period 1983 to 1985, as the table in the appendix shows. The best year was 1983 when Sutton Harriers were in the top division of both Northern Leagues with the women finishing 2nd and the men finishing 2nd equal with Hull Spartan on league points, but being placed 3rd on total match points. That year the women's team was invited to the National League Qualifier, but they were unsuccessful in their bid for National League status.

At this point in its history, the club was poised to move on to greater things and if it had gone on to National League status perhaps the history of athletics in St Helens might have been significantly different. Unfortunately, the club did not make that next step for two main reasons. Firstly, a number of athletes, coaches and club officials had reached the stage in life when family and career commitments came first. Consequently they had less time for their athletics. Secondly, developments at Sutton High had stalled, with the local authority in dispute with its contractors over the completion of the track at Sutton High Sports Centre. At that stage this was only a cinder track, and not until September 1995 was it opened as an all-weather surface. In the meantime the club had to struggle on with the limited facilities available in St Helens while other new tracks in the area were of the all-weather type.

Sutton's Versatile Athletes

Since a league team is only as strong as its weakest link, the secret of success must be to cover all events. To achieve this a team needs quality athletes to score well in their specialist disciplines, good all-rounders who can cover a number of events, and willing reserves who will compete when required.

Over the years Sutton Harriers have had all of these, and a number of leaders who have inspired team members to perform to the limit.

Sutton's early days, in Men's League athletics, were dominated by the all-rounders who tried their hand at everything, discovering unknown skills in triple jumping, hurdling and hammer-throwing. Among these were Tom Hackett, Jim Parish, Roger McCall, Mike Ahearne and Peter Code. Tom was one of the older generation of Sutton Harriers who along with Austin Tipping started a tradition of fathers and sons competing in the same team. Tom's son Mike was an outstanding 400 metre runner while Steve and Anthony Tipping gained many points for the club over the years, with Anthony in particular starring as a discus thrower. The high spots of the father-and-son combinations were the two occasions when the club won the A and B strings of an event. This first occurred when Jim and Mark Parish won both long jump events at Kirkby and the second when Jim and Steve Hull won both 5000 metre races at Stretford. (This latter event happened in the colours of St Helens Sutton AC, but each had started his running career with Sutton Harriers).

The club's distance running traditions transferred to the track with many star performances over the longer distances. A number of athletes competed over the years, but the greatest club servant of them all was Frank Rimmer, an inspirational club captain who led from the front with some fine performances in the steeplechase, as well as being prepared to try his hand at any event to gain points for the club.

Frank Rimmer

The St.Helens Athletic Community have been stunned by the tragic death last Friday of 36 year old Sutton Harriers club secretary Mr.Frank Rimmer.

Mr.Rimmer of Brownheath Ave. Birchley was involved in a collision with a lorry while trying to arrange a field trip in Wrexham for pupils of the Deanery High School, Wigan where he taught.

A popular athlete, he had been a member of Sutton Harriers for the past 20 years, and was highly regarded as an athlete, and administrator. He was renowned for his front running tactics, and gained numerous awards in the Sutton ranks. In later years he turned to administration, and became club secretary.

Educated at West Park School and Dundee University he held an M.A.Degree in Geography, and has been married for seven months to his wife Kath, who is expecting their first child.

Chairman of Sutton Harriers, Mr.Frank Costello, commented: 'Above all he was a clubman through and through, whose loyalty, and unswerving devotion to the club, and the sport he loved provided an example to us all.

His was a vision shared with others of creating at Sutton a climate where athletics could flourish where enjoyment and friendship were paramount, and individuals were encouraged to realise their potential.'

He added: 'He worked towards this end, and had little time for those who detracted from his ideals, or were motivated by dogma or selfishness. This was a vision that became reality, and the Sutton club provides a living monument to his memory.'

St.Helens Reporter 5th June 1987

Other fine steeplechasers to represent Sutton Harriers included Jim Crehan (Sue's husband), and Neil Smart (her brother), Bernard Lloyd and Alan Jones. Neil also won the UK 3000 metres steeplechase title and represented Great Britain on the track. Although Alan Jones left the town for a career in the RAF he returned where possible to compete for Sutton Harriers and represented the Service on the track and for cross-country, following in the footsteps of Bill McMinnis.

In the middle distance track events Ray Vose and Neil Smart graduated from being successful colts to the senior team, with Ray Vose having a league career of over 20 years, since he competes for St Helens Sutton AC in the new millennium.

The sprint events were boosted in the late seventies by the arrival of the Gaskell brothers, Mike and Martin, who joined the club from Liverpool Pembroke AC. As well as being good sprinters and hurdlers themselves, their contribution as coaches brought the best out of young stars such as Sean White and Steve Hanley, who all combined to produce fast times for the 4x100 metres relay.

Despite the limited facilities available for specialist training Sutton Harriers gained useful league points in the field events. In the throws Anthony Tipping and Mike Ahearne started with the club as youngsters and developed into 40 metre plus discus throwers, while the best jumpers were Peter Code in the pole vault, John Byrne in the high jump and Lynton Boardman in the long and triple jumps. John won the Lancashire high jump title and Lynton went on to gain junior international honours in the long jump.

All league meetings end with the 4x400 metres relay and no review of Sutton Harriers' performances in the Northern Men's League would be complete without mentioning those who contributed some brilliant 400 metre relay runs. These include sprinters such as Mike Gaskell and Sean White moving up in distance, runners such as Frank Rimmer and Jim Crehan moving down, and specialist 400 metre and middle distance men such as Mike Hackett, Mark Ashley, Mark Case, Martin Gaskell, Ray Vose, Iain Adams and Neil Smart, all of whom put in sparkling runs for the club. Anyone who witnessed the matches with Rotherham Harriers in the early 1980s will never forget Sutton's Martin Gaskell and Rotherham's Peter Elliott running the last leg of the 4x400 metres relay stride for stride, with honours equally divided over the season. Peter went on to win a silver medal in the 1988 Olympics 1500 metres and is nowadays much involved with the Great North Run.

The Women's League is for all age groups, but for Sutton Harriers in the early days it was the depth in the younger age groups that was the club's strength and it was rewarding to watch these young athletes work through the age groups and come to represent the club at senior level.

The middle distance races were always good scoring events for the club with athletes such as Sue Crehan, Julie Knowles, Sue Barton, Tracey Lavelle, Ann Williams, Lyn Vose, Susan Woods, Debbie Fairclough and Linda Hannaby, who all won a good number of races for the club. Sue Crehan and Ann Williams went on to represent Great Britain in the Olympic Games but by that time they were both members of Sale Harriers. Ann won a silver medal in the 800 metres in the 1990 Commonwealth Games in New Zealand.

Over the years the club also produced a number of good sprinters. Gaynor Thompson, Jenny Taylor and Denise Smart (Sue Crehan's youngest sister) being probably the best, whilst the women too had their all-rounders, with Lesley Norcross and Susan Lunt probably the most versatile. Lesley was a fine high jumper who formed a winning partnership with Ann Williams in their younger days.

As with the men's teams the women's, too, had strong family ties. Following on from the Tipping father-and-sons team was the Tipping mother-and-daughters team, as Margaret competed together with daughters Ann and Jane. This time, it was taken one stage further as Margaret's sister Pat Fitzgerald and her daughter Joanne also took part. Indeed it was a regular event for Margaret and Pat to score well in the senior throws and for Jane and Joanne to pick up points in the under 15 throws.

That a contributor to *Athletics Weekly* should ask if having six members of a family (the Tippings) competing in different events at different venues on the same day, constituted a record, ties in with Margaret's description of them as a very sporty family.

'Austin and I,' she recalls, 'met in the Harriers in 1951 and we trained regularly at Ruskin Drive and Allanson Street. Austin was an out and out sprinter, 100, 200, 400 yards. I liked sprinting, hurdling, relay running and I was a good thrower. There were few opportunities for throwing in those days.*

On our engagement day, we went to Liverpool and bought the ring, had a celebration lunch, and hurried home for an athletics match at Ruskin Drive against a team from the Burtonwood Airbase. Austin ran against an outstanding sprinter D Snow in the 100 yards, and although doing even time, was placed second. However, in the 220 yards, on a circular grass track with no lanes marked, Austin won. Apparently Americans had not been taught to use their elbows in such circumstances! I competed in the discus. Just as we were about to commence, we noticed a huge wasps' nest hanging from the trees on the long pitch at Ruskin Drive. So we calmly picked up our gear, went to the opposite side of the field and marked out a new circle on the grass. I doubt if they would do that today. I was worried all though the event in case I damaged my new engagement ring.

We married in August 1956 and I stopped training 5 months before our first child, Stephen, was born in October 1957. That August, heavily pregnant, I had gone to Manchester White City Stadium (a dog-racing Mecca), to watch Austin run in the Northern Counties 220 yards, I think it was. Standing in the stands near a group of men I heard them saying, "10-1 the field - bar Tipping". I was amazed to hear them betting as it was illegal. Austin told me later that in handicap events and championships the bookies would approach the possible winners and ask, "Are you going?" which meant "Are you going to try to win?" If the answer was "No", then they would alter their odds.

The young Tippings took to various events. Anne was the star. She was a naturally fast runner, who didn't need much training at all. Roy Ashley looked after them at that time. Anne was the Lancashire Schools' Champion in 1974 and was given the same time as the winner of the English Schools' 100 metres Championship, although placed 2nd. She was 4th in the 3 AAA's metres under 15's. A serious back injury spoilt what would undoubtedly have been an international career.

Stephen was a steeplechaser and high jumper. Anthony took to discus and shot, and was Club Champion for many years. Jane was Merseyside Schools' Champion at shot, and also a very good pentathlete. She had county honours in discus. Christopher was a good sprinter, but preferred gymnastics and hockey, whilst Jonathan, a good all-rounder, only entered once for the Club's Boys' Championship and won it.

When Anthony competed at the English Schools Championships, at Kirkby, and finished 4th in the Senior Discus, a Senior coach caught up with him as he was going to get his medal. He asked who was his coach. Anthony replied "My Mum". The coach, rather bemused, asked "No, I mean where do you train?" Anthony replied, "on my Nanna's park, on 4 paving stones". That was the only availability he had for either a coach or a discus training area.'

E J (Eddie) Stubbs

(Club President 1947 - 1988)

Though he was born in Speakman Road, Dentons Green, in October 1905, it was in fact in Ealing, London, that Edward James (Eddie) Stubbs grew up. Having left school he qualified as an estate agent and chartered surveyor, and as a chartered auctioneer, and at the same time pursued his interest in sport, in particular by joining London Polytechnic Harriers - a major athletics club - competing against runners of Chariots of Fire calibre.

Shortly after qualifying he returned to St Helens to become a partner with his uncle, Edward Burrows, in the estate agents, Grayson (his mother was a Grayson) and Burrows, which could trace its origin back to 1843.

He made immediate contact with Sutton Harriers and in December 1928 was elected a member of the club, turning out for the senior teams in both the West Lancs and the Northern Championships a few weeks later.

Eddie Stubbs could not have foreseen that, within twelve months, not only would he be running as a Harrier, but also have begun two years as Club Secretary, and, following the sudden tragic death, due to long-suffered war injuries, of the Club Treasurer, Robert Fowles (son of Reuben Fowles and cousin to 'Ham' Finney), have taken on that role as well.

As Secretary - and post WorldWar II as Club President - his invariably encouraging reviews of the club's achievements reveal his enthusiasm for athletics and for the Harriers. A busy man - work pressures even deprived him of his honeymoon - he served the club in quiet ways:- auditing accounts, meeting the drinks' and guests' bills at an annual dinner, providing prizes, giving occasional sums to help the committee defray runners' travelling costs.

His help was invaluable when possible permanent HQ sites were being sought and considered, and when the Harriers were truly homeless after World War II it was their President, Eddie Stubbs, who found them a temporary base at the Old Powder Works off Normans Lane, and made Grayson and Burrows' premises available for committee meetings.

Everyone was encouraged by Eddie's cheerful presence at club events - from training sessions to championships. He was no passive supporter, as his daughter Lynn Lawton's reminiscences show. However, perhaps more important even than his enthusiastic encouragement from beside the course, urging Harriers on, was his desire to nurture the latent athletic skills of the younger members of the club.

Reflections of an All-Rounder

No longer a teenager, the former all-rounder Lesley-Ann Norcross has recently been reflecting on the short and long-term benefits of having been a Harrier.

'Had I known what I know today I would have exploited to my heart's content the many opportunities open to me during those 11 years between 1973 and 1984 spent with the Sutton Harriers. In retrospect, I'd like to think that today I'd be a much fitter and pleasingly wealthier woman if I had followed through those opportunities to fruition. In reality though, I have no regrets, only extremely pleasant memories of the valuable experiences, the many skills learnt and, most importantly, the laughs shared along the way. I believe these memories are worth sharing if, at least, I'm able to highlight the added value gained both short and long-term from the experiences.

Here, pictured at a club prize presentation in 1982, over half a century since he joined the Harriers, E.J.Stubbs, the Club President, stands amidst some of the club's officers and its successful youngsters.

I guess my introduction to athletics came from my own family. My father and his own father had both been 'runners' and so I guess the interest and encouragement had come from within the home. My drive to pursue my athletics throughout both primary and secondary school came from within. Most of my school friends were also keen; in particular my dear friend Ann Williams who went on to great things. I enjoyed all types of sport. In fact, in those early days I was extremely interested and involved in gymnastics, swimming, horse-riding, squash and cycling, but my athletics seemed to take up most of my time.

On joining the Sutton Harriers I was introduced to a running coach, Dr Phil Thomas, and a number of other members of the team. I was asked to gather with other new recruits in the main meeting room of the clubhouse headquarters near to Sherdley Park. My first evening was spent running around the perimeter of the park with the rest of the team. Training evenings were held in all weathers: in those days there was no such thing as a cancelled evening due to snow, thunder or rain. When the visibility was extremely poor we would train on the roads around the area, potholes and all! Obviously in the early days I'd walk most of the way; however I was able to keep up with the rest of the field after a while. In the first few years in training I learnt how to pace myself, how to compete and work with others and, of course, how to be a good loser. This I soon got used to. Today these skills have come in very handy indeed in the workplace.

Most weekends during the year were spent in competition around the country. There was probably no city in the UK that the club had not visited at some point during its existence. Edinburgh, Newcastle, London, Coventry, Birmingham, Leeds and Bradford were a number of the places I visited with fond memories.

I remember travelling to nearby Kirkby one weekend to compete in a county championship event at the Kirkby Sports Stadium and taking part in a number of track and field events over the course of the day. My last race was the Ladies' 3000 metres. I turned up on the start line to realise that I was the only competitor. Seemingly, the other females had pulled out at the last minute owing to unforeseen circumstances. The funniest thing was the newspaper write-up the following week headlined "Norcross left the field standing". The fact that there was no one else competing alongside me made this easily achievable! Dr Phil Thomas certainly had a way with words in those days!

After a number of years running with the Harriers I began to realise how hard work through very difficult and painful training sessions could pay-off. I don't mean "pay-off" in terms of winning because in reality I often didn't win. I'm actually referring to the "pay-off" in terms of a boost to my self-confidence, my physical fitness and the overwhelming feeling of achievement in just taking part. The Harriers taught us all how to put training plans together over each week and how to implement these plans. In retrospect, I realize what I failed to learn at first was how to prioritise and balance - how to balance home life and school. School for me during the 70s was not exciting, and I guess lacked the pressures that currently exist in today's environment. My excuse these days for developing my career belatedly is that I was a late developer!

I can imagine, for me, as for most people of my own age, the changes seen over the past twenty years have been remarkable; especially regarding the current economic and political climate and pressures placed upon us by the social architectures of our working and home environments. By these I mean the competition for recognition, reward and promotion as a result of hard work in the work place, the bureaucracy and internal and external politics, plus the processes inflicted upon us that occasionally make our working and home lives less enjoyable.

How do we cope, then? Well, if as Darwin held, it's about 'survival of the fittest' successful survival tactics must be learnt. I used to wonder what Darwin actually meant. A number of years ago, I remember believing that the focus of his theory was on physical fitness alone. At the time I failed to realise that in fact it was more than just physical well-being: it was about the body and mind as a whole. Today, as Global Clinical Programme Manager within Research and Development working for GSK, I can appreciate what role the Harriers and my athletics had to play in the development of my own body and mind and in developing those survival tactics. I can now identify where my attitude and some of those valuable skills originated, especially my sense of humour.

When I think back to those days with the Harriers, the most important conclusion for me is the fact that I really didn't need to be in a classroom or lecture theatre at university to develop my body and mind. Part of this was achieved quite successfully by taking part in sport and other outdoor activities beyond the school and university gates. Don't get me wrong. I realise my school and university days were extremely important in my obtaining valuable qualifications which have allowed me to get where I am today. However, the teaching received from these establishments alone could not have taught me such skills as how to work and interact with others under extreme pressures, how to balance both work and pleasure and how to time-manage. There are numerous organisations around today who run personal development programmes, using basic team-building concepts, skills and philosophies that are inherent in athletics and sports clubs around the country, such as the Sutton Harriers. I would encourage anyone to make the most of these opportunities as early as possible as their short and long-term benefits are invaluable!'

Susan Smart and her sister Karen joined Sutton Harriers in 1970, having been introduced to the club by teacher and Sutton Harriers coach, Roy Ashley. Susan was talented from the start and Roy told her she had the ability with training and hard work to become a future Olympic athlete. Under

his watchful eye she trained steadily and represented Lancashire at cross-country and track She was a member of the Lancashire Schools' team that won the English Schools' Cross-Country Championship in 1972 and actually finished 6th in that race.

When she went away to college in 1976 her studies curtailed any athletics but upon completing them in 1980 she returned to competition. Sutton Harriers were getting a team together for the Northern Women's League. Sue was not very fit at this time but turned out for the club in the 3000 metres although she didn't have much success at first. She was now coached by her husband, Jim Crehan, whom she had married in 1977 whilst at college, and over the next six years steadily improved and was a major strength in the club, together with Ann Williams and other Sutton girls at that time.

Susan would run the 800 metres, 3000 metres followed by the 1500 metres, and was at such a level, even in Division 1 of the Northern Women's League, that she would win all these races in national class time.

During the summer of 1983 she started to run longer distances with success and won the Ladies' Section of the Sale Harriers Half Marathon. She later, together with her husband Jim, ran the New York Marathon which she completed in the excellent time of 2 hours 50 mins 49secs. She finished 3rd in the Northern Women's Cross-Country at Clarke Gardens, Liverpool, and won many Merseyside Cross-Country Championships even though she did not really relish cross-country. In subsequent years she won the Northern Cross-Country Championship, the Inter-Area Cross-Country Championship and finished 2nd in the Inter-Counties as well as 5th in the National Cross-Country Championships.

In 1984 Sue showed she could perform to a high standard on the track, and international honours followed. She started the season in the Merseyside County Championships at Victoria Park, Warrington, winning the 800 metres, 1500 metres and 5000 metres all within a couple of hours, setting new record times in both the 1500 metres and 5000 metres events. She finished 3rd in the WAAA 5000 metres and was a finalist in the 1500 metres.

At the UK Championships in Cwmbran with a time in the 3000 metres of 9 mins 19 secs she qualified to compete in the Olympic trial over that distance at Crystal Palace. This race was won by Zola Budd. Sue later in the year finished 3rd in the WAAA 10,000 metres, and achieved international honours when she was selected to run the 3000 metres for England in Dublin. However, she still found time to run on the road and finished 2nd in the Ladies' Section of the St Helens Half-Marathon.

At Cosford in 1985 she won the WAAA Indoor 3000 metres and later represented England in the 3000 metres. She won the WAAA 10,000 metres Championship and was then selected for Great Britain against Hungary in the 3000 metres to partner Zola Budd, who broke the record for the distance. Sue did not forget about road running and during 1985 won the Ladies' Section in the St

Helens' and the Sale Harriers' half marathons, as well as a 20 km road race in Paris which had 14,000 runners and finished at the Eiffel Tower.

The following year Sue left Sutton Harriers to join Sale Harriers in order to compete at a higher level and with better training facilities. Whilst with Sale Harriers in 1987 she won the WAAA 10,000 metres Championship and set a new English record for that distance at the Bislett Games in Oslo, behind Ingrid Christianson, the world record holder at the time. She went on to represent Great Britain in the 10,000 metres at the World Athletic Championships in Rome and the following year was 3rd in the WAAA London Marathon in a time of 2hrs 36mins 10secs, which earned her selection for the Marathon in the Seoul Olympics.

On the road Sue represented Great Britain three times in the World 15 km Championships in Portugal, Monaco and Australia. Certainly Susan's ability, hard work and training had brought reality to Roy Ashley's 1970 forecast.

Ann Williams

Born on 20th August, 1965, Ann began her running career in primary school when she was nine. It was her father who felt she had the potential to become a runner and so at the age of ten she joined Pilkington Recreation Athletic Club. She quickly established herself as a future champion. In 1977 she won the Merseyside Schools' under 13 girls' cross-country title and the following year the under 15 girls' cross-country title. During 1978 she also had success on the track, winning the Merseyside Schools' under 15 girls' 800 metres Championship.

Ann joined Sutton Harriers early in 1979 and during that year concentrated on 400 metres with considerable success, gaining selection for the English Catholic Schools' team at the European Catholic Schools' tournament in Ireland. Her breakthrough into top class athletics came in 1982 when, a six-

teen-year-old, she won the English Schools' 400 metres Intermediate Girl's Championship in a record time of 55 seconds, and also the NCWAAA Junior 800 metres Championship. Ann's fine achievements that season were rewarded by selection to run for Great Britain against West Germany at Birmingham, just one week before her seventeenth birthday, and also to represent England in the Home Countries International at Middlesborough three weeks later.

She was again chosen to run for Great Britain in the 4x400 metres relay at an indoor meeting against France in January 1984. Ann was the first woman in the history of Sutton Harriers to gain international selection.

As a Harrier, in addition to being a reliable individual performer over distances ranging from 200 to 1500 metres for club league fixtures, Ann was also an essential part of many relay teams. Together with Tracy Lavelle, Lesley Norcross and Bernadette Hanley, they finished a creditable fifth place in the 1980 4 x 800 metres National Intermediate Women's Relay Championship at Birmingham. Two years later, in 1982, Ann, Helen McEvoy, Lesley Norcross and Lyn Vose were placed second in the National Women's Relay 4 x 800 metres Championship, again at Birmingham.

However, despite many fine runs over 400 metres, Ann's real future lay in running the 800 metres and 1500 metres events, and in order to compete at a higher level, as well as to train on proper tracks, Ann resigned from Sutton Harriers on 28th February, 1985 to join Sale Harriers.

Whilst with Sale Ann appeared for Great Britain and for England in most major athletics championship events, including the Olympic Games, the Commonwealth Games, and the World and European Championships. She won a silver medal in the Commonwealth Games 800 metres in New Zealand in 1990 when finishing second to Diane Modahl. After giving birth to a son in 1998, and conscious of a niggling back injury, Ann was reluctantly forced to call time on a long and successful running career.

Ann always trained in and around the St Helens area, as well as with Sale Harriers. Even in the late 1980s and 1990s, when competing for Great Britain, she would train regularly with the senior men at Sutton Harriers, going for 7 to 10 mile runs on Thursday evenings. The runs were hard and very competitive and provided an important part of her winter training. Ian White, Nev White, Neil Smart, Stan Irlam and Jimmy Hull all provided good hard runs and Ann never really forgot where her athletics roots were.

* * * * *

League competition still constitutes the main summer event for athletes and, like their Harrier predecessors, today's members of St Helens Sutton AC continue to participate in the Northern League.

Chapter 11

BALANCING THE BOOKS

Managing the club's finances has always been a challenging responsibility. In the early days of the club's history the office of treasurer changed frequently. There were six different treasurers between 1899 and 1908, including Sammy Colville and 'Ham' Finney. The minute book for that period gives an insight into the prices of some everyday items, together with the cost of membership and of club expenses.

1901 Membership card of Charles Rigby

Money was not plentiful and expenditure, such as authorising 4d (1½p) for brandy when a member was taken ill, was carefully recorded. The fund-raising 'Smoking Concert' of November 1899 was reported in the press. A most 'enjoyable evening', it helped fund the forthcoming Christmas Handicap.

Sadly there are no details of the club supper and the ball held in 1901 - but there does survive a list of the twenty-three local gentlemen to whom requests for financial help ('subscriptions') were to be made on specially printed official notepaper. Thus, listed among colliery managers, local farmers and well-known publicans were Lord Derby, Richard Pilkington, Arthur Sinclair (of Waterdale), Joseph Beecham and Henry Seton-Carr, MP for St Helens.

In 1901 the club annual subscriptions were fixed at 2s (10p) for those over seventeen and 1s (5p) for those under. Whilst help was provided towards team members' travelling costs, 12s (60p), for example, in April 1902 to be shared by the six runners competing in Manchester, entrants for the Christmas Handicap paid 6d (2½p) each, and boy spectators 1d (½ p).

SUTTON HARRIERS CYCLING & ATHLETIC CLUB.
Balance Sheet Season 1909-10.

RECEIPTS.	£	s.	d.	EXPENDITURE.	£	s.	d.
Messrs Greenall, Whitley & Co.	1	1	0	Costumes	2	8	0
W. Bell, Esq.	1	1	0	Sweater	0	4	11
Col. W. L. Pilkington	1	1	0	Northern Counties Subscription and Entrance Fee	0	15	6
T. Boardman, Esq.	0	10	6	Liverpool & District ,,	0	15	0
H. Hibbert, Esq.	0	10	0	National ,,	2	0	0
Mrs. Lightfoot	0	10	0	St. Helens & District ,,	0	8	0
H. Hewitt, Esq.	0	10	6	National Cyclists' Union ,,	0	12	6
Ald. H. B. Bates	0	10	0	Expenses to Bebington Liverpool & Dist. Championship	1	7	5
S. Royle, Esq.	0	10	0	,, Derby National	4	0	3
T. Glover, Esq., M.P.	0	5	0	,, Rainford St. Helens & Dist.	0	11	6
S. Ingram, Esq.	0	5	0	,, Haydock Northern	0	15	8
Coun. T. Abbott	0	5	0	,, Stanley Marathon Race	0	6	6
G. Brown, Esq.	0	5	0	Hire of Ground for Championship	1	1	0
P. Jeffery, Esq.	0	5	0	Prizes Club Championship 5 miles	1	15	0
J. H. Fletcher, Esq.	0	5	0	,, ,, 10 miles	3	8	0
W. Kilmury, Esp.	0	5	0	,, Marathon Race	0	12	6
H. Stephenson, Esq.	0	5	0	,, 2 Club Medals	0	15	0
W. Whittaker, Esq.	0	5	0	,, Novice Handicap	1	4	6
F. Plews, Esq.	0	5	0	Expenses to Lancaster	1	14	0
Rev. F. S. C. Crane	0	5	0	Wreath for H. J. Taylor, V.P.	0	4	6
W. Longton, Esq.	0	7	6	Delegates Expenses to Liverpool	0	11	0
T. R. Prodger, Esq.	0	5	0	,, Manchester	0	10	0
J. Fowles, Esq.	0	5	0	Ancle Band, Bandages and Vaseline	0	6	0½
R. P. Beards, Esq.	0	5	0	Tin Trunk	0	6	6
G. H. Reid, Esq.	0	5	0	Repairs to Punch Ball	0	11	3
Members' Subscriptions	8	5	6	Expenses at Winwick	0	3	0
Profit on 2 Cinderellas	3	8	6	Insurance of Rudge-Whitworth Cup	0	5	0
Profit on Easter Dance	0	13	6	Track Prize	0	15	0
Collected in Boxes	1	8	8	Washing Towels and Sweaters	0	3	10
Entrance Fees, Christmas Handicap	0	13	6	Embrocation	0	6	6
,, 10 miles Club Championship	0	7	0	Sundries	0	5	9
Sale of Costumes	1	2	0	Printing	2	12	9
Receipts 5 miles Club Championship	2	0	5	Christmas Handicap Prizes	5	16	6
,, 10 ,, ,,	3	0	5	Re-instatement Forms	0	15	0
Profit on Saloon to Derby	0	2	0	Postages	1	7	1
Re-instatement Form	0	8	0	Balance in hand	0	0	6½
Subscriptions for Christmas Handicap	5	15	0				
Balance in hand season 1908-9	2	10	11				
	£39	18	5		£39	18	5

Audited and found correct August 20th, 1910.   Signed—F. J. WHITTLE.

Prizes agreed for that event were 25s (£1.25), 15s (75p), 7s 6d (37½ p), 5s (25p) and 2s 6d (12 ½ p). A year later, 1903, when it was decided to engage a policeman for two hours at a cost of 9d (nearly 4p), the prizes were in kind:- a turkey, valued at 12s (60p), a goose at 10s (50p), a second goose at 8s (40p), ham at 7s (35p), 6 lb pork at 4s 6d (22½ p), a duck at 4s (20p) and two rabbits donated by F Peachey, one of the handicappers. These were generous prizes, well worth winning, when one real-ises that the old age pension, introduced in 1909 for the over 70s was five shillings (25p) per week, and that the average weekly wage for male industrial employees stood at £1.10s (£1.50) in 1914.

Interestingly, just over eighty years later, when annual subs were £11 for seniors and £5 for jun-iors, the first prize at the 1986 Christmas Handicap was still a turkey (valued at £10)!

Hints at hard times and at raising money emerge from committee minutes during 1933, when it was decided that six members should be taken to Lancaster with the teams *'for their great work in raising funds by whist drives'*, and on another occasion that *'all runners in work should pay 6d (2½p) to-wards train fare'*. Expenses were inevitably incurred in entering teams for events, sending delegates to cross-country athletics association meetings. There were fares to subsidise, as when the club's Manchester-Blackpool Relay team travelled by workman's fare to Manchester and contributed 2s 6d (12½ p) each to the subsequent charabanc.

A successful season like 1936-7 did not necessarily reap financial rewards, as the following letter to potential patrons, drafted the following year by Bill Glover, then Club Secretary, reveals:

'Dear Sir,

On behalf of my club, I am again making an appeal to our generous patrons, to help us to meet the heavy financial burden we are called upon to bear in order that our teams may compete in the various champion-ships.

This season is an exceptionally heavy one as the Northern Counties Championships, in which we usu-ally have three teams qualifed to compete (Youths, Juniors & Seniors) are being held at Stockton on Tees, and the English Championships are being held at Reading, and we will be sending our strongest team down for this.

As you are probably aware, last season we had a very successful season, winning the St.Helens and District Youths and Senior Championship, the West Lancs Junior and Senior, and Northern Counties Senior Championships, and we finished 3rd in the National to Birchfield Harriers and Belgrave Harriers. This season we are hoping to improve on this performance, and, knowing how nobly you have responded to our appeals in the past, I am sure that you will again give the lads every encouragement by once again helping to send the team to the venues.

Thanking you most heartily for past favours.'

The income and expenditure totals of Sutton Harriers' athletic section in 1938-9 (the last season before World War II broke out) shown opposite come from that season's balance sheet, drawn up by the Club Treasurer, Richard Whittle.

In an era in which £1 = 20 shillings and 240 pence, rather then our 100p, and a shilling at 12 pence had not been converted to 5p, but would have bought six Mars bars, the items listed deserve attention. Fund-raising efforts and the existence of a building account are revealed, whilst tucked among the usual items of expenditure are the sum granted Arthur Williams so that he could rep-resent Wales, and the amount outlayed on a wreath for the club's first President and long-standing patron, Michael Hughes.

BALANCE SHEET 1938-9

ATHLETIC SECTION

Income		Expenditure	
Sutton	10 - 0	W L CCA Subscription	1 - 1 - 0
Mr Wakefield Sen	2 - 0	W Lanc Entry Fees	1 - 0 - 6
Mr & Mrs McMinnis	10 - 0	National Entry Fee	1 - 1 - 0
Mr E Harrison	5 - 0	Northern AAA Sub	1 - 1 - 0
Mr F Baines	5 - 0	Northern Youths Entry	2 - 6
Mr R Whittle	10 - 6	St Helens & Dist Sub	10 - 0
Mr H Arnold	5 - 0	St Helens & Dist Entry Fees	12 - 6
Collection for Wreath	5 - 0	Track Team Entries	1 - 10 - 9
Raffle per Mr S Strettle	1 - 14 - 0	Fare to Leyland re Course	2 - 6
Raffel per Mr T Lea	15 - 0	Leeds 2 Meetings	17 - 6
Bank Interest	4 - 3	Manchester / Meetings N C C	5 - 0
Deposits, Gas & Elec	2 - 0 - 0	Liverpool 3 meetings W L CCA	3 - 3
Profits from Dances	16 - 0	Liverpool 4 meetings N C AAA	6 - 6
Balance in Bank 1938	11 - 7 - 6	Postages	9 - 6
Members Subs	1 - 10 - 0	Envelopes	1 - 0
Transferred from Building a/c	2 - 13 - 3	Team Expenses Championships	1 - 18 - 6
	23 - 12 - 6	Manchester - Blackpool Relay	3 - 0 - 0
		Refreshments Visitors	11 - 6
		Coke & Coal	5 - 6
		Soap	1 - 8
		Grant to A Williams International	15 - 0
		Wreath Col M Hughes	10 - 0
		Trainers Expenses	13 - 0
		General Rate	1 - 15 - 6
		Elec	1 - 5 - 4
		Gas	1 - 4 - 0
		Water	1 - 7 - 8
		Grant J Forshaw Wedding Present	4 - 0
		Printing Dances	15 - 0
		Return of Waterloo Trophy	1 - 4
		Loss on Handbooks	1 - 6
		Pins Etc	6
			23 - 14 - 6

The 1970s and 80s witnessed a significant expansion of the club, with a considerable influx of members, especially in the junior sections. There were fifty-seven paid-up members in 1972-3 and subscriptions totalled £56.98. By 1986 membership had increased to over a hundred and fifty with £992.50 being paid in membership fees.

The same decades also saw the construction of the club's first brick-built headquarters in Chester Lane, replacing the wooden building erected in 1958 and extended half a dozen years later.

Building work began in 1973 and was completed in 1986. The whole project cost £23,325.34, of which £14,228.34 was raised by the club. The remainder came from donations and grants provided by the Sports Council and St Helens Metropolitan Borough Council.

One of the most important sources of revenue was the '100 Club' which raised over £5000 between 1975 and 1976. Sponsored runs were good fund-raisers, contributing nearly £1800 during that period. These included the 75th Anniversary St Helens to London Relay and a 24-hour relay around Sherdley Park. Money was also raised through social events and the Christmas dances at St Anne's, Sutton, organised by Joe and Barbara White, were very popular occasions. Refreshment sales provided valuable revenue. In 1986 the profit from sales was £355, boosted by the club's hosting of the Northern Cross-Country Championships in Sherdley Park that February. Raffles, jumble sales and car-boot sales also brought in extra revenue.

Rebuilding the club headquarters was a major project. The upkeep of that building required extra money, as did the running of the weekly athletic activities of a large and thriving club. In 1972 the cost of rent, rates, insurance, gas, electricity and water was £66.72. By 1987 that had risen to £1291.75. Team entry fees in 1972 were £19.44 and in 1987 £126.08. Affiliation fees rose from £10.10 to £104.75. However, travel costs stayed more or less the same at £30, owing to the policy of filling coaches and covering costs.

The 1970s and 80s saw huge amounts of money going into athletics, with large appearance fees, sponsorship and prize money. Televised events also provided a large income for the sport. However, very little of that money filtered down to the club level. In spite of that, Sutton Harriers did experience a period of considerable growth and prosperity, which contributed significantly to the club's successes during that time.

Tony Walsh
Treasurer 1972-1987

Chapter 12

CHESTER LANE AND BEYOND

In the later 1950s Sutton Harriers' search for a permanent home took a positive turn with the leasing from the Council of derelict land at Chester Lane, Marshalls Cross. This was to become the club's headquarters for almost forty years.

External view of the Green Hut

A disused clay-hole occupied almost half its area and, given permission to open up the site for suitable tipping, the lengthy process of infilling and then rough levelling the surface commenced.

Rather more speedily the club's new HQ came into being. Progress began with plans submitted by Tom Fillingham, the then Club Treasurer, residing at the time at 77 French Street, Thatto Heath. These were submitted on the 27th July, 1958 and described the proposed development as 'a sectional timber building with brick wc and urinal'. Building regulation approval was conveyed by notice from St Helens Council on the 21st August 1958 with planning permission following on the 29th.

Many former members will re-member the 'Green Hut', as it was affectionately known. Complete with built in under-seat storage, array of coat hooks (adorned by various items of athletics apparel), Belfast sink and ample supply of cold water, it represented a mas-sive step forward in providing a permanent home for the club. Its crowning glory came in the shape of the tin bath, a rare delight for those who managed to get to it first. Thereafter this became a blackened mud bath. Under these

Internal view of the Green Hut showing the shower facilities

arrangements, youngsters were quickly to realise the advantage of running first.

Located amongst many items of discarded 'athletic apparel' upon one coat hook in the corner was the club's spare jock strap. Rumoured to having once belonged to Eddie Edwards, it was to provide support to those in need. Many will also remember the spectacle of queueing to use the detached wc. This facility was at a premium prior to any race and long queues were often observed as athletes sought urgent relief. Characteristic of its time was the nail behind the door, complete with six-inch carefully cut squares of old newspapers. Besides serving an essential purpose these demonstrated the breadth of readership amongst the club's membership.

August 1964 brought the opportunity to extend the 'Green Hut', and as Tom McIntyre vividly recounts (with apologies to Flanders and Swann) :

'Twas on a Sunday morning that Sutton Harriers called . . .'

'In August 1964 an intrepid party of Sutton Harriers' members descended on Lea Green Colliery - one of many collieries to be closed down in the South-West Lancashire coalfield. The aim of the expedition was to move a large wooden structure which was to be added to the already existing building in Chester Lane. This structure was available at no cost to Sutton Harriers - a godsend for almost any social or sporting club which did not have too much money, or resources to buy a building for club purposes.

Dismantling, removal, transporting and re-assembling took place in one day! Yes, it was done in one day, a daunting task for the artisans, who were Fred McMinnis, Tom Fillingham, Jack Chidlow, and Eddie Edwards. It was also a challenge to the 'DO IT YOURSELF' capabilities of those involved. It meant an early start that Sunday morning, with all hands to the pump. Firstly, the building had to be carefully dismantled in sections, each being given an identification number for its re-assembly. The sections had to be moved manually with much muscle power. There wasn't any available handling equipment such as fork lift trucks, or mini cranes, and in 1964 there were no tool hire firms in the community.

Such tools as we had were brought by club members from their sheds and garages, comprising shovels, spades, picks, rakes, brushes, sledge and other types of hammer, spanners, screwdrivers, ropes and any item at all that would assist.

When the dismantling was done, an articulated lorry from Philip Priestner Haulage Co, of Moore in Cheshire, appeared. Club member Peter had persuaded his brother Philip to volunteer his services without charge, a gesture for which the club were most grateful. Without his transport the club might not have been able to carry out this transfer. The sections were lifted manually on to the lorry, and transported to Chester Lane. A section of the group who had gone from Club HQ to Lea Green Colliery came back on the lorry wherever they could find space to sit or stand, clinging on to ropes or whatever they could find. On arriving back at Chester Lane all of this 'happy band' looked as though they had just finished the 6am-2pm early shift below ground, hewing out the black gold called coal!

The day of course was made a little less arduous by numerous 'breaks' for refreshments. Most members had brought with them their own selection of foodstuffs and various liquids (all non-alcoholic). Stop that laughing. It's true! However the club provided another choice of eatables, and drinks. The kitchen staff of course, were lady members and parents who, with their constant supply of refreshments, and cries of 'Tea, or coffee, up!', certainly worked as hard as the 'tradesmen and labourers'.

Believe it or not the erection of this section of our 'new' extension to the existing wooden building ('the Green Hut') was completed by the early evening of that day - by when there really wasn't any time to sit back and admire our 'engineering' feat. But the atmosphere was of a job well done and we exuded a coal-dusty air of genuine satisfaction.'

This mammoth effort resulted in the available space being broadly doubled. Ironically, it was this additional section which was to deteriorate first, so that by the early 1970s parts of the structure were dangerous and incapable of economic repair. This provided the stimulus for a much more ambitious project which through phased development was to cover the period 1973 to 1986.

To begin with, plans were submitted to the Council on the 14th November 1973 by E A (Ted) Johnson, the then Chairman. Described as a 'toilet and shower block' the brick-built structure provided much improved facilities, adjoining the 'Green Hut' and accessible from it. With materials 'scrounged' from local suppliers - hardcore from Pickavances, concrete from Quickmix, bricks from Roughdales and timber from Laithwaites, and ably put together by a team of members led by Alf Thompson, the building was produced at a fraction of its true value. This was to prove crucial to the funding of further work. Also crucial was the support gained at that time from the local Sports Council through the form of a grant for 50% of the value of the work. This translated to a contribution of £1664. The club found itself in the enviable position of having completed the work, whilst retaining a healthy bank balance. In turn, this was to provide the encouragement to do more.

Supported by additional fund-raising events orchestrated by Treasurer, Tony Walsh, which included the 75th Anniversary St.Helens to London Relay described earlier, resources were gradually assembled to the point where the club was able to embark upon the next phase of development in mid 1977. This involved the removal in its entirety of the by then totally dilapidated 'Green Hut', which on June 18th 1974 had featured in this article in the *St Helens Newspaper and Advertiser* .

Harriers - A Famous Club Dying of Shame -

by David Hodgkinson

'It could be called a cabin in the clearing. Only it's not. The cabin would be better described as a derelict disaster, the clearing nothing more than a dirt-ridden slag heap. It is tucked behind an overgrown clump of bushes on waste land just off the main road out of St.Helens - a wooden monument to decay.

Yet this shambles of a shack is the home of one of Britain's best-known athletic clubs, Sutton Harriers. "Go anywhere in the country," coach Roy Ashley tells me, "and people involved in athletics know Sutton Harriers." But these friends from as far south as Southampton and as far north as Nairn are never invited back to Sutton. "It's like the last outpost to Hell," commented one member. Sutton Harriers' clubhouse must be seen to be believed. It's like a glimpse into the dark and distant past.

Committeeman John Hodgetts gave me a conducted tour

The building - described as "temporary" over 20 years ago - lies on a stretch of waste land at Marshalls Cross, hard by Sherdley Park. The first thing that strikes you about it is how desolate the place looks - abandoned, neglected. A brick building stands by its side, the words T Rex emblazoned across it in tired chalk. "That's the toilet," says John. I look in ... and hurry out with a shudder.

Clambering over a couple of man-made hillocks, I get a close look at the side of the cabin - every one of six windows boarded up. "Vandals. They've been a scourge to the club for years," says John. The building is in two parts: the original, painted green, and a second section bought in the late 60s from the NCB. Part of this second stage bulges out as if in the later stages of pregnancy. The timber is rotted and bowed. There are more gaps and holes in it than a colander.

We stepped inside. It was like dropping into a time machine that whisked us right back to the eighteenth century. "This is the men's changing room - and shower," said my guide. Cold, damp, unwelcoming. The shower? An antiquated water geyser set over a concrete base which could have been dragged up from the foundations. "Most people just wash as best they can out of a bucket," said John.

There is a girls' changing room-cum-kitchen. "Vandals broke in here some time ago and burst the water pipes. The place was in a terrible mess," he continued. Most of the inner walls, crumbling with old age, are kept together with large pieces of cardboard boxes.

The last room of this forbidding place is for general use. Light flickers in through a series of gaps and holes; there are no windows, as such, any more. You might think you were in Colditz ... or Cannery Row. John Hodgetts, who joined the Harriers two years ago, looked up at the ceiling. "It gets wet in here", he said. "It's cold as well". There is heating - one or two electric appliances - and there is lighting. But they don't help to lift the gloom that fills the place like an eerie tomb.

Members of Sutton Harriers are dedicated athletes. They have to be. They are paid-up members of a club which can offer them scant facilities, a club now celebrating its 75th anniversary.

Don't get the idea that Sutton Harriers are content with their lot. They are not. For 75 years they have fought to build their club into something worth shouting about. The finishing tape is still, sadly, a marathon away. "We tried to get a grant from the council," said John. "They offered 30 per cent. But where do we get the other 70 per cent from?" Subscriptions hardly pay for the lighting, heating and rates. Then there are affiliation fees, coach-fees to events up and down the country.

Now Harriers are making a determined effort again. This year sees the launching of a five-year plan to rebuild. Work has already begun on a shower/toilet block, work started by members who have dug the foundations themselves. And appeals have gone out to firms in St.Helens for help. Over 60 have been sent: already six have been returned. Total of funds raised so far: £62. 'The club are also planning their St.Helens to London relay for July 6 and 7, when 40 members of the club will run in relay to deliver a petition to 10 DowningStreet. "We want people in St.Helens to notice us," say the members.

Sutton is an established club, a famous club with a glittering history of big names and star successes, particularly in cross-country. The club won a hat-trick of national cross-country championships in 1949, 1950 and 1951.

But you can't live on past glories forever.'

Instead of the 'Green Hut' there was to be a 60ft x 30ft brick building, providing community room, kitchen, meeting rooms, male and female changing rooms, storage and links to the shower and toilet block.

With unemployment running at a high level the opportunity arose to secure help through the Government-sponsored Community Industry Initiative, which provided training and learning opportunities for young unqualified people. As labour was supplied free, the club's commitment was to fund material costs. Steady if unspectacular progress saw the brickwork completed to roof height by Autumn 1977. With the onset of winter, the club members resolved to finish the project themselves, under the guidance of Joe White. His expert leadership, extending over many weekends, saw the task eventually completed in early 1978 - a major achievement for an independent club.

Very quickly the club-house established its reputation as an excellent facility, and its proximity to Sherdley Park and the popularity of the racing terrain within the park made Sutton an obvious choice for regional events. In turn, the revenue derived from catering income through the staging of these events, including sales of the famous 'woolly back soup' helped to replenish reduced coffers and restore balances to healthy levels.

Continual expansion of the membership caused the committee to look at options for development. This led to further extension to provide additional changing accommodation in 1984.

Other demands on club officials' time meant this could only be undertaken professionally. Tenders received amounted to £13,600,which after negotiations reduced to £12,800 - well beyond the club's resources. Approaches to the Sports Council were to prove fruitful in the securing of a grant of £5,000. With work commencing in 1985 the appointed contractor, Robert Clarke of Liverpool, completed the job in the spring of 1986,despite the efforts of poor ground conditions and exposed gas pipes to hinder progress and add to costs. The extension's successful completion brought to an end a building development programme spanning some 13 years.

It is to the credit of the club and its talented members, that a dream became reality, thereby completing a process started some 30 years previously by the gifted leaders of that period.

A New Era

Early in 1989 the committee's attention was drawn to Sutton Harriers' impending centenary (1999!), with a view to producing a history of the club. The idea received no further mention, for attention was focussing elsewhere. Of more immediate concern was fund-raising, and a 24-hour sponsored run was considered. Then, also at Sherdley Park, there was the NW Women's Cross-Country event to be hosted.

For some of the committee a bolt from the blue arrived in October when, under *'Any Other Business'*, it was suggested that *'in the interests of the club in general, the ladies' section in particular and for the long-term future of athletics in St Helens an unofficial approach be made to Pilkington AC to discuss the possibility of a merger between the two clubs'.*

What had prompted such an idea?

The demise of handicapping and the advent of league athletics, though welcome, had had mixed consequences for clubs and for individual athletes. Whilst high fliers could have the satisfaction of competing against others of the same calibre, was the enthusiasm of the less able dampened as they could no longer compete with the best? Faced with meagre training facilities the ambitious and talented were understandably likely to transfer their membership to clubs with more to offer. Anyone who had competed in Europe knew what first-class facilities could and should be like. When a St Helens party - including many Harriers - competed in Stuttgart (St.Helens' partner town) in 1975, they discovered an abundance of tartan tracks, whereas in Lancashire only two existed.

Meanwhile, television had brought top-class performances into one's living room, and inevitably this had subtly pressured clubs towards maximising their top athletes' achievements and providing them with optimum facilities.

For an individual club doing this could well be impossible and it began to be seen that strength, and indeed survival, lay in clubs amalgamating. In fact, history was repeating itself. As early as 1877 three clubs had joined together to form the Cheshire Tally Ho Hare and Hounds Club. In Leeds, in 1967, three clubs fused to become Leeds City. Manchester and District Lads' Club, Northern Counties Senior Cross-Country Champions 1963-8, merged with the track-oriented Manchester Athletic Club (to which Norman Ashcroft had once belonged) in the 1970s, and 1997 would see Liverpool Pembroke AC joining forces with Sefton Harriers.

Thus Sutton Harriers made tentative non-committal approaches to Pilkington AC, and St.Helens AC, a club some ten years old using Queens Park, Boundary Road, became involved as well. Representatives of the three clubs met. Their feeling was that in the interests of athletics in St Helens a merger of the three seemed inevitable. Notices and an informal talk advised members of Sutton Harriers of the discussions and what lay behind them.

In March 1990 members learnt Pilkington AC had voted against a merger. Discussion went ahead with St Helens AC and eventually, at a special club meeting held on the 19th July, the 36 members present voted unanimously in favour of a merger with St.Helens AC. As one member commented on that occasion, the general trend in many towns and cities was towards one large strong club.

Athletes at the Sutton Harriers sign on the last day of Sutton (St Helens) Harriers & Athletic Club

Sutton Harriers' committee met again a week later to make plans for the end of August. The John Orrell Mile was run on the 23rd. On the 30th, at the final athletics meeting of Sutton (St Helens) Harriers and Athletic Club, the Tom Fillingham 5000 metres was followed by the presentation of the year's awards.

The last day of Sutton Harriers & Athletic Club

Two days, later, on Saturday September 1st 1990 the St Helens Sutton Athletic Club came into being.

At the new club's first meeting, during which Steve Anders was elected Club Captain and Frank Costello Club Chairman, members realised from a hand-out some of the forethought that had accompanied the merger. Sutton Harriers' Chester Lane clubhouse would be their HQ; subscriptions would be £12 for adults and £6 for juniors; there was to be a new strip - a white vest with red and black vertical panels and either matching or red shorts.

Days later, on September 9th, the newly-named club took part in its first competition, in an invitation two-mile race at Kirkby Stadium, Liverpool as part of a track and field meeting held to celebrate Liverpool Pembroke AC's centenary year. The team of Steve Anders 3rd, Arthur Deane 11th, Paul Cliff 17th, and Gary White 19th, was placed 4th overall.

Throughout September and October that year St Helens Sutton AC competed in several road relays, including one at Bewsey in Warrington hosted by Warrington AC, for which they turned out no fewer than six teams. However the 'F' team on that day would have been incomplete but for the inclusion of Brian Renshall, who had only turned up to watch but, against his better judgement at the age of 49, and not having competed for five years, was 'persuaded' to run. Brian recalls, '*I had to borrow running shoes, shorts and vest and eventually took over twenty-six minutes to run 3¾ miles. Mind you, that did include going off course!*' Another who ran that day at the age of 48 and still going strong was Peter Roberts, one of the club's most successful runners in the 1960s. Peter ran in the 'E' team and recorded a very respectable time of 22 mins 42 secs.

The inclusion of the former St Helens AC athletes, such as Steve Anders and Arthur Dean, considerably strengthened the team, as was shown in the Lancashire Road Relay at Southport on October 13th, when they finished 5th, their highest position for many years. In the cross-country season the new club were turning out up to twenty runners in the senior races of the Liverpool and District League. At Croxteth Park, on November 7th, the seniors finished just outside the medals in 4th place, but had the consolation of seeing Steve Anders grabbing the 3rd individual place. Meanwhile the juniors came 2nd in their event, thanks to Steve Jacques 2nd, Paul Cliff 3rd, Scott Cargill 14th and Chris Kane 19th, whilst Ian Edwards was 2nd in the Boys' race. The outcome of the second League event, at Victoria Park, Warrington, on December 1st, was probably the best since Sutton's glory days of the 1960s, as the seniors won their team race, the boys, not to be outdone, won theirs, and the colts finished second.

The final League placings for the 1990-1 cross-country season, taken over three races, saw St Helens Sutton AC's senior team finish in 3rd position, just eleven points behind Liverpool Harriers, Liverpool Pembroke being the comfortable winners.

The regional championships were also contested, the high point being the senior men's team's 3rd place in the Liverpool & District Championships at Arrowe Park, Wirral, behind Liverpool Pembroke AC and Warrington AC. On the same day Ian Edwards came 2nd in the Boys' race whilst Steve Hull (whose father Jim ran in the senior team) was placed 5th in the Youths' race. Although not competing on that day, Steve's brother Stuart was also a member of the club and it was not unusual to see all three running over cross-country, road and track. The same could be said of the White family. Joe White, a Sutton stalwart for many years, became actively involved in coaching (Ian Edwards being one of his first charges) as well as serving on the committee. Joe was also organiser of the Harriers' annual Christmas dance, thanks to his involvement at St Ann's Social Club in Sutton, and was a past master at procuring men and materials whenever the clubhouse, changing rooms etc needed repairs or refurbishments. His three sons, Ian, Nev and Phil, all joined Sutton Harriers and like their father gave years of dedicated service. In fact, following the merger, Nev became vice-captain whilst Joe remained on the committee.

Ian Edwards

Ian joined Sutton Harriers in 1988 when he was 11 years old. His elder brother Gareth, was already running for the club and Ian decided to tag along, just to see what it was all about. Initially he was coached by Joe White who very quickly realised that he had a special talent on his hands. One of Ian's early successes came when he finished 9th in the Liverpool and District Cross-Country Championship in the Colts (11 to 13 year olds) event in 1988. Such was Ian's ability Joe suggested that it would be to his benefit if he were to move up to the group of athletes coached by Frank Costello. Although this meant that Ian would be

training with older boys Joe was confident that he would be more than capable of holding his own, apart from which he was so much better than anyone in his training group he was getting very little benefit from training with them. Frank took Ian under his wing and the relationship was to last for six years, culminating in Ian being awarded a junior international vest. His successes were many in both cross-country and track and he was at home on either surface.

According to Frank Costello, '*Ian made a wonderful contribution to Sutton Harriers and his spirit, courage and commitment made him a joy to coach. Undoubtedly he was the outstanding middle-distance talent within the area and the best young athlete amongst many whom I coached. He was not only naturally talented but had a great capacity for hard work and endeavour, along with immense courage and self belief. He was (and is) an absolute example of all that is good in to-day's younger generation*'.

There can be little argument that in terms of achievement at major championships Ian Edwards was the finest male athlete to represent Sutton Harriers since Ken Wilcock 30 years previously, even though his career effectively ended at junior level.

Ian's major cross-country performances included winning three Liverpool and District Championships, in 1989 as a colt, and in both 1993 and 1994 as a youth. In 1989 he followed coming 1st in the West Lancs Championship as a colt by achieving 7th place in the Inter-Counties Championship. Two years later he was the winner of the Lancashire Championship Boy's event. In 1995, aged 17 and running as a junior, he came 5th in the Northern, and in the International Championships in Luxembourg finished 11th and 2nd English counter.

On the track in 1991, having won the Lancashire 1500 metres boy's event, Ian came 2nd in the Northern 3000 metres in 9 mins 18 secs, which placed him 2nd in the national ratings. Then in 1993, in the youths' 3000 metres at the Northern, his 9 mins 01 secs gained him second place.

Meanwhile, as well as winning numerous races locally at both club and school level throughout the age ranges, Ian was also a constant on the victors' rostrums at the annual Skipton and Heaton Park cross-country races.

So, what happened to him? At the time Ian was awarded his junior international vest he was studying for his 'A' levels with a view to going to university and taking up a degree course in dentistry, and as he recently explained: *'I realised that to progress into senior international ranks, and be able to compete at the highest level and be successful, I would almost certainly have to become a full-time athlete. This would have meant trying to obtain funding and also asking my parents to support me financially. Given that athletics can be a very short-lived career, especially if you get injured, I decided that long term I had to pursue a career in dentistry, especially as I was already experiencing problems with my back which were hindering both my my training and racing. I thoroughly enjoyed my time with Sutton Harriers and would like to thank all those that helped me in my achievements, especially Frank Costello who gave up so much of his time to coach me and to whom I owe any success I may have achieved.'*

Ian did indeed go on successfully to study dentistry and is now working at Manchester University Hospital.

Based on their individual performances in league and championship races, the first cross-country champions for the new club were:- Danny Cromption (Colts), Stuart Hull (Boys), Steve Hull (Youths), Paul Cliff (Juniors) and Geoff Rawlinson (Seniors). The inclusion of the former St Helens AC athletes, having made the senior team far more competitive, seemed to augur well for the forthcoming track and field, season, which was to be preceded by the usual round of road races.

Sadly, the club's expectations were dashed, for the 1991 track and field season proved a disappointment. By running two senior teams in the Northern Men's League, one in Division 2C the other in Division 4NW, the club's resources proved to be over-stretched. Reporting on the situation that September, team manager Tony Walsh questioned the wisdom of the club having two teams in the Northern League. *'Whilst a number of athletes have gained valuable experience in the 'B' Team, and there has been good team spirit, too often, there have been insufficient athletes, particularly in field events, and more importantly, the 'A' team has suffered due to conflicting interests.'* To enter a single team seemed wiser, as was proved the following season when, with only one team competing in division 3C, promotion was won and St Helens Sutton AC could return to Division 2C.

Although detailed information is in short supply, the ladies' section, whilst relatively small compared to the men's, was undoubtedly active. Like the men they competed in all the local cross-country and track and field leagues, as well as taking part in a variety of road races. Records show that in September 1992, for instance, in the club's track and field championships, in which participants competed in the 100 metres, 800 metres, long jump and shot putt, Kerrie Gent was the Under 11's winner, Nicola Appleton won the Under 13's event whilst Michelle Murray triumphed in the Under 15's age group. The following year, Michelle went on to represent Merseyside in the Inter-Counties Track & Field Championships over 200 metres, and was also a finalist at the English Schools' Championships over the same distance. Her mother, Ann, was later to become the Club Secretary.

The Christmas Handicap in December 1993 was unique in that no fewer than five members of the Langley family took part:- Club Treasurer, Peter Langley, his wife, Vera, and their two sons, Christopher and Anthony, all entered the two-lap (2½ miles) race held in Sherdley Park, while their daughter Kerry ran in the Junior one-lap event, being placed third. A family occasion indeed! The race winner was Julie Ball from the Under 15's age group, chased home by the diminutive but highly talented Holly O'Connor from the Under 11's, who was just five seconds behind. Holly had a precocious talent but sadly failed to realise her obvious potential, dropping out of athletics in her early teens. Stephanie Cliff (whose brother Paul was a regular member of the men's team) was another talented individual who joined the club at an early age and, coached by Joe White, went on to win county honours. Having moved to the Wirral Stephenie continued to train and compete with the club, until she found travelling too arduous and re-gretfully had to retire. Another mainstay of the ladies' section, Celia Fitzsimmons, is still competing in the senior age groups, where she has won several honours.

Addressing members at St Helens Sutton AC's inaugural meeting in September 1990, Frank Costello, the Club Chairman had said, '*The new Club has exciting challenges ahead and if the friendliness and commitment which characterised the merger talks can be continued and built upon, we will have a very successful future. Changes will obviously take place, and it is important to realise from the outset that the Club will be what we all make it, and a willingness to participate and co-operate will be needed, together with more than a little patience at times.*'

Time proved him right. The club had it successes, but sadly many of the former St Helens AC ath-letes failed to settle with the new club, moving on to join Liverpool Harriers barely fifteen months after amalgamation. Meanwhile, nearby at Sutton High Leisure Centre it seemed that the long-promised 'all weather track' was indeed to materialise. Considering how its members might best use such an as-set led to as momentous a change for the club as had been the merger itself.

Chester Lane had been Sutton Harriers' base since 1958 and its brick-built clubroom and changing facilities had become St Helens Sutton AC's headquarters and centre for events. However, apart from rates, insurance, electricity and other charges, upkeep of the building, with its flat roof, could well prove costly. Moreover, with increasing road traffic it seemed unwise for the club's junior members to go to and fro between the clubhouse and training sessions at the Leisure Centre, particularly on dark winter evenings.

By late August 1995 the track's construction problems (in particular the spectator bank on the home straight which had taken some time to stabilize), had been solved. Thus on September 5th, and not without heart-searching for many members, St Helens Sutton AC officially moved trackside to the Leisure Centre. Representatives of St Helens MBC, the Sports Council, the North of England AA and St Helens Sutton AC were present at the track's opening meeting. Primary school races were held, followed by the club's annual John Orrell one-mile handicap race, which was won by Peter Code.

Severe weather was to interrupt the cross-country programme in the following months, but things went better in 1996-7. That season the senior team finished 6th overall in the Liverpool and District League, 5th in the Merseyside Championships and 4th in the Liverpool and District Championships. Full teams completed both the Northern and National Championships, despite these being held at Durham and Havant (Hants) respectively. Clashes with other races on two of three occasions marred the club's entry into the Cheshire Cross-Country League; whilst entry into the Mid Lancs League was under consideration. Ian White's 142 points deservedly made him Club Champion with Brian Beilby's 128 and Andy O'Connor's 107 points gaining them their 2nd and 3rd places.

Established at the Leisure Centre, the club took to hosting a number of meetings, including the McDonald's Boys' League, McDonald's Girls' League, Northern Men's League and the Cheshire League Open Meeting until, in 1998, following problems with track maintenance and safety issues surrounding the throwing and jumping areas, it was decided the future meetings would be held at Warrington's Victoria Park track until the matters could be resolved. By then, rather than let the

Chester Lane building stand empty, needing insurance, and a possible target for vandals, it was decided to sell the former clubhouse, and to retain the money realised, in the hands of designated trustees, as a nest egg for the club for future development.

Credit for steering the club through the momentous changes of the 1990s undoubtedly lay with the committee, former Harriers like Frank Costello, Frank Rimmer, Tony Walsh, Joe White, Roger McColl, Brian Renshall and Peter Langley, some of who had given over thirty years of sterling service. On the athletics side, thanks for their contributions were certainly due to Jim Hull, Ian and Nev White, Jeff Coates, Ken Williams, Peter Code, Tony Raffle, John Irwin, Stan Erlam and Ray Vose.

By 1999 the club, changed in name but largely Harrier at heart, was well established in its new home at the Sutton High Leisure Centre and, despite the failed amalgamation with St Helens AC, problems with the track in its early years and the ups and downs usually associated with the running of an athletics club, was ready to enter the new millenium supporting and competing at all levels of local and regional athletics.

Of those who were involved in the running of the club following the amalgamation in 1990 only the Club President, Bill McMinnis remained in office. Both Roger McColl and Tony Walsh lived outside the area and found travelling onerous, whilst Tony's work as a local councillor was taking up much of his time. Both, however, continued to volunteer their services as track and field officials in local track meetings. Meanwhile, work commitments eventually meant that Peter Langley and Frank Costello had to stand down, and Joe White and Brian Renshall had also to call it a day.

Nevertheless, no one being indispensable, new people stepped into the breach, amongst whom were long-time members John Irwin and Ray Vose, who continue to give invaluable service to the club which had its origin way back in 1899, when the acorn that turned into a mighty oak was planted in Sutton.

Chapter 13
LIST OF OFFICERS & HONOURS
Officers
Where dates are known

Secretary

1899	G Horton		1939	J Appleton
1900	W E Brownlee		1946-52	H Wilson
1901-02	J Moss		1952-63	J Burke
1903-07	C Rigby		1964-71	N Ashcroft
1908-10	H Finney		1972	P R Thomas
1911-14	S Colville		1973-74	R Adams
1919-20	S Colville		1975-78	R McCall
1921	J Morris		1979	B Morrison
1921-28	R Fowles		1980-81	R McCall
1929-30	E J Stubbs		1982	M Gaskell
1931	W Parry		1983-87	F Rimmer
1931	W F Glover		1987-94	B Renshall
1932-33	E Owen		1995-96	A Murray
1934	W Parry		1997-98	P Davenport
1935-36	W F Glover		1999-	S Appleton
1937	J Forshaw			
1938-39	W F Glover			

Treasurer

1899	J Armstrong		1932-37	J Morris
1900	P Smith		1938-39	R Whittle
1901-3	A Royle		1945-53	J Forshaw
1904	S Colville		1954	T Fillingham
1905	H S Finney		1955	J Burke
1906	S Colville		1956-60	T Fillingham
1907	J Catterall		1961	R Priestner
1908-14	C Rigby		1962-71	T Fillingham
1919-21	C Rigby		1972-86	A Walsh
1922-24	S Colville		1987-97	P Langley
1925	J Morris		1998-99	J Irwin
1926-28	R Fowles			
1929-31	E J Stubbs			

Chairman

1947	W McMinnis (Snr)
1948-55	M Morris
1956	T Fillingham
1957-58	P Burrows
1959-60	F McMinnis
1961	P Priestner
1962-74	F McMinnis

President

1899	Capt M Hughes
1900	A Royle
1901-06	Capt M Hughes
1907	H B Bate
1908-14	Councillor W Bell
1919-25	Councillor W Bell
1926-36	C Rigby
1937-39	R Whittle
1946-88	E J Stubbs
1989-	W McMinnis

Club Captain

1899	J Painter
1899-1903	S Colville
1904	J Morris
1904	H Wilcox
1905	J Morris
1906	S Welding
1907	J Bailey
1908-10	F J Whittle
1911-14	J Morris
1919-21	E Harrison
1922	J Hughes
1923	T Edwards
1924	A McKinnon
1925-29	E J Morris
1930	W Heyes
1931-2	W Burrows
1933-34	J Meadows
1935	A Worral
1936-39	A Tyrer
1945-47	A Tyrer
1948-56	F McMinnis
1957-58	K J Wilcock
1959-60	P Priestner
1961-62	T Prescott
1963-65	R Ashley
1966	J McLoughlin
1967	J McLoughlin (CC)
	B Renshall (Track)
1968-70	D Costello
1971	C Johnson
1972-73	J McLoughlin
1974	J Crehan
1975-79	F Rimmer
1980-82	F Rimmer (CC)
	M K Gaskell (Track)
1983-86	B Renshall
1987-90	N White
1991	S Anders

Ladies' Captain

Rita Almond	1951-1954
Doreen Fitzgerald	1955
Barbara Billington	1956
Margaret Astell	1957
Pam Thompson	1958-1959
Elaine Porter	1962

Individual Representative Honours

CROSS-COUNTRY INTERNATIONAL

ENGLAND

Charles J Straw	1906/1909
Sam Welding	1905/06/07/08/11
Albert Worrall	1928
Tommy Lee	1937
Alf Tyrer	1939
Tom Fillingham	1947
Fred McMinnis	1948
Mick Maleedy	1949
Bill McMinnis	1953
Ian Edwards	(Junior) 1995

EIRE

Gordon Edgar	1938

WALES

Arthur Williams	1935/36/37/38

AREA / COUNTY

Alf Tyrer	NCAA 1947/8
	Lancs 1947/48
	Cheshire 1949
Tom Fillingham	NCAA 1947/48/49
	Lancs 1947/48/49/50/51
Fred McMinnis	NCAA 1947/48/49
	Lancs 1947/48/49/50
Bill McMinnis	NCAA 1949
	Lancs 1947/48/50/51/53
Joe Harrison	NCAA 1947
	Lancs 1947/48/49
Mick Maleedy	NCAA 1948/49
	Lancs 1950
Jack Chidlow	Lancs 1949
Bert Tebb	Lancs 1958
Bob Meadows	Lancs 1960
Steve James	Cheshire 1969/70/71
Ron Barlow	Cheshire 1969
	Lancs 1970/1
Brian Woodford	Cheshire 1969
Jim Crehan	Lancs 1971(Y) 1974(J) 1987
Alan Jones Lancs	1986
Ian Edwards	Lancs (Boys) 1991

CROSS-COUNTRY & ROAD (MEN)

INTERNATIONAL CROSS-COUNTRY CHAMPION

Charles J Straw	1908

ENGLISH NATIONAL CHAMPION

Charles J Straw	1908

NORTHERN CROSS-COUNTRY CHAMPION

Charles J Straw	1908
Sam Welding	1907
Alf Tyrer	1939
Fred McMinnis	1948

WEST LANCASHIRE CROSS-COUNTRY CHAMPION

Sam Welding	1907
Arthur Welding	1923
Jim Kelly	1924
Arthur Williams	1935/36/37/38
Alf Tyrer	1939
Tom Fillingham	1947
Fred McMinnis	1948/49
Bill McMinnis	1953
Ron Barlow	1971
Jim Crehan	1986

LIVERPOOL & DISTRICT CHAMPION

Peter Roberts	1968 & 1971

R.A.F. & INTER-SERVICES CHAMPION

Bill McMinnis	1951

JUNIOR CROSS COUNTRY CHAMPIONS

WEST LANCASHIRE

Tom Lee	1935
Peter McGovern	1937
Mick Maleedy	1948 & 1949
John McLoughlin	1966

LIVERPOOL & DISTRICT

Ian Edwards	1993/94

ST. HELENS & DISTRICT

Ernie Wakefield	1933
Peter McGovern	1936
Tom Fillingham	1937/38/39

YOUTHS' CHAMPIONS (CROSS-COUNTRY)
WEST LANCASHIRE

Ernie Wakefield	1933
Tom Fillingham	1939
John McLoughlin	1965

BOYS' CHAMPIONS (CROSS-COUNTRY)
WEST LANCASHIRE

Les Laithwaite	1952
John McLoughlin	1962

LIVERPOOL & DISTRICT

Frank Jeffries	1958
John McLoughlin	1962
Iain Adams	1975
Ian Edwards	1991

LANCASHIRE

John McLoughlin	1962

COLTS' CHAMPIONS (CROSS-COUNTRY)
WEST LANCASHIRE

Ian Edwards	1989

LIVERPOOL & DISTRICT

Ian Edwards	1989

MARATHON RUNNING
AAA NATIONAL

Bill McMinnis	1955

NORTHERN

Alf Tyrer	1947/48
Bill McMinnis	1953

CHESHIRE

Peter Priestner	1960

20 MILE ROAD RUNNING CHAMPION
LANCASHIRE

Bill McMinnis	1957

CHESHIRE

Peter Priestner	1960
Brian Woodford	1969

CROSS-COUNTRY - WOMEN
MERSEYSIDE COUNTY WOMEN'S CROSS-COUNTRY CHAMPION

Susan Smart	1976

INTERMEDIATE CHAMPION

Ann Williams	1980
Lyn Vose	1981

JUNIOR CHAMPION

Tracy Lavelle	1979
Debbie Pinnington	1982

GIRLS' CHAMPION

Lyn Vose	1978
Debbie Pennington	1980
Linda Hannaby	1981/82

ENGLISH NATIONAL CHAMPIONS:

Men: Seniors	1906, 1947, 1948, 1949, 1950, 1951
Youths	1950
Women: Girls	1979

NORTHERN CHAMPIONS

Men: Seniors	1937, 1939, 1947, 1948, 1949, 1950, 1951
Juniors	1904, 1935
Youths	1933, 1950
Boys	1951

WEST LANCASHIRE CHAMPIONS:

Men: Seniors	1912, 1924, 1929, 1932, 1933, 1935, 1936, 1937, 1938, 1947, 1948, 1949, 1950, 1951, 1952, 1953, 1955, 1969, 1970, 1971
Juniors	1920, 1925, 1931, 1933, 1934, 1935, 1937, 1949, 1951, 1953, 1965, 1966, 1976, 1977
Youths	1932, 1933, 1938, 1952, 1953

MERSEYSIDE COUNTY WOMEN'S CHAMPIONS

Seniors	1981, 1982
Intermediate	1975, 1980, 1981
Juniors	1979, 1980
Girls	1976, 1977, 1978, 1981

INDIVIDUAL REPRESENTATIVE HONOURS

TRACK, FIELD AND ROAD
INTERNATIONAL
GREAT BRITAIN AND NI

Bill McMinnis	1955
Ken Wilcock	1961/2
Ann Williams	1982 (Junior), 1983 & 1984
Lynton Boardman	1984 (Junior)
Sue Crehan	1985
Neil Smart	1989

EIRE

Jim Kelly	1924 (Olympic Games)

JERSEY

Mike Stafford 1958	(Empire Games)

ENGLAND

Ken Wilcock	1961/62
Ann Williams	(Junior) 1981/82, 1983
Sue Crehan	1984/85
Lynton Boardman	(Junior) 1984

AREA / COUNTY

Alf Tyrer	Lancs 1939
Gordon Edgar	Lancs 1939
Fred McMinnis	Lancs 1939
Tom Hackett	NCAA 1951
	Lancs 1950/51
Austin Tipping	AAA 1953
	Lancs 1950/51/52/55/56
	Civil Service 1950/51/52
Ted Ashley Cheshire	1950/51/52
Ken Wilcock	AAA 1960/61/62
	NCAA 1956/57/58/59/60/61/62
	Lancs 1956/57/58/59/60/61/62
Joe Harrison	Lancs 1957/59
Bill McMinnis	Lancs 1957
Gordon Yale	Lancs 1959
Trevor Simms	Lancs (Junior) 1956
Ian Adams	NCAA (Junior) 1979
	Lancs (Youth) 1977
	Lancs (Junior) 1979
Steve Wilson	NCAA 1981/82
Martin Gaskell	NCAA 1980
	Lancs 1982/83
Alan Jones	NCAA 1982
	C.S. 1982
Paul Cliff	Lancs 1990
Neil Smart	Lancs 1985
Lynton Boardman	AAA 1984
Phil Fearnly	Lancs (Junior) 1986
Jim Crehan	Lancs 1985

INDIVIDUAL HONOURS
TRACK, FIELD AND ROAD

Gordon Edgar	NCAA 6 miles Champion 1938
Bill McMinnis	AAA Marathon Champion 1955
	NCAA Marathon Champion 1953/54
Alf Tyrer	NCAA Marathon Champion 1946/7
Margaret Astell	Women's AAA 80 yards and 100 yards Junior Champion 1952
Jimmy Doyle	English Schools (Under 16) 440 yards Champion 1950
Margaret King	Women's NCAA Long Jump Champion 1951

Jenny Welding	Women's NCAA Junior High Jump Champion 1952
Rosemary Whetton	Women's NCAA Junior Long Jump Champion 1952
Ken Wilcock	NCAA 440 yards Champion 1958/60/61/62
	NCAA Junior 440 yards Champion 1953
John Byrne	NCAA Youths' High Jump Champion 1981
Jackie Cotton	WAAA Junior Pentathlon Champion 1984
	NCWAAA Junior Javelin Champion 1984
Sue Crehan	NCWAAA 1500 metres Champion 1984
	WAAA indoor 3000 metres Champion 1985
	WAAA 10,000 metres Champion 1985
Ann Williams	English Schools 400 metres Champion 1982
	NCWAAA 400 metres Champion 1981
Neil Smart	UK Championships 3000 metres Steeplechase Champion 1989
Lynton Boardman	AAA Junior Champion Long Jump 1984
Paul Hamilton	NCAA A Youths' 400 metres Champion 1984

WINNERS - RELAY CHAMPIONSHIPS

MEN'S:

NCAAA	4 x 110 Yards 1954
NCAAA	One Mile Medley 1954-55
Lancashire County AAA	
	Road Relay Championship 1951
	4 x 110 yds 1953
	4 x 440 yds 1953
	4 x 440 yds (Jnr) 1953

WOMEN'S

NCWAA	4 x 110 yds 1950-52-53-55
	660 yds 1951-53-54
	4 x 110 yds (Jnr) 1951
Lancashire County WAAA	4 x 110 yds 1951-6

THE JOHN ORRELL MEMORIAL CUP

Donated by Mr Frederick Orrell and Mr J H Orrell to Sutton Harriers and Athletic Club (St Helens)
on June 11th 1951 for annual competition

Year	Winner	Year	Winner	Year	Winner
1951	J Doyle	1968	D Costello	1985	C M Gaskell
1952	K Wilcock	1969	J Crehan	1986	K Roe
1953	J Doyle	1970	J Crehan	1987	
1954	B Tebb	1971	D King	1988	
1955	B Tebb	1972	S James	1989	D Service
1956	B Parton	1973	J Crehan	1990	N Salleyman
1957	H Holland	1974	T McIntyre	1991	
1958	K Wilcock	1975	B Grundy	1992	W Whitley
1959	M Rylatt	1976	A McGauley	1993	P Robinson
1960	R Meadows	1977	G Colquitt	1994	J Cottam
1961	J McLoughlin	1978	N White	1995	P Code
1962	J Moffatt	1979	C M Gaskell	1996	S Erlam
1963	J McLoughlin	1980	C O'Shaughnessy	1997	I White
1964	B Renshall	1981	S Rimmer	1998	Not Held
1965	P Roberts	1982	S White	1999	M Arnott
1966	M Griffiths	1983	A M Gaskell		
1967	K Owen	1984	M Robson		

Ken Wilcock winning the John Orrell Mile in 1952

SUTTON ROAD RACE

	SENIOR INDIVIDUAL		SENIOR TEAM	UNDER 20	VETERAN (TEAM/ INDIVIDUAL)
	(Roughdale Trophy)		(Geoff Harwood Trophy)	(Burtonwood Trophy)	(Alf Cowell Trophy)
1959	J Highton (Liverpool Pembroke)		Liverpool Pembroke AC		
1960	G North (Blackpool & Fylde)		Blackpool & Fylde AC		
1961	M Freary (Bolton United)		Bolton United Harriers		
1962	B Woolford (Wallasey)		Liverpool Pembroke AC		
1963	R Barlow (Wallasey)	34.29	Wallasey AC		
1964	R Hill (Bolton United)	33.58	Manchester & District H		
1965	J McLoughlin (Sutton Harriers)	34.33	North Staffs & Stone		
1966	J Jackson (North Staffs)	33.21	Manchester & District H		
1967	M Craven (Kendal AC)		Longwood Harriers		
1968	E Haslem (Bolton United)	34.20	Manchester & District H		
1969	R Hill (Bolton United)	34.01	Sutton Harriers & AC		
1970	R Hill (Bolton United)		City of Stoke AC		
1971	A Birks (City of Stoke)		City of Stoke AC		
1972	J Jackson (City of Stoke)		Sale Harriers		
1973	F Davies (Liverpool Harriers)	35.24	Wirral AC	K Carroll (Liverpool Pembroke)	
1974	R Wilde (Manchester & District)		Liverpool Harriers	L Valentine (Sale Harriers)	
1975	J Calvert (Blackburn Harriers)		Wirral AC	L Valentine (Sale Harriers)	
1976	R Wilde (Manchester & District)	34.04	Liverpool Harriers	Phil Gaytor (Sale Harriers)	

NEW COURSE

1977	D Brennan (Warrington AC)	35.22	City of Stoke AC	M Watts (Notts AC)	
1978	K Harrison (Stretford AC)	35.27	Liverpool Pembroke AC	N Holliday (Warrington AC)	Liverpool Pembroke
1979	J Woods (Liverpool Harriers)	36.20	Liverpool Harriers	S Ellison (Liverpool Harriers)	Liverpool Pembroke
1980	H Jones (Ranelgh/Liverpool Uni)	34.32	Manchester Harriers	C Dagnall (Liverpool Harriers)	Bolton United
1981	S Anders (St Helens AC)	36.11	St Helens AC	C Dagnall (Liverpool Harriers)	Bolton United
1982	S Anders (St Helens AC)	35.38	Sale Harriers	B Currier (Liverpool Harriers)	Liverpool Pembroke
1983	M McLoughlin (Liv. Pembroke)	35.06	Liverpool Pembroke AC	A Kay (Bolton United)	M Flynn (Liverpool Pembroke)
1984	M McLoughlin (Liv. Pembroke)	35.24	Liverpool Harriers	A Kay (Bolton United)	L Carroll (Wirral AC)
1985	P Campbell (Bolton United)		Sutton Harriers & AC	P Fearnley (Sutton Harriers)	P Roberts (Sutton Harriers)
1986	A Carey (Warrington AC)		Sutton Harriers & AC	S Hobday (Altrincham AC)	M Flynn (Liverpool Pembroke)
1987	J Asshworth (Keughley)	35.36	Liverpool Harriers	S Jones (Sale Harriers)	M Flynn (Liverpool Pembroke)
1988	N Rimmer (Sale Harriers)		Sale Harriers (GM Building Systems Trophy)	S Jones (Sale Harriers)	S Erlm (Sutton Harriers)
1989	N Rimmer (Sale Harriers)	38.10	Liverpool Harriers	J Calland (St Helens Striders)	K O'Toole (Liverpool Pembroke)
1990	N Smart (Sale Harriers)		Sutton Hariers & AC		

10K

1991	O Ludago (Tanzania)	30.14	Sale Harriers		
1992	N Smart (Sale Harriers)	31.00	Sefton Harriers	M Woolrich (Helsby)	